PSYCHOLOGY LIBRARY EDITIONS:
COMPARATIVE PSYCHOLOGY

Volume 13

NONVERBAL COMMUNICATION

NONVERBAL COMMUNICATION

Where Nature Meets Culture

Edited by
ULLICA SEGERSTRÅLE AND PETER MOLNÁR

Routledge
Taylor & Francis Group

LONDON AND NEW YORK

First published in 1997 by Lawrence Erlbaum Associates, Inc.

This edition first published in 2018
by Routledge
2 Park Square, Milton Park, Abingdon, Oxon OX14 4RN

and by Routledge
711 Third Avenue, New York, NY 10017

Routledge is an imprint of the Taylor & Francis Group, an informa business

© 1997 by Lawrence Erlbaum Associates, Inc.

British Library Cataloguing in Publication Data
A catalogue record for this book is available from the British Library

ISBN: 978-1-138-50329-8 (Set)
ISBN: 978-1-351-12878-0 (Set) (ebk)
ISBN: 978-0-8153-7327-8 (Volume 13) (hbk)
ISBN: 978-0-8153-7396-4 (Volume 13) (pbk)
ISBN: 978-1-351-24313-1 (Volume 13) (ebk)

Nonverbal Communication
Where Nature Meets Culture

Edited by

Ullica Segerstråle
Illinois Institute of Technology
Chicago, Illinois

Peter Molnár
Semmelweis University Medical School
Budapest, Hungary

LEA LAWRENCE ERLBAUM ASSOCIATES, PUBLISHERS
1997   Mahwah, New Jersey

Lawrence Erlbaum Associates, Inc., Publishers
10 Industrial Avenue
Mahwah, New Jersey 07430

Library of Congress Cataloging-in-Publication Data

Nonverbal communication : where nature meets culture / edited by Ullica Segerstråle, Peter Molnár.
    p. cm.
    Chiefly papers presented at a conference held at the Center for Interdisciplinary Research (ZiF), Bielefeld, Germany, March 1992.
    Includes bibliographical references and indexes.
    ISBN 0-8058-2179-1 (alk. paper)
    1. Nonverbal communication (Psychology) 2. Emotions. 3. Ethology, Comparative. I. Segerstråle, Ullica Christina. II. Molnár, P., 1942–
    BF637.N66N66   1996
    153.6'9—dc20   96–2148
                              CIP

Printed in the United States of America
10 9 8 7 6 5 4 3 2

Contents

PART III THE SOCIAL ROLE OF NONVERBAL COMMUNICATION AND EMOTIONS: EVOLUTIONARY INFERENCES

PART IV NONVERBAL COMMUNICATION AS A MEDIATOR BETWEEN NATURE AND CULTURE

PREFACE

The search for the biological foundations of human culture inevitably leads to nonverbal communication. Superficial intuition suggests that nonverbal communication is a *sine qua non* for the evolution of sociality. Without it, the diversity and sophistication of today's social systems would be unimaginable. However, there is the opposite hypothesis that the evolution of nonverbal communication may in part be the result of our being thoroughly social entities: Our sociality itself may have amplified the evolution of a capacity we share with other primates but developed to a degree unequaled by any other species.

As far as language is concerned, these issues have been subject to fascinating research in linguistics, paleoanthropology, and other fields. However, the fundamental question of the causation of sociality and thus, ultimately, of human culture, remains contested between disciplinary territorial claims of biology and the social sciences. Quite obviously, the presumed interdependence of the evolution of nonverbal communication as a biological capacity and the evolution of its significance for human culture calls for an interdisciplinary effort to explore the processes involved on both a phylogenetic and an ontogenetic level. One promising approach is the study of similarities and differences of nonverbal communication among humans and nonhumans (above all primates).

Advances in the realm of the evolution of nonverbal communication as presented in this volume will certainly contribute to further insights into the intricacies of the biological and the social. Inevitably, new problems and questions will also arise. Interdisciplinarity, for that matter, is not a new answer to old questions; rather, it is a new framework, considered to provide a more plausible "language" in which to pose questions and evaluate the answers.

With a few exceptions, the following volume documents a conference at the Center for Interdisciplinary Research (ZiF), Bielefeld, which took place in March 1992. This conference was organized within the framework of a research group working on the overarching theme of "Biological Foundations of Human Culture." Throughout the academic year 1991–1992 scholars of areas as different and far apart as biology, psychology, sociology, anthropology, economics, primatology, history, and philosophy of science presented and discussed recent approaches toward a biologically and sociologically founded understanding of human culture. In outlining plausible pluralistic accounts of such phenomena as the evolution of social intelligence, psychological dispositions such as trust and the detection of cheating, or basic social institutions such as the family, the group explicitly avoided biological and sociological reductionisms. This pluralistic perspective was considered a prerequisite of the project as a whole by all its participants, and it made it possible to bring the diverse disciplinary approaches into fruitful dialogue. The results of the project are published in three books, of which this is one.

In my dual role as convener of the research group and executive director of the ZiF, I want to thank Peter Molnár and Ullica Segerstråle for organizing the conference and editing this volume, Signe Preuschoft for helping organize the conference, and Sabine Maasen for assuming a major share of the burden of editing and preparing this book for publication. Thanks also go to the staff of the ZiF, notably Lilo Jegerlehner, for her indispensable technical assistance.

Peter Weingart

1

NONVERBAL COMMUNICATION: CROSSING THE BOUNDARY BETWEEN CULTURE AND NATURE

Ullica Segerstråle
Illinois Institute of Technology, Chicago

Peter Molnár
Semmelweis University Medical School, Budapest

NONVERBAL COMMUNICATION AS AN INTERFACE BETWEEN SOCIAL SCIENCE AND BIOLOGY

One of the basic aims of this book is to convince the reader of the utter artificiality of the supposed opposition between culture and biology. This opposition has a long tradition in academia, and it is perhaps no surprise that some recent controversies such as the sociobiology debate have been conducted within the standard framework of nature versus nurture. However, such a contrast is not only artificial, but it also represents a biologically quite outdated way of thinking. At least since the modern synthesis during the first half of the 20th century, the paradigm of gene–environment interactionism has prevailed within biology—if this had been adopted also by social scientists, their obvious conclusion would long since have been that it is not a question of nature versus nurture, but of both at the same time. Unfortunately, the prevailing division of labor in academia and a lingering "biophobia" in the social sciences have made a rapprochement difficult for those who study human

1

behavior from a biological and a social scientific perspective. However, we believe that the field of nonverbal communication is a strategic site for demonstrating the inextricable interrelationship between nature and culture in human behavior. We hope that the chapters presented in this volume will persuade social scientists that much of the new research now going on in the life sciences could be of direct relevance to their own most fundamental theoretical quests.

Nonverbal communication is a field that encompasses a wide variety of disciplines within both the social and natural sciences. If there ever was a field that could be labeled "the missing link" between the social and natural sciences, this would be it. Nonverbal communication is not only naturally multidisciplinary, it also approaches the multifaceted connections between biology and culture from a broad spectrum of intellectual angles. In fact, the typically interdisciplinary interests of students of nonverbal communication sometimes make it hard to classify these researchers as belonging to either natural or social science. This is particularly true because epistemological and methodological views in this field freely cross the supposed divide between the two cultures. At present, relevant research goes on in a range of academic disciplines, from neurophysiology, psychophysiology, behavioral ecology, and ethology to social psychology, psychiatry, anthropology, sociology, and linguistics.

Despite an overlap of interests and methodological approaches, students of nonverbal phenomena in different disciplines may not always be aware of one another's research. The academic organization of fields and specialties encourages relatively narrow specialization, and publications are typically directed to an expert audience. Based on our conviction that nonverbal communication might serve as a model for the much-needed rapprochement between the natural and social sciences, we requested the assistance of the Zentrum für interdisziplinäre Forschung (ZiF) to provide an opportunity for us to organize a conference on this topic as part of the group project Biological Foundations of Human Culture. With the support of ZiF, we were able to invite the foremost students of nonverbal communication from a wide variety of fields to share their recent recearch with each other and our group in nontechnical language. This book is an edited version of the papers presented at the conference "Nonverbal Communication and the Genesis of Culture," held at ZiF in March 1992. We hope that this book will convey some of the interdisciplinary spirit and many individual "aha!" experiences of that conference.

The opposition to biology in the social sciences has a long tradition. For some, it may even seem that resisting biological explanations of human behavior ought to be the epistemological *raison d'être* for a social scientist. However, such a view represents a relatively recent paradigm in the social sciences. It should be pointed out that ever since their beginning, the social sciences have had an off-again, on-again relationship with biology. Thus, there have existed periods when social scientists have felt quite free to seek explanations for human behavior in biological factors. For instance, at the beginning of the 20th century, evolutionary biology was taken as a basis for many social scientific theories. Interestingly, at that time, biological arguments were used for both conservative and progressive social policy programs. However, the social sciences' involvement with biology later followed a (mistaken) view of human genetics as Mendelian, which got them implicated in contemporary racial theorizing and eugenics. After World War II, the tide turned again. Several factors contributed to a decline of the biological paradigm and a shift to environmentalism in the social sciences: the realization that earlier assumptions about the inheritance of human traits could not be biologically supported any longer, the revulsion to Nazi doctrine, and the emerging cultural relativist paradigm promoted by Boas and his students. Ever since World War II, particularly after the famous 1952 UNESCO statement on race, the environmentalist paradigm has prevailed. This means that for the last four decades, biology has been not only black-boxed but black-listed. However, we believe that it is now high time that for intellectual reasons social scientists take a new look at the biological sciences and the potential insights they may provide for social scientific theorizing.

It seems clear, however, that the initiative for a reconciliation between biology and the social sciences would have to come from the latter. A good example of how not to try to integrate biology and the social sciences was probably Wilson's (1975) suggestion to "biologize" the social sciences, judging from the strong reaction his *Sociobiology* provoked (e.g., Leach, 1981; Sahlins, 1976; Wiegele, 1979). Indeed, overselling biology to the social sciences may trigger all kinds of epistemological and political resistance, particularly because any consideration of biological factors tends to be immediately labeled "reductionism" or "biological determinism" (see, e.g., Segerstråle, 1992). However, an additional reason for social scientists' lack of sympathy for sociobiology may well have been the different time scales involved in social scientific and evolutionary biological theorizing. Sociobiological reasoning deals with long-range evolutionary scenarios and adaptive explanations for particular behaviors. Such a way of thinking is quite alien to social scientists, who deal with contemporary or at most historical behaviors. Therefore, among biological fields, the closest field to the social sciences is probably ethology. Interestingly, this discipline has not been overtly recognized as relevant to the social sciences (even though ethological notions have been smuggled in through the back door in the footnotes of sociologists such as Goffman, 1972; see also Collins, 1975, for an explicit interest in ethology).

It should be noted, however, that not all types of biological arguments have been rejected by social scientists. At least three biological givens seem to have been largely incorporated as part of the social scientific body of knowledge: the "hard-wiredness" of the human capacity for language, the existence of critical periods in language development, and the importance of social interaction for normal human development. This at least opens up the possibility that social scientists might also be interested in further studies concerning the biological basis of human communicative abilities, including the results of today's sophisticated psychophysiological and neurophysiological research. Indeed, what emerges today is an increasingly complex picture of human communicative ability as simultaneously biologically and socioculturally influenced, with a few capacities apparently more biologically "hardwired" than others (and therefore probably crucial as communicational building blocks): face recognition, imitation, emotional communication, and the capacity for language. This is dealt with in more detail later.

OVERCOMING THE FALSE DICHOTOMY BETWEEN NATURE AND NURTURE

Nonverbal communication has not been sufficiently appreciated in the social sciences so far. The main reason is probably that the social sciences have tended to strongly emphasize the unique human capacity for language (i.e., symbolic communication). However, considering that nonverbal communication is obviously an important everyday phenomenon—there have been estimates that up to two thirds of our behavior in dyadic interaction is nonverbal (Birdwhistell in Knapp, 1978, p. 30)—it is high time for the important insights from this field to get integrated in the social scientific domain. It is safe to say that much of our de facto understanding of one another—and of total strangers—is rooted in our nonverbal abilities and their relationships to our shared human neurology and physiology. This everyday experience seems to have been played down in much abstract social science discourse. In sociology, the most notable exception is the symbolic interactionist school, represented by Mead (1934), who introduced the notion of a "conversation of gestures" to explain the origin of the social Self (G. H. Mead, 1934). Later on, the role of nonverbal communication has been recognized particularly within the traditions of microsociology (Collins, 1975, 1981; Goffman, 1959, 1972; Scheff, 1990) and ethnomethodology (Garfinkel, 1967), and occasionally in more general social theory (e.g., Giddens, 1984).

Another reason for the relative invisibility of nonverbal communication within the social sciences is the particular history of this type of research, originating in fields outside the mainstream. One of the two main orientations of early nonverbal communication research, beginning in the mid-1950s, resulted from a collaboration among structural linguists, psychiatrists and anthropologists who were inspired by the new developments in information theory and cybernetics. The representatives of this "structural" approach or "context analysis" were interested in the organization of behavior, patterns of interaction, and the like. Because it drew inspiration from anthropological linguistics in the Sapir–Whorf tradition (Sapir, 1949; Whorf, 1956), this strand of early nonverbal research saw itself as falling on the "culture" side of a hypothetical academic divide. For instance, Birdwhistell (1970), the founder of kinesics (the language of body movement), insisted on the total determination of nonverbal behavior by culture or language group. The same was true for Hall, the founder of proxemics (the language of space), who extended the linguistic relativity thesis to cultural differences in conceptions of space and time (E. T. Hall, 1959, 1966).

Meanwhile, research on the nature side in nonverbal communication concentrated on finding evidence of human behavioral universals. Ultimately, this line of research derives from Darwin's (1872/1965) famous *The Expression of the Emotions in Man and Animals* (Ekman, 1973). The evidence here came from several sources: primatological studies indicating homologies between primate and human facial expressions (Chevalier-Skolnikoff, 1973; van Hooff, 1972); human ethological research on facial expressions of blind, deaf, and later even thalidomide children (Eibl-Eibesfeldt, 1973, 1989); identification of cultural universals (Eibl-Eibesfeldt, 1972, 1989); and cross-cultural research on facial expressions (Ekman, 1973; Ekman & Friesen, 1969,

1975, 1978; Ekman & Keltner, chap. 2, this volume; Izard, 1977; Tomkins, 1962; Zajonc, 1980). Still another important type of research involves the psychophysiology of the human face (Dimberg, 1982; Öhman & Dimberg, 1978).

Until recently, these two main strands of research saw themselves as, and were also presented as, representing serious alternative viewpoints (see, e.g., Knapp, 1978). Now it is no longer possible to postulate a simple either–or situation when it comes to culture and biology. Additional evidence has accumulated to tip the balance in favor of the biological foundations of nonverbal behavior, or, more correctly, toward an answer that inseparably involves both culture and biology (see also Hinde, 1987; Reynolds, 1980). This volume is designed to make this point as explicitly as possible. Furthermore, today the dividing lines between nonverbal and language communication appear much less defined than before. The same is true for the distinction between human and animal communication. Language experts are increasingly turning to preverbal communication for clues to the infant's linguistic development. Meanwhile, there is accumulating evidence of symbolic or proto-symbolic communication in animals, although the extent to which this is really the case still remains controversial (these topics are more extensively covered in Velichkovsky & Rumbaugh, 1996).

It is also important to argue for the complementarity between different types of research on behavior across the disciplinary divide. We have in mind Tinbergen's (1963) famous "Four Questions". Tinbergen argued that "why" questions concerning behavior can be equally legitimately asked at four different levels: the phylogenetic, ontogenetic, physiological, and functional ones. (From such a perspective, e.g., evolutionary biologists cannot claim that theirs is the ultimate answer to the "why" of a particular behavior). Within the field of nonverbal communication, this means that we might talk about such things as the evolutionary preparedness for sending and receiving, the ontogenetic development of interpersonal communication skills in infancy, the physiological concomitants of various types of nonverbal interactions, and the social function of particular nonverbal messages. An alternative way to see the four questions would be to regard them as representing four different aspects of the same problem, requiring not four responses but only one complex interdisciplinary answer. This is also what we hope to demonstrate in this volume, where in every chapter the authors were encouraged to examine the interconnections between nature and culture and between levels within their own specific field of research.

The book is divided into four parts. Part I is devoted to human universals, a long-standing issue of contention in the nature–nurture debate and obviously of central importance to nonverbal communication. Part II focuses on developmental aspects of nonverbal behavior, and Part III on evolutionary ones. However, the authors of the chapters in Parts II and III have many common research interests, as will become apparent. Both parts also emphasize the central importance of the social and cultural context. Part IV, the final section of this book, addresses the relationship between nonverbal communication and culture from a variety of perspectives and suggests how social scientific theorizing may benefit from recent insights in nonverbal research.

HUMAN UNIVERSALS: FROM BEHAVIOR MANIFESTATIONS TO PREDISPOSITIONS

It is now clear that some of the early conceptions of alternative cultural and biological explanations for nonverbal behavior were based on mistaken assumptions. Among other things, earlier researchers did not make the crucial distinction between voluntary and involuntary expression of emotion, nor consider the possibility that culture could "order" persons to mask their true emotions (Ekman & Keltner, chap. 2, this volume). In fact, the whole situation regarding human universals is now being re-evaluated. Particularly, it seems that the original Sapir–Whorf thesis of linguistic relativism (i.e., that our language determines our categories of thought) is becoming increasingly untenable. (Interestingly, one prominent anthropologist working within the linguistic anthropological tradition admitted this already some time ago; E. T. Hall, 1977, 31). There is now mounting evidence for the *de facto* existence of universals in cases where earlier anthropologists proclaimed fundamental cultural differences. Moreover, earlier anthropological studies have recently been criticized for errors or exaggerations (see, e.g., Brown, 1991; Cosmides, Tooby, & Barkow, 1992; R. Fox, 1989). In this process of reevaluation, it is probably psychology rather than anthropology that provides the most significant new research. For instance, regarding the disputed existence of a universal color scheme, sophisticated methods now point to a prelinguistic tendency to divide up the continuous color spectrum into discrete colors (e.g., Bornstein, 1976, 1996; Harnad, 1996; for overviews of anthropological and psychological findings see Brown, 1991; Shepard, 1992).

However, despite these new efforts to set the record straight, the whole discussion of universals may be on the wrong track. Because it was focused on particular behaviors, earlier anthropologists could always mobilize some culture that did not fit the human ethologists' claims about universals, and meanwhile criticize the latter for selective documentation. Now again it seems that it is the cultural anthropologists' turn to be scrutinized for errors. It is not clear that an easy reconciliation can be reached. In this situation, perhaps a useful alternative to looking for the manifestations of particular behavioral universals across cultures would be to concentrate instead on universal human predispositions for nonverbal communication. Thus, the new emphasis would now be on the elementary building blocks for interactional skills and the process of their development in infancy. Such a focus would allow for real observable cultural differences yet maintain a panhuman foundation.

Current research in nonverbal communication and neurophysiology shows an increasingly complex picture of human communicative ability as both biologically and socioculturally influenced. However, it seems that there are a few capacities that are apparently more biologically "hard-wired" than others. Let us briefly look at them.

The most important clue to human communication may well be in the face. The face is surprisingly well prepared for nonverbal communication. Already at birth, all of the important muscles needed for emotional expressions are well developed (Ekman, 1982). There are studies of newborn infants, including infants born with damaged cortex or without cortex, that show that they react to various stimuli (sweet, sour, bitter, taste, etc.) in a clearly identifiable way (J. E. Steiner, 1979). Research has also shown the great speed with which the all-important mother–infant bond is formed through newborns' preferential tracking of facelike stimuli (e.g., Johnson, Dziurawiec, Ellis, & Morton, 1991). (This bond can be described as the "machine" for the infant's emotional and linguistic development.) Earlier studies have already shown mimicking to be a particularly important inborn response (Field, Woodson, Greenberg, & Cohen, 1982; McDougall, 1908; Meltzoff, 1985; Meltzoff & Moore, 1977). For instance, the heart rate connected with mimicking in neonates indicates that this is indeed a directly triggered response, not connected to any conscious activity (see Molnár, 1990). However, mimicking in turn gives rise to particular physiological responses in the infant and is thus related to its emotional development. Studies also continue demonstrating an innate fear reaction to negative faces in young infants, even to faces drawn as asymmetrical lines (Dimberg, chap. 3, this volume), with physiological responses similar to other well-known fear reactions (e.g., to snakes; Öhman, 1986; Sackett, 1966). Overall, we seem to have an inborn very rapid encoding and decoding capacity for facial emotional messages; that is, we are naturally capable senders and receivers (Dimberg, chap. 3, this volume). Maybe the most intriguing piece of evidential support for the central role of the face in human communication is that an area of the brain appears to be specifically devoted to facial recognition (Geschwind, 1979). "Face neurons" have recently been reported for facial recognition in monkeys (Perrett, Rolls, & Caan, 1982; R. Weiss, 1988; Young & Yamane, 1992) and in sheep (Kendrick & Baldwin, 1987).

For those who are skeptical of the existence of universal emotions, new responses have now been provided by Ekman and his colleagues. The newest research on crosscultural universals in facial expressions of emotions shows a connection of facial display with physiology (as measured, e.g., by galvanic skin response or heart rate) and with regional activity of the brain. It is now reported that the same physiological effect (or brain activity) is also achieved when research subjects are instructed to put together a facial expression muscle by muscle (Ekman & Keltner, chap. 2, this volume; Ekman, Levenson, & Friesen, 1983; Levenson, Ekman, & Heider, 1992). Meanwhile, in response to those who argue for a purely cultural or personal control of emotions, it has been shown that humans have, after all, a limited capacity for successfully masking their emotions. Humans are particularly good at distinguishing authentic from inauthentic smiles, as the external eye muscle involved in the so-called Duchenne smile typical of genuine happiness is not under voluntary control (Ekman, 1985; Ekman & Friesen, 1982; Ekman & Keltner, chap. 2, this volume). Some criticism of the research on universal emotions has suggested that it has focused too much on those basic emotions that can reliably be identified in the face (happiness, sadness, surprise, fear, anger, and disgust). There are now studies underway of universals that also involve body movement, particularly a tell-tale movement sequence indicating embarrassment (Ekman & Keltner, chap. 2, this volume).

Further evidence that the dispositions for interpersonal interaction in different nonverbal channels (face, voice, touch, etc.) are relatively hard-wired comes from research on grooming behavior (Suomi, chap. 7, this volume). Grooming is ubiquitous both in animals and humans–including German university students–but may recently have become "repressed" in Western culture (as manifested by the hairdresser and barber professions; Schiefenhövel, chap. 4, this volume). To the list of universal ritualized gestures collected over the years by the Eibl-Eibesfeldt school of human ethology (e.g., the famous eyebrow flash, a greeting that also indicates surprise or fear), two new candidates have now been added: the "nose wrinkle" as a gesture for slight social distancing and the "disgust face" as a strong signal of social repulsion. The suggestion is that both these ritualized gestures involve muscle movements that originally had to do with bad smells or vomiting, respectively (Schiefenhövel, chap. 4, this volume). Schiefenhövel explains the human capacity for cross-cultural understanding as grounded in our common anatomical-emotional history, a result of the fact that, morphologically, nature tends to utilize already existing organs for necessary new functions.

THE IMPORTANCE OF THE SOCIAL CONTEXT FOR THE DEVELOPMENT OF NONVERBAL SKILLS

Ever since Harlow's (1959) famous monkey experiments, in which infant monkeys preferred a terrycloth "mother" to a milk-providing wire "mother," Spitz' (1965) research on human infants, and Bowlby's (1969) studies of attachment and loss, the hard-wiredness of the mother–infant bond (i.e., our basic predisposition for affective sociality), has been clear (see Suomi, chap. 7, this volume). In fact, this is one of the tenets of social scientists. Further detailed studies of early mother–infant bonding show the role of nonverbal communication in the development of the infant's social skills, particularly through the infant's increasing realization of the social meaning of the smile (Schneider, chap. 6, this volume). Here, a new research finding is the important guiding role of parents in turning the biological infant into a cultural being (H. Papoušek & M. Papoušek, chap. 5, this volume).

Developmental research on monkeys also shows the continued role of the parent as a trainer of the infant's social capabilities. A dramatic example of how a nurturing environment may overcome a genetic handicap is the case of congenitally shy infant monkeys. Under the care of a nurturing foster mother, monkeys with such a shyness trait may in fact turn into superior social performers. There is also a clear link between stressful situations and elevated ACTH hormone levels for these genetically shy monkeys (Suomi, chap. 7, this volume).

In humans, this early bonding apparently helps prepare the way for the infant's later language development. Studies have shown that neonates not only lock into the gaze of their mothers, but also move rhythmically to the sounds of the mother's voice (Brazelton, Koslowski, & Main, 1974; Condon & Sander, 1974; H. Papoušek & M. Papoušek, chap. 5, this volume; Trevarthen, 1984). It even seems that infants at a very early stage learn to distinguish the sounds of their mother tongue from the sounds of other languages (Kuhl, Williams, & Lacerda, 1992). Indeed, preverbal communication is of increasing interest for students of language communication (see Velichkovsky & Rumbaugh, 1996).

THE CONVERGENCE OF APPROACHES IN HUMAN AND ANIMAL NONVERBAL COMMUNICATION STUDIES

It has already earlier been forcefully argued that it is a mistake to believe that human messages are typically cognitive and intentional whereas animal signals are typically expressive and involuntary (e.g., Marler, 1984). Now ingenious naturalistic and laboratory experiments with tape recorders and video cameras have further strengthened the thesis that animal signals may in fact function as rudimentary symbolic communication systems. In vervet monkeys, the alarm calls corresponding to threats from eagles, leopards, and snakes are all context sensitive (Cheney & Seyfarth, 1990; Marler & Evans, chap. 8, this volume). There is also an interesting parallel: In the same way that in children the meaning of words becomes more specified during the course of semantic development, vervet monkeys first show a generalized responsiveness to moving aerial stimuli, which is then sharpened by experience to correspond to one particular eagle species among many (Marler & Evans, chap. 8, this volume).

Furthermore, animal alarm calls are subject to an "audience effect"—they are not made if there is no obvious recipient (Marler & Evans, chap. 8, this volume). Working within a similar framework, Schneider looked at the audience effect in the smiles of young children. He found that in task-oriented situations, children's smiles could take on different natures: They were either of an expressive or communicative kind, depending on whether or not someone was watching (Schneider, chap. 6, this volume).

Considering that human ethologists tend to draw parallels between nonverbal behavior in humans and primates, it is interesting to have primatologists warn that we cannot always assume homology between facial expressions when comparing primate and human facial displays (S. Preuschoft & van Hooff, chap. 9, this volume). Even though phylogenetically, human smiles and laughter can be seen as modifications of the primate "silent bared-teeth" and "relaxed open-mouth" displays (originally denoting a fear grin or a friendly play face, respectively), primates may use smiles and laughter instrumentally (e.g., as appeasement strategies). Moreover, this varies with different primate species and societies (here "the power assymetry hypothesis" states that it is the social organization of the society that determines the particular forms these evolutionarily "emancipated" displays will take: Despotic societies are dependent on a clear distinction between displays for sub-mission and friendliness, whereas in egalitarian societies the distinction is blurred). In addition to social ecological explanations of this type, there appears to be an increasing interest in primate Machiavellianism, too, these days (D. S. Wilson, Near, & Miller, 1993). Thus, it seems that also when it comes to intentional behavior, animals are brought closer to humans.

Finally, it is possible to regard both nonverbal and language com-munication as evolutionary adaptations to particular ecological condi-tions. An "informed speculation" goes as follows (Maryanski, chap. 10, this volume). Instead of considering spoken language a mysterious property of humans, it might be seen as the end result of a series of changes of primate sensory modalities that first evolved in an arboreal zone and were later selectively modified during the adaptation of homi-nids to an open-country zone. After bipedalism had open up the vocal tract, there were good evolutionary reasons why the next step was bringing the vocal-auditory channel under cortical control (vision and touch already were). Cortical control made voluntary sounds possible. In turn, the vocal sounds under volitional control got connected with a cultural tradition involving symbols and intergenerational transmission (Maryanski, chap. 10, this volume).

THE ROLE OF NONVERBAL COMMUNICATION
FOR UNDERSTANDING HUMAN BEHAVIOR

How can these various research results on nonverbal communication, particularly the communciation of emotion, help us better understand human interaction? In the first place, it can be said that our everyday intuitions have been substantiated. Emotions are indeed easily perceived and felt, which gives us a basis for empathic understanding across languages and cultures. The "contagiousness" of some emotions suggests that emotions may indeed sweep through masses of people who are in close visual or physical contact (see Schiefenhövel, chap. 4, this volume). This is, in fact, a well-known social psychological process, which is probably directly connected to various collective phenomena, including Durkheim's famous *conscience collective*.

Furthermore, we can relatively easily detect nonverbal signs of deception, or even embarrassment (Ekman, 1985; Ekman & Keltner, chap. 2, this volume). Trying on the hat of the evolutionary biologist, we may ask: Can this be given an evolutionary explanation? One argument is that detection of lying may be important for the evolution of cooperation. It is important for us to know whom we can trust in order to establish long-term relationships with such persons. Meanwhile, one good indicator that we will be able to take a person on his or her word is that the person is an obviously bad liar. This can be assessed from telltale signs (Frank, chap. 15, this volume). What is interesting in this account is that nonverbal communication of genuine emotions, rather than the deceptive strategies typically favored in sociobiological reasoning (e.g., Krebs & Dawkins, 1978), is postulated as important for the evolution of social behavior.

We may also be able to spot lying because we are used to congruence between channels of communication (a phenomenon documented by Condon & Ogston, 1966, among others). In this case, it would make us sensitive to incongruence between the verbal and nonverbal channels, or between stated and felt commitment. Indeed, recent research in neuroscience suggests that the brain appears to have the ability to constantly cross-check information within itself. One model for this cross-checking capacity is provided by the famous model of the triune brain (MacLean, 1990). Here more ancient parts of the brain (the mammalian limbic system, which regulates emotions, and the Reptile complex, which is connected to primitive fight or flight behavior) are in constant communication with the neocortex.

It is true that nonverbal expression and body language form only a small part of the broad repertoire that humans have for communicating emotions or regulating status and power in interpersonal relationships (Heller, chap. 13, this volume). However, it may be an important tool for culture to work with. Human posture is a concrete example of nonverbal communication as a joint product of nature and culture. Here the natural constraints of the anatomy combine with the work requirements for particular professional groups, producing such things as backache (Heller, chap. 13, this volume). Another example of nonverbal communication as a mediator between nature and culture is the postulated transmission of culture-specific emotional attitudes by childrearing practices (Goldschmidt, chap. 12, this volume). These cultural practices interacting with the natural processes of child development may push personality development in a particular direction, emphasizing particular cultural sentiments and thus contributing to the production of a particular national character. Exploring the possible mechanisms involved here, Goldschmidt quotes earlier anthropological work on Balinese culture by Bateson and Mead (1942) and does a reanalysis of his own earlier study of the Sebei in Uganda, where he relates the "idle hands and absent eyes" of Sebei mothers to the typical lack of affective ties in Sebei society (Goldschmidt, chap. 10, this volume).

At the most general level, a way of summarizing the basic message of the conference for the social sciences could be the following: Nonverbal processes of emotional communication are inseparable from cognitive processes and play a crucial role in human social interaction at all four relevant levels; that is, the evolutionary, developmental, physiological and functional ones. Humans are phylogenetically predisposed to react emotionally to facial expressions, constantly switching roles as senders and receivers of nonverbal signals. When we see an expressed emotion, we mirror it, and it seems that this in turn elicits a physiological response and the appropriate feeling in us. This explains the ubiquity of empathy in interpersonal interaction. In turn, this process lies at the basis of social communication. We are biologically preprogrammed for sociality and continuously monitor one another for emotional cues that serve as guides to future interaction.

THE BIOLOGICAL GROUNDING
OF SOCIAL CONSTRUCTION

Despite the seemingly increasing convergence between nature and nurture in nonverbal communication studies, the battle for an interactional approach is not yet won. Recently, there has been a resurgence of the militant cultural perspective, this time under the label of the social construction of emotions (e.g., Harré, 1986). The argument here is that people learn to label a state of general physiological arousal based on categories obtained from their culture. (The physiological arousal as such is not in question.) In its structure, the social constructivist claim appears quite similar to the previous linguistic relativist thesis of the cultural determination of our categories of thought, except that here we are dealing with emotions rather than cognitions. A good example of the possibility of radical cultural or temporal conventionalism in nonverbal communication is the code of silence in medieval monasteries, in which ostensibly "obvious" gestures and signs may have quite unexpected meanings. As to the social conventions typical for an epoch, interesting information can be derived from studying postures and gestures in medieval pictures (Nitschke, chap.14, this volume). Interestingly, however, even here there appears to be a limited range of possibilities.

There is no doubt that culture has a major say in the case of nonverbal communication. We are interested here merely in pointing out the following:

1. There seems to exist a biological basis for cultural influences to work with; that is, some capabilities are hard-wired and others develop particularly easily. This should come as no surprise to those who accept the idea of our innate capacity for language, critical periods for learning, or the idea of stages of development.

2. There are crossculturally understandable basic emotions and a universal basis for human empathy. This is another unsurprising point, it seems, considering humans' proven abilities to travel and get by without knowing languages.

3. Finally, although it is certainly possible to manage emotions to some extent (see, e.g., Hochschild, 1983), emotions cannot always be successfully brought under conscious control. More than a decade ago, in his remarkable attempt to bridge the gap between the Two Cultures, Reynolds (1980) stated that even though we con-

struct our social reality in our minds, cultures have to work within the limits of human physical capability, and that stress is one of many examples of a conflict between the body and the exigencies of modern culture.

Interestingly, one of the most adamant current spokesmen against the social construction of emotions is a sociologist, Theodore Kemper (1978, 1987, 1990), a leading figure in the recent field of the sociology of emotions. In support of his position, he quoted physiological data (studies of epinephrine and norepinephrine levels, serotonin, and activity patterns in the nervous systems). Turner (chap. 11, this volume) provides a suggestive overview of the function and possible evolutionary rationale of nonverbal and emotional communication for human society. He suggests, among other things, that the development of emotional communication in humans was a necessary prerequisite for social bonding among asocial hominids (see Maryanski & J. H. Turner, 1992).

Perhaps the best route for combatting exaggerated claims of the social construction of emotions may be to point to the close interrelation between cognition and emotion. Indeed, the cognitive revolution's overemphasis on the linguistic capabilities of humans makes it seem worthwhile to try to re-establish a central role of emotion as a guide for cognition (e.g., Plutchik, 1984; Zajonc, 1980). To the extent one is willing to accept the reality of cognitive biases in human reasoning (Nisbett & Ross, 1980; Tversky & Kahneman, 1974), it seems but a step toward accepting the existence of basic emotional biases, too. There is exciting research going on in this area (e.g., Barkow, Cosmides, & Tooby, 1992). The question is what form these predispositions need to take; for example, do we need to postulate the existence of ready-made Darwinian algorithms for problem solving (Tooby & Cosmides, 1989, 1990), or should we settle instead for a minimalist approach, whereby it would suffice to postulate the existence of an initial inborn emotional bias for or against particular stimuli, which would thereafter be instrumental in the development of neural networks in the brain, mental maps, and so on—in short, for the cognitive development of the mind (Edelman, 1992)?

The excitement of current research in nonverbal communication reinforces our belief that this is a strategic site for addressing the multilevel interaction between biology and culture. Our belief is that once it again becomes commonplace to consider the biological makeup of humans as an element in social scientific explanations, a whole range of new theoretical possibilities will open up. We see as our task as editors to try to bring this sense of opportunity to the reader. At the very least, we hope to be able to convince social scientists to start considering the vast body of empirical data on nonverbal communication that is now accumulating within various fields, including the sophisticated findings from psychophysiology and neurobiology.

Even though it seems that the academic climate today is moving away from the extreme cultural determinism of recent years, it may still be necessary to add the following caveat. The fact that we are interested in looking closely at biological, social, and psychological factors does not mean that we are suggesting any kind of "reduction" of the social sciences to biology. We want rather to refute the misconception that biology is something monolithic, threatening and deterministic, or something that automatically precludes or excludes culture. If anything, we want to point to the necessary grounding of our social and cultural capabilities in biological givens, and elucidate how these biological factors are systematically co-opted for cultural purposes, particularly for human interpersonal communication. In our view, nonverbal communication is not only a pedagogically useful site for concretely demonstrating the multilevel links between nature and nurture, it is the place where nature meets culture.

ACKNOWLEDGMENT

It is our sad duty here to inform readers of the untimely death of Klaus Schneider as this volume was going to press.

The participants of the conference will remember Klaus Schneider as a distinguished scholar and an esteemed colleague.

REFERENCES

Barkow, J. H., Cosmides, L., & Tooby, J. (1992). *The adapted mind: Evolutionary psychology and the generation of culture.* New York: Oxford University Press.

Bateson, G., & Mead, M. (1942). *Balinese character: A photographic analysis.* New York: New York Academy of Sciences.

Birdwhistell, R. (1970). *Kinesics and context.* Philadelphia: University of Pennsylvania Press.

Bornstein, M. H. (1976). Infants' recognition memory for hue. *Developmental Psychology, 12,* 185–191.

Bornstein, M. H. (1996). Origins of communication in infancy. In B. M. Velichkovsky & D. M. Rumbaugh (Eds.), *Communicating meaning: The evolution and development of language* (pp. 139–172). Mahwah, NJ: Lawrence Erlbaum Associates.

Bowlby, J. (1969). *Attachment and loss*. New York: Basic Books.

Brazelton, T. B., Koslowski, B., & Main, M. (1974). The origins of reciprocity: The early mother–infant interaction. In M. Lewis & L. A. Rosenblum (Eds.), *Origins of behavior. Vol. I: The effect of the infant on its caregiver* (pp. 49–76). New York: Wiley.

Brown, D. E. (1991). *Human universals*. Philadelphia: Temple University Press.

Cheney, D. L., & Seyfarth, R. M. (1990). *How monkeys see the world: Inside the mind of another species*. Chicago: Chicago University Press.

Chevalier-Skolnikoff, S. (1973). Facial expressions of emotions in non-human primates. In P. Ekman (Ed.), *Darwin and facial expression* (pp. 11–89). New York: Academic Press.

Collins, R. (1975). *Conflict sociology*. New York: Academic Press.

Collins, R. (1981). On the micro-foundations of macro-sociology. *American Journal of Sociology, 86,* 984–1014.

Condon, W. S., & Sander L. W. (1974). Neonate movement is synchronized with adult speech: Interactional participation and language acquisition. *Science, 183,* 99–101.

Condon, W. S., & Ogston, W. D. (1966). Sound film analysis of normal and pathological behavior patterns. *Journal of Nervous and Mental Disease, 143,* 338–347.

Cosmides, L., Tooby, J., & Barkow, J. (1992). The psychological foundations of culture. In J. H. Barkow, L. Cosmides, & J. Tooby (Eds.), *The adapted mind: Evolutionary psychology and the generation of culture* (pp. 19–136). New York: Oxford University Press.

Darwin, C. (1872). *The expression of the emotions in man and animals*. London: John Murray. Chicago: University of Chicago Press, 1965.

Dimberg, U. (1982). Facial reactions to facial expression. *Psychophysiology, 19,* 643–647.

Edelman, G. (1992). *Bright air, brilliant fire: On the matter of the mind*. New York: Basic Books.

Eibl-Eibesfeldt, I. (1972). Similarities and differences between cultures in expressive movements. In R. A. Hinde (Ed.), *Nonverbal communication* (pp. 297–314). Cambridge, UK: Cambridge University Press.

Eibl-Eibesfeldt, I. (1973). The expressive behavior of the deaf-and-blind born. In M. von Cranach & I. Vine (Eds.), *Social communication and movement* (pp. 163–194). London: Academic Press.

Eibl-Eibesfeldt, I. (1989). *Human ethology*. New York: Aldine de Gruyter.

Ekman, P. (Ed.) (1973). *Darwin and facial expression*. New York: Academic Press.

Ekman, P. (1982). *Emotions in the human face*. Cambridge, UK: Cambridge University Press.

Ekman, P. (1985). *Telling lies: Clues to deceit in the marketplace, marriage, and politics*. New York: Norton.

Ekman, P., & Friesen, W. V. (1969). The repertoire of non-verbal behaviour: Categories, origins, usage and coding. *Semiotica, 1,* 49–98.

Ekman, P., & Friesen, W. V. (1975). *Unmasking the face: A guide to recognising emotions from facial clues*. Englewood Cliffs, NJ: Prentice-Hall.

Ekman, P., & Friesen, W. V. (1978). *Facial action coding system: A technique for the measurement of facial movement*. Palo Alto, CA: Consulting Psychologists Press.

Ekman, P., & Friesen, W. V. (1982). Felt, false and miserable smiles. *Journal of Nonverbal Behavior, 6,* 238–252.

Ekman, P., Levenson, R. W., & Friesen, W. V. (1983). Autonomic nervous system activity distinguishes among emotions. *Science, 221,* 1208–1210.

Field, T. M., Woodson, R., Greenberg, R., & Cohen, D. (1982). Discrimination and imitation of facial expressions by neonates. *Science, 218,* 179–181.

Fox, R. (1989). *The search for society: Quest for a biosocial science of morality.* New Brunswick, NJ: Rutgers University Press.

Garfinkel, A. (1967). *Studies in ethnomethodology.* Englewood Cliffs, NJ: Prentice-Hall.

Geschwind, N. (1979). Specialization in the human brain. *Scientific American, 241,* 180–201.

Giddens, A. (1984). *The constitution of society.* Berkeley: University of California Press.

Goffman, E. (1959). *The presentation of self in everyday life.* Harmondsworth, UK: Penguin.

Goffman, E. (1972). *Relations in public.* New York: Harper Colophon.

Hall, E. T. (1959). *The silent language.* New York: Fawcett.

Hall, E. T. (1966). *The hidden dimension.* New York: Doubleday.

Hall, E. T. (1977). *Beyond culture.* Garden City, NY: Anchor Press, Doubleday.

Harlow, H. (1959). Love in infant monkeys. *Scientific American, 20,* 2–8.

Harnad, S. (1996). The origin of words: A psychophysical approach. In B. M. Velichkovsky & D. M. Rumbaugh (Eds.), *Communicating meaning: The evolution and development of language* (pp. 27–44). *Mahwah, NJ: Lawrence Erlbaum Associates.*

Harré, R. (Ed.). (1986). *The social construction of emotions.* Oxford, UK: Basil Blackwell.

Hinde, R. A. (1987). *Individuals, relationships and culture: Links between ethology and the social sciences.* Cambridge, UK: Cambridge University Press.

Hochschild, A. (1983). *The managed heart: The commercialization of human feeling.* Berkeley: University of California Press.

Hooff, van, J. A. R. A. M. (1972). A comparative approach to the phylogeny of laughter and smiling. In R. A. Hinde (Ed.), *Nonverbal communication* (pp. 209–241). Cambridge, UK: Cambridge University Press.

Izard, C. E. (1977). *Human emotions.* New York: Plenum.

Johnson, M. H., Dziurawiec, S., Ellis, H., & Morton, J. (1991). Newborns' preferential tracking of face-like stimuli and its subsequent decline. *Cognition, 40,* 1–19.

Kemper, T. D. (1978). *A social interactional theory of emotions.* New York: Wiley.

Kemper, T. D. (1987). How many emotions are there? Wedding the social and the autonomic components. *American Journal of Sociology, 93,* 263–289.

Kemper, T. D. (1990). *Research agendas in the sociology of emotions.* Albany: SUNY Press.

Kendrick, K., & Baldwin, B. (1987). Cells in temporal cortex of conscious sheep can respond preferentially to sight of faces. *Science, 236,* 448–450.

Knapp, M. L. (1978). *Nonverbal communication in human interaction.* New York: Holt, Rinehart & Winston.

Krebs, J. R., & Dawkins, R. (1978). Animal signals: Information or manipulation? In J. R. Krebs & N. B. Davies (Eds.), *Behavioural ecology: An evolutionary approach* (pp. 282-309). Oxford, UK: Blackwell.

Kuhl, P. K., Williams, K. A., & Lacerda, F. (1992). Linguistic experience alters phonetic perception in infants by 6 months of age. *Science, 255,* 606–608.

Leach, E. (1981). Sociobiology and anthropology: Wedding or rape? *Nature, 291,* 267–268.

Levenson, R. W., Ekman, P., & Heider, K. (1992). Emotion and autonomic nervous system activity in the Minangkabau of West Sumatra. *Journal of Personality and Social Psychology, 62,* 972–988.

MacLean, P. D. (1990). *The triune brain in evolution.* New York: Plenum.

Marler, P. (1984). Animal communication: Affect or cognition? In K. R. Scherer & P. Ekman (Eds.), *Approaches to emotion* (pp. 345–365). Hillsdale, NJ: Lawrence Erlbaum Associates.

Maryanski, A. R., & Turner, J. H. (1992). *The social cage: Human nature and the evolution of society.* Stanford, CA: Stanford University Press.

McDougall, W. (1908). *Introduction to social psychology.* London: Methuen.

Mead, G, H. (1934). *Mind, self and society.* Chicago: University of Chicago Press.

Meltzoff, A. N. (1985). The roots of social and cognitive development: Models of man's original nature. In T. M. Field & N. Fox (Eds.), *Social perception in infants* (pp. 1–30). Norwood, NJ: Ablex.

Meltzoff, A, N., & Moore, K. M. (1977). Imitation of facial and manual gestures in human neonates. *Science, 198*, 75–78.

Molnár, P. (1990). A kapaszkodasi reflex humanetologiai megkozelitese (A human ethology explanation of clinging reflex). *Pszichologia, 3*, 441–446.

Nisbett, R., & Ross, L. (1980). *Human inference: Strategies and shortcomings of social judgment.* Englewood Cliffs, NJ: Prentice-Hall.

Öhman, A. (1986). Face the beast and fear the face: Animal and racial fears as prototypes for evolutionary analyses for emotion. *Psychophysiology, 23*, 123–145.

Öhman, A., & Dimberg, U. (1978). Facial expressions as conditioned stimuli for electrodermal response: A case study of "preparedness." *Journal of Personality and Social Psychology, 36*, 1251–1258.

Perrett, D., Rolls, E., & Caan, W. (1982). Visual neurons responsive to faces in monkey temporal cortex. *Experimental Brain Research, 47*, 329–342.

Plutchik, R. (1984). Emotions: A general psychoevolutionary theory. In K. R. Scherer & P. Ekman (Eds.), *Approaches to emotion* (pp. 197–219). Hillsdale, NJ: Lawrence Erlbaum Associates.

Reynolds, V. (1980). *The biology of human action.* Oxford, UK: Freeman.

Sackett, G. (1966). Monkeys reared in isolation with pictures as visual input: Evidence for an innate releasing mechanism. *Science, 154*, 1468–1473.

Sahlins, M. D. (1976). *The use and abuse of biology: An anthropological critique of sociobiology.* Ann Arbor: University of Michigan Press.

Sapir, E. (1949). *Selected writings in language, culture and personality.* Berkeley: University of California Press.

Scheff, T. J. (1990). *Microsociology: Discourse, emotion and social structure.* Chicago: University of Chicago Press.

Segerstråle, U. (1992). Reductionism, "bad science" and politics: A critique of anti-reductionist reasoning. *Politics and the Life Sciences, 11* (2), 199–214.

Shepard, R. N. (1992). The perceptual organization of colors: An adaptation to regularities of the terrestrial world? In J. H. Barkow, L. Cosmides, & J. Tooby (Eds.), *The adapted mind: Evolutionary psychology and the generation of culture* (pp. 495–532). New York: Oxford University Press.

Spitz, R. (1965). *The first year of life: A study of normal and deviant development of object relations.* New York: International Universities Press.

Steiner, J. E. (1979). Human facial expressions in response to taste and smell stimulation. *Advances in Child Development and Behavior, 13*, 257–295.

Tinbergen, N. (1963). On aims and method of ethology. *Zeitschrift für Tierpsychologie, 20*, 410–433.

Tomkins, S. S. (1962). *Affect, imagery, consciousness: Vol. 1. The positive affects.* New York: Springer-Verlag.

Tooby, J., & Cosmides, L. (1989). Evolutionary psychology and the generation of culture, Part I. Theoretical considerations. *Ethology and Sociobiology, 10*, 29–49.

Tooby, J., & Cosmides, L. (1990). The past explains the present: Emotional adaptations and the structure of ancestral environments. *Ethology and Sociobiology, 11*, 375–424.

Trevarthen, C. (1984). Emotions in infancy: Regulators of contact and relationships with persons. In K. R. Scherer & P. Ekman (Eds.), *Approaches to emotion* (pp. 129–157). Hillsdale, NJ: Lawrence Erlbaum Associates.

Tversky, A., & Kahneman, D. (1974). Judgment under uncertainty: Heuristics and biases. *Science, 183*, 1124–1131.

Velichkovsky, B. M., & Rumbaugh, D. M. (Eds.) (1996). *Communicating meaning: The evolution and development of language.* Mahwah, NJ: Lawrence Erlbaum Associates.

Weiss, R. (1988, November 19). Discriminating neurons pick the right face (monkey temporal lobe facial recognition cells; work of Michael E. Hasselmo and Gordon Bayliss). *Science News, 134,* 326.

Whorf, B. L. (1956). *Language, thought and reality.* Cambridge, MA: MIT Press.

Wiegele, T. C. (Ed.). (1979). *Biopolitics: Search for a more human political science.* Boulder, CO: Westview Press.

Wilson, D. S., Near, D. C., & Miller, R. (1993, August). *Machiavellianism: A synthesis of the evolutionary and psychological literatures.* Paper presented at the fifth annual meeting of the Human Behavior and Evolution Society, Binghamton, NY.

Wilson, E. O. (1975). *Sociobiology: The new synthesis.* Cambridge, MA: Harvard University Press.

Young, M. P., & Yamane, S. (1992). Sparse population coding of faces in the inferotemporal cortex (macaques). *Science, 256,* 1327–1331.

Zajonc, R. (1980). Feeling and thinking: Preferences need no inferences. *American Psychologist, 35,* 151–175.

PART I

New Findings on the Universality
of Human Nonverbal
Communication

The first part of this book is devoted to human universals. After an earlier impasse between the two opposing camps in nonverbal communication—the anthropological linguists, who emphasized the cultural determination of nonverbal behavior, and the cross-cultural psychologists, psychophysiologists, and human ethologists who argued for the universality of basic emotions and behaviors—the balance now seems to have shifted toward the universalists. However, they are typically more interested in demonstrating the universal human capabilities for communication than the universality of particular behaviors; they, too, recognize the role of cultural tradition.

Paul Ekman and Dacher Keltner report on the studies on facial expressions coming out of Ekman's UCSF laboratory as well as Ekman's many ongoing collaborative projects. The psychophysiological approach to nonverbal communication is represented by Ulf Dimberg, working within the tradition of Arne Öhman in psychology at Uppsala University. A decade ago they together outlined an evolutionary perspective on human social behavior (Öhman & Dimberg, 1984), a forerunner to later efforts by evolutionary psychologists (e.g., Tooby & Cosmides, 1989, 1990). We also get an update on studies within the human ethological tradition by Wulf Schiefenhövel, an anthropologist and medical doctor, and a collaborator of Eibl-Eibesfeldt at the Max-Planck Institute near Munich.

Ekman and Keltner review famous earlier theories championing cultural specificity in nonverbal communication (Birdwhistell, 1970; Klineberg, 1938; LaBarre, 1947) and suggest that these theorists did not distinguish between voluntary and involuntary emotional expressions. Meanwhile, recent research shows that it is possible to distinguish the smile of true enjoyment from that of other types of smiles, and also a telltale smile of embarrassment from a smile of amusement. Also, it seems that voluntary facial movements are capable of generating changes in the activity of the nervous systems, suggesting a direct link between facial expressions and physiology.

In the second chapter Dimberg presents evidence to support his claim that from an evolutionary perspective, humans are preprogrammed to act both as senders and receivers in emotional face-to-face communications. The appropriate response patterns appearing in relation to facial expressions of emotion are extremely fast: They can be detected by electrographic techniques as early as $1/3$ of a second after stimulus onset, revealing the presence of fast operating affect programs. He also presents data supporting the notion of an inborn preference for human faces (or facelike features) in newborns, as well as an easily triggered fear reaction to negative faces.

Schiefenhövel discusses the evolutionary rationale for the likelihood of universals in human nonverbal behavior: our common anatomy and the tendency of evolution to utilize already available mor-

25

phological features for new functions. He explains the "nose wrinkle" and the "disgust face" as ritualized gestures, whereby muscles involved in actual bodily functions are utilized to convey a new cultural meaning of social disapproval. He also addresses the ubiquitous phenomenon of social grooming and the physiological, evolutionary, and social advantages of this behavior. Here he draws on his own anthropological research in the Trobriand Islands, New Guinea, and Germany, as well as recent hospital studies (Strecke, 1991). As an interactional process, grooming is of potentially central importance for understanding the effects of emotions on social structure (e.g., Gordon, 1990). Finally, recent "cultural repression" of grooming in the West shows how culture may, in fact, redirect human nature.

REFERENCES

Birdwhistell, R. (1970). *Kinesics and context.* Philadelphia: University of Pennsylvania Press.

Gordon, S. L. (1990). Social structural effects on emotions. In T. Kemper (Ed.), *Research agendas in the sociology of emotions* (pp. 145–179). Albany: SUNY Press.

Klineberg, O. (1938). Emotional expression in Chinese literature. Journal of Abnormal and Social Psychology, 33, 517–520.

LaBarre, W. (1947). The cultural basis of emotions and gestures. Journal of Personality, 16, 49–68.

Öhman, A., & Dimberg, U. (1984). An evolutionary perspective on human social behavior. In W. M. Waid (Ed.), *Sociophysiology.* New York: Springer-Verlag.

Strecke, D. (1991). Psychophysiologische Effekte der Körperberührung bei Patienten auf einer Intensivstation (Psychophysiological effects of body contact on patients in intensive care) . Diplomarbeit. München: Technische Universität.

Tooby, J., & Cosmides, L. (1989). Evolutionary psychology and the generation of culture. Part I. Theoretical considerations. Ethology and Sociobiology, 10, 29-49.

Tooby, J., & Cosmides, L. (1990). The past explains the present: Emotional adaptations and the structure of ancestral environments. Ethology and Sociobiology, 11, 375-424.

2

UNIVERSAL FACIAL EXPRESSIONS OF EMOTION: AN OLD CONTROVERSY AND NEW FINDINGS

Paul Ekman
University of California, San Francisco

Dacher Keltner
University of California, Berkeley

More than a century ago, Darwin published his work *The Expression of the Emotions in Man and Animals* (1872), 13 years after his revolutionary *The Origin of the Species* (1859). Darwin claimed that we cannot understand human emotional expression without understanding the expressions of animals; for, he argued, our emotional expressions are in large part determined by our evolution.

Amazingly, Darwin's book had very little influence up until 20 years ago. The empirical research on facial expressions of emotion following Darwin's expression book was quite episodic. A number of recent trends, however, have contributed to the resurgence of interest in facial expression in the last 20 years. These include the work of Tomkins (1962, 1963), who provided a theoretical rationale for studying the face as a means for learning about personality and emotion; the application of ethological methods and concepts to human behavior, with emphasis placed on the biological bases of behavior and commonalities in social behavior across cultures; developmental psychologists' investigation of attachment, mother–infant interaction, and the development of emotion; and new methods for measuring the face. These trends have generated research that indicates there are universals in facial expressions of emotion. Before describing that evidence, the cultural specificity view of facial expressions of emotion, which dominated the field up until recently, is first discussed.

THE CULTURE-SPECIFIC VIEWPOINT

A. Theorists

Three theorists were extremely influential in anthropology and psychology for a number of decades, arguing that the information signaled by facial expressions is specific to each culture. None provided much evidence, but their views merit consideration both for historical reasons and to elucidate certain theoretical issues they ignored that are relevant to understanding the signal value of facial expressions.

"What is shown on the face is written there by culture." Klineberg claimed he never made that statement, although it was attributed to him. He did argue, in a more tentative way, for that view. Commenting on an anthropologist's account of how people arriving in a village wore a fierce look rather than a smile, Klineberg (1940) said:

> Not only may joy be expressed without a smile, but in addition the smile may be used in a variety of situations a smile may mean contempt, incredulity, affection … [quoting from Lafacadio Hearn's observation of the Japanese] Samurai women were required, like the women of Sparta, to show signs of joy on hearing that their husbands or sons had fallen in battle. (pp. 194f).

Birdwhistell (1970), an anthropologist with training in linguistics, dance, and dance notation, was another influential advocate of this view. He claimed that facial expressions are part of what he termed *kinesics*, which can best be viewed as another language, with the same type of units and organization as spoken language.

> Early in my research on human body motion, influenced by Darwin and by my own preoccupation with human universals, I attempted to study the human smile. Not only did I find that a number of my subjects "smiled" when they were subjected to what seemed to be a positive environment but some "smiled" in an aversive one (p. 29f). This search for universals was culture bound. There are probably no

universal symbols of emotional state. We can expect them [emotional expressions] to be learned and patterned according to the particular structure of particular societies. (p. 126)

Klineberg and Birdwhistell's observations highlight both a methodological and conceptual problem. First consider the methodological problem that is due to the use of imprecise behavioral description. The term *smile* unfortunately covers too many different facial expressions. Ekman and Friesen (1976) distinguished dozens of such smiling expressions, each of which involves the deployment of different sets of muscle actions. Each of these smiles differs in appearance, although in each the lip corners are drawn upward. The evidence to be described later about smiling shows that when different forms of smiling are distinguished, they are found to occur in quite different circumstances. Two forms of smiling occur in other than pleasant situations, another occurs when politeness is called for, another when enjoyment is experienced, and another when embarrassment is experienced.

It is confusing to call these all smiling, implying that they are a singular, unified category of behavior. When these different lip-corner-up appearances are treated by the observer as one entity, then, it will appear, as it did to Klineberg and Birdwhistell, that the smile has no common meaning. It is only by understanding the anatomy of facial action, by experience in the close description of facial behavior, that such errors in describing facial behavior can be avoided. The problem of treating smiles as a unitary category is especially acute when observations are made in real time without the opportunity to review the behavior repeatedly and at slowed motion, and when the observations are made by a single observer, so there is no capability to check on interobserver reliability. Imprecise terms such as *frown, grimace,* and *scowl,* like smile, encourage observers to miss what may be important distinctions.

The conceptual problem underlying the claims of Klineberg and Birdwhistell is their failure to consider the possibility that differences in observed facial expression may be due to culturally imposed attempts to manage universal expressions. They treated facial expression as if it is a totally involuntary system, not capable of being voluntarily controlled. Ekman and Friesen (1969) coined the phrase *display rules* to refer to such norms about who can show which emotion to whom, and when. People learn to interfere, they proposed, with facial expressions of emotion. The observation that Klineberg cited of the fierce look during a greeting could, from this vantage point, be due to a display rule to mask the appearance of happiness. Similarly, the smiling appearance of the grieving Samurai women could be a display rule to cover any sadness or distress with the appearance of polite smiling.

It would be quite damaging to the conclusion that there are universal expressions of emotion if there were clear evidence that when people are in a negative affect situation (experiencing pain, sadness, disgust, fear, or anger), they show an expression in which the lip corners go up—but only if the following other explanations can be ruled out:

1. The subject who shows this smiling countenance does not believe that negative feelings must be masked with a simulated, deliberate smile.

2. The smile is not a comment added by the subject to signal that the negative experience can be endured (a grin-and-bear-it smile, or what Ekman and Friesen called a "miserable smile").

3. The smile incorporates the features that Ekman and Friesen have found to occur when enjoyment is experienced (see following description), as distinct from polite or masking smiles.

There is no such evidence.

LaBarre (1947) made his major argument against universality 9 years after Klineberg. He failed to distinguish facial expressions of emotion from gestures, as seen in his statement "there is no natural language of emotional gesture" (p. 55). The distinction between gesture and emotional expression is not an easy one, but it is necessary, because gestures are socially learned and culturally variable, whereas there is strong evidence that facial expressions of emotion are not. Ekman and Friesen (1969) subdivided gestures into what they termed *illustrators*, movements that punctuate or help to illustrate simultaneous speech, and *emblems*, a term first suggested by Efron (1941), which refers to movements that have a direct verbal translation, a dictionary definition known to all members of a culture or subculture.

Any message can be conveyed by an emblem, including factual information, commands, attitudes, and—here is the complication—feelings. The latter Ekman called *referential expressions*, expressions that refer to emotions, performed in a way that signals that the emotion is not felt when the expression is made. The message conveyed by an emotional expression is, by definition, a feeling of the moment, providing information about likely antecedent events, consequent events, and so on. Ekman (1979) gave a more complete explanation of the differences between referential and emotional expressions.

It would take us too far afield to discuss thoroughly the differences between emblems, illustrators, and conversational regulators (which collectively Ekman [1979] called *conversational signals*) as compared to emotional expressions. It is sufficient to draw attention to the fact that every facial movement is not an emotional expression. Although many conversational signals involve the hands, some do involve the face. Facial action is not dedicated solely to emotional expression. Brow raising, brow lowering, and a number of different types of actions that pull the lip corners up are among the most common conversational signals. LaBarre failed to clearly make these distinctions.

Darwin also was not completely consistent in this regard. Darwin was primarily concerned with emotional expressions, which he considered innately determined and thereby universal. Although he mentioned a few emblems that he considered universal, he acknowledged that most were culture specific. LaBarre, on the other hand, focused primarily on emblems, although he included some emotional expressions and referential expressions.

UNIVERSAL FACIAL EXPRESSIONS

In the early 1970s there were two challenges to the culture-specific view of facial expressions of emotion: a critical re-evaluation of the experiments that had supported that position (Ekman, Friesen, & Ellsworth, 1972); and, more importantly, new cross-cultural data. Izard (1971), and also Friesen and Ekman conducted similar studies of literate cultures, working independently but at the same time.

In each culture, subjects were presented with photographs of posed Caucasian facial expressions similar to those presented in Fig. 2.1. Subjects were asked to choose the emotion term that best matched the emotion shown in the photograph. Although Izard and Ekman each showed different photographs, gave the subjects somewhat different lists of emotion terms, and examined people in different cultures, both obtained consistent evidence of agreement across more than a dozen Western and non-Western literate cultures in the labeling of enjoyment, anger, fear, sadness, disgust, and surprise facial expressions.

In order to rule out the possibility that such agreement could be due to members of every culture having learned expressions from a shared mass media input, Ekman and Friesen also studied a visually isolated preliterate culture in New Guinea (Ekman & Friesen, 1971; Ekman,

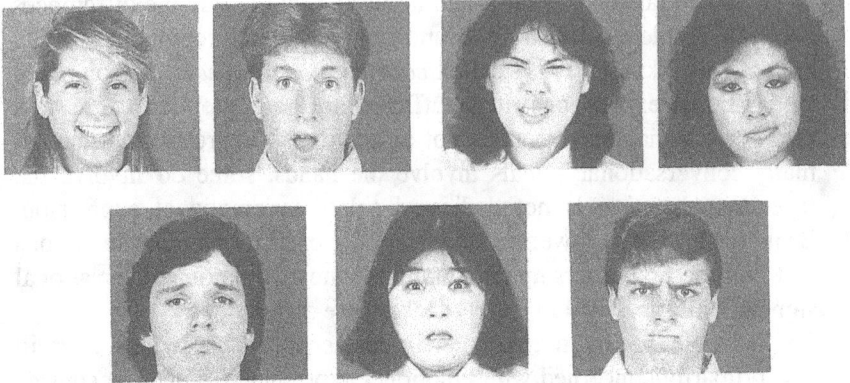

Fig. 2.1. Starting in the upper left corner and moving clockwise, the emotions posed are: happiness, surprise, disgust, contempt, anger, fear, and sadness.

Sorenson, & Friesen, 1969). They replicated their literate culture findings, as did Heider and Rosch (as reported in Ekman, 1972) a few years later in another visually isolated culture in what is now West Irian. Although surprise expressions were distinguished from anger, fear, sadness, disgust and enjoyment expressions in both preliterate cultures, surprise was not distinguished from fear expressions in one of the preliterate, visually isolated cultures. Ekman and Friesen also reversed the research design and found that when New Guineans posed facial expressions they were understandable to Western observers.

To reconcile these findings of universality with the many reports by cultural anthropologists of culture-specific facial expressions, Ekman and Friesen (1969) postulated display rules to describe what they presumed cultures teach their members about the management of expression in social contexts. Cultural variations in display rules could explain how universal expressions might be modified in social situations to create the impression of culture-specific facial expressions of emotion. They tested this idea in a study comparing the spontaneous expressions of Japanese and Americans observed in response to films evocative of fear and disgust. In each country subjects were videotaped when they were alone (and presumably no display rules should operate) and when they were with another person. As predicted, there was no difference between cultures in the expressions shown when the subjects thought they were alone. When an authority figure was present, however, the Japanese masked negative expressions with the semblance of smile more than the Americans.

Ekman, Friesen, and Izard interpreted the evidence as showing universal facial expressions as posited by Tomkins, Plutchik (1962), and (much earlier), by Darwin (1872). Consistent with this evolutionary view of expression were other reports of similarities in expression in other primates and early appearance developmentally. Recently, there have been challenges to the claim of universality in facial expressions of emotion. Lutz and G. M. White (1986) cited anthropologists who regarded emotions as social constructions and reported cultures in which the emotions proposed as universal are neither named nor expressed. Unfortunately such reports are not substantiated by quantitative methods or protected against the potential for bias or error when the information is obtained by the single observer who formulated the hypothesis under study. There are no replicated findings, with safeguards against bias and data on interobserver reliability, that a facial expression signifies entirely different emotions in two cultures.

Ortony and T. J. Turner (1990) provided a different challenge, speculating that it is only the components of expressions and not the full emotional expressions that are universal. However, there is no evidence to support their contention, and their claims contradict what is known about the muscular basis for facial expression (Ekman, 1992). Their challenge to the evidence on universals in expression was born out of their desire to reject the theoretical position that there are any emotions that should be considered basic. Their stance required them also to dismiss developmental, phylogenetic, and physiological evidence consistent with an evolutionary view of facial expressions of emotion.

A new line of studies has identified one way in which cultures do differ in regard to facial expression. Ekman et al. (1987) reported evidence of cultural differences in the perception of the strength of an emotion rather than which emotion is shown in a facial expression. Japanese participants made less intense attributions than did Americans regardless of the emotion shown or whether the person showing the emotion was Japanese or American, male or female (Matsumoto & Ekman, 1989). This difference appears to be specific to the interpretation of facial expressions of emotions, because it was not found in the judgment of either nonfacial emotional stimuli or facial nonemotional stimuli (Matsumoto, 1991).

A number of empirical questions remain about universals in facial expression. We do not know how many expressions for each emotion are universal, for no one has systematically explored a variety of expressions for each emotion in multiple cultures. Nor is there certain knowledge about whether there are other emotions that have universal expressions. There is some evidence, but it is contradictory, for universal facial expressions for contempt, interest, shame, and guilt. Little is also known about cross-cultural differences in display rules, as a function of gender, role, age, and social context (but see recent work by Matsumoto, 1990).

FACIAL ACTION GENERATES EMOTION PHYSIOLOGY

Most emotion theorists emphasize the involuntary nature of emotional experience, ignoring those instances in which people choose to generate an emotion through reminiscence or by adopting the physical actions associated with a particular emotion (e.g., speaking more softly to deintensify anger or smiling to generate enjoyment). Facial expression from this vantage point is seen as one of a number of emotional responses that is generated centrally when an emotion is called forth by an event, memory, image, and so on.

A new role for facial expression was found in the collaboration between Ekman, Friesen and Levenson of the University of California at Berkeley (Ekman, Levenson, & Friesen, 1983). Voluntarily performing certain facial muscular actions generated involuntary changes in autonomic nervous system (ANS) activity (for review, see Levenson, 1994). Subjects were not asked to pose emotions, but instead to follow muscle-by-muscle instructions to configure their face into one of the expressions that had been found to be universal. For example, rather than ask a subject to pose anger, instructions stated: "Pull your eyebrows down and together, raise your upper eyelid and tighten your lower eyelid, narrow your lips and press them together." There was greater heart rate acceleration and increased skin conductance when subjects made the expressions for negative emotions (anger, disgust, and fear) as compared to the positive emotion of happiness. There was greater heart rate acceleration when subjects made the expression for anger, fear and sadness as compared to disgust, and increased finger temperature in anger as compared to fear.

This work has since been replicated in three more experiments (Levenson, Carstensen, Friesen, & Ekman, 1991; Levenson, Ekman, & Friesen, 1990), and a number of a possible artifacts that could have been responsible for this phenomenon have been ruled out: It occurs when subjects cannot see their own faces or the face of the person giving the instructions; it is not an artifact of somatic muscle activity; and, it is not due to differences in the difficulty of making the different facial configurations. The finding that voluntary facial action generates different patterns of ANS activity was also replicated in an older population (Levenson et al., 1991). Recently an experiment was conducted in another culture to determine whether these findings are specific to Americans, or are more general. A cultural group was selected—the Minangkabau of Sumatra—who differ from Western societies in language, religion (fundamentalist Moslem), and social organization (they are matrilineal, with inheritance through the mother's side of the family). The findings replicated (Levenson, Ekman, Heider, & Friesen, 1992) suggesting that this phenomenon may be pancultural.

There are several issues that are relevant to the fact that voluntary facial action generated physiological changes. The nature of the physiological changes themselves and their likely functions have been discussed elsewhere (Ekman, 1984; Ekman et al., 1983; Levenson et al., 1990). First is the consideration of whether these voluntary facial muscular performances generate emotion or only the physiology of emotion. The problem in answering this question is what to use as the criterion for emotion. Ekman and Levenson could not use either the face, which generated the response, nor the physiological changes that occurred when the facial actions were made because they wanted to know whether an emotion was experienced when these physiological changes were generated. Instead they had to rely on self-report, which is notoriously vulnerable to demand characteristics. They tried to minimize that by asking an open-ended question, and by also including in that question a probe about any physical sensations or memories. Few sensations or memories were reported, whereas on 78% of the trials, the subjects reported feeling an emotion. When subjects reported actually feeling the emotion associated with the expression they made, the ANS distinctions among the negative emotions were more pronounced. Clearly, considerably more research is needed to be certain that people actually are experiencing emotions in this task. Different self-report procedures should be used, perhaps also with manipulations about expectations, to learn how subjects construe the physiological changes that occur when they make the facial muscular actions.

A question can also be raised about whether the changes in ANS activity generated when subjects make the different facial expressions are unique to this specific task or would occur when emotion is brought about by more usual means. This raises the general question about whether ANS patterning is emotion specific or context specific (see a recent discussion by Stemmler, 1989). Ekman (1984) has proposed that the changes in both physiology and expression are emotion specific, but the results on this issue in the first study (Ekman et al., 1983) were not clear cut. They found both similarities and differences in the specific ANS patterns generated by the voluntary facial action task and by a task in which subjects were instructed to relive past emotional experience. Recently Ekman and Levenson (Levenson et al., 1991) obtained more consistent results, finding the same distinctions among negative emotions in ANS activity in both the voluntary facial action task and in the relived emotion task. Work now in progress is comparing the ANS activity that occurs with these two tasks and a task in which emotions are aroused by viewing short motion picture films.

The same question—are any observed patterns of activity emotion specific or task specific—can be asked about any emotional response, not just ANS physiology. Although there has been no specific study aimed at answering this question for facial activity, there is considerable evidence suggesting that the facial configuration (the specific pattern of facial muscular activity) is more emotion specific than task specific, whereas attempts to control the expression, the timing of the configurational changes, and the extent of activity all reflect the specifics of how the emotion was brought about. In work in progress, Ekman and Levenson are directly examining this issue for the face as well.

Before turning to the question of how voluntarily making different facial configurations generates different patterns of physiology, the focus is broadened to consider central nervous system (CNS) as well as ANS physiology, drawing on new findings in a collaboration between Ekman and Davidson, from the University of Wisconsin. Exactly the same task was employed, in which subjects followed muscle-by-muscle instructions to create different facial configurations. R. J. Davidson and his colleagues measured left and right frontal, temporal, and parietal electroencephalogram (EEG) activity. Different patterns of EEG activity occurred when subjects made the muscular movements that had been found universally for the emotions of happiness, anger, fear, sadness, and disgust. These findings await replication.

There are three quite different explanations of how voluntary facial action generates emotion-specific physiology. The first explanation posits a central, hard-wired connection between the motor cortex and other areas of the brain involved in directing the physiological changes that occur during emotion. Usually when emotions are aroused by the perception of a social event, a set of central commands produce patterned emotion-specific changes in multiple systems, including (but not limited to) such peripheral systems as facial expressions, vocalizations, skeletal muscular settings, and ANS activity. When there is no emotion operative, as in the described experiments, but one set of those commands is generated deliberately, the established emotion networks transmit the same patterned information, thereby generating the other emotion-specific response changes. The initiating actions need not be a facial expression; emotion-specific vocalizations, or respiratory patterns, for example, should do just as well.

A second group of alternative explanations could propose that any connection between expression and physiological change is learned and not hard-wired. The extreme version of this viewpoint sees emotions as totally socially constructed, and has no reason to expect that there always will be both an expression and a unique pattern of physiology in every emotion, let alone any connection between the two. Emotion-specific ANS activity might only be learned in those cultures that teach their members specific adaptive behaviors for an emotion, and there would be no reason for every culture to do so, or if they did, to teach the same adaptive pattern. If anger exists in two cultures, and it certainly need not in every culture, there would be no necessary reason that anger would be associated with fighting and the physiology that subserves such actions in any two cultures. Nor would there be any reason for expressions to be learned and associated with any physiology. Levenson and Ekman's findings (Levenson et al., 1991) of the same emotion-specific ANS physiology, and the capability for voluntary facial action to generate that activity, in a Moslem, matrilineal, Indonesian culture challenge such a radical social constructivist view. A more moderate social learning position, which allowed for universals in both expression and in physiology, might still claim that the link between the two is learned and not hard-wired, established through repeated co-occurrence.

A third set of alternative explanations emphasizes peripheral feedback from the facial actions themselves, rather than a central connection between the brain areas that direct those facial movements and other brain areas. This view includes variations in terms of whether it is feedback from the muscles, skin, or temperature changes and whether it is hard-wired or requires learning. This explanation is consistent with the views of Izard, Laird, Tomkins, and Zajonc.

For now, there is no clear empirical basis for a definitive choice among these explanations. Studies of people with facial paralysis who have no possibility of peripheral facial action or feedback will hopefully challenge that explanation. If there is a direct central connection, and if these people know how to deliberately and accurately make their facial muscles contract, then the patterned changes in their physiology should be observed, even though no facial action occurs. That study is not yet complete, and the results may be ambiguous. The findings may be negative not because the mechanism is not a central one, but because these patients may not be able to follow the instructions to attempt to contract specific facial muscles. We have no way to verify, as we can with normal subjects, that they actually produced the required facial muscle configuration.

THE SMILE OF ENJOYMENT

Failing to recognize that there are different types of smiling that may have different meanings has confused both psychologists and anthropologists. The appearance of smiling of some form in unpleasant circumstances led anthropologists such as Birdwhistell (1970) and La-Barre (1947) to proclaim that facial expressions are culture specific. Within psychology, the conclusion that facial expressions do not provide much accurate information about emotion—the position taken in W. A. Hunt's (1941) and Bruner and Tagiuri's (1954) influential literature reviews—relied heavily on experiments in which subjects smiled in unpleasant circumstances. The classic study by Landis (1924) found that subjects smiled as often when observing a rat being decapitated as when listening to music.

More recently, studies of interpersonal deception have obtained contradictory findings on smiling (see review by M. G. Frank, Ekman, & Friesen, 1993). The confusion might have been avoided if scientists in this century had read the French neuroanatomist Duchenne de Boulogne, who wrote in 1862. Although this work was not translated into English until recently (Duchenne, 1990), Darwin had described Duchenne's ideas about smiling in his own book on expression. Duchenne said that the smile of enjoyment could be distinguished from deliberately produced smiles by considering two facial muscles: zygomatic major, which pulls the lip corners up obliquely, and orbicularis oculi, which orbits the eye pulling the skin from the cheeks and forehead toward the eyeball. "The first [zygomatic major] obeys the will but the second [orbicularis oculi] is only put in play by the sweet emotions of the soul; the fake joy, the deceitful laugh, cannot provoke the contraction of this latter muscle" (p. 126). "[This muscle] does not obey the will; it is only brought into play by a true feeling... Its inertia in smiling unmasks a false friend" (p. 72).

Duchenne's observation is consistent with the finding that most people cannot voluntarily contract the outer portion of the muscle that orbits the eye, and would therefore not be able to include this action when they deliberately smile (Ekman, Roper, & J. C. Hager, 1980). Duchenne had not distinguished between the inner and outer part of the orbicularis oculi muscle, but Ekman and colleagues found that most people can voluntarily contract the inner portion of the orbicularis oculi muscle. They therefore modified Duchenne's formulation considering just the actions of the outer part of this muscle crucial for distinguishing the smile of enjoyment from other forms of smiling.

Ekman and Friesen (1982) also suggested that enjoyment smiles could be distinguished from other forms of smiling by the presence of certain other muscles, and by the symmetry and the timing of the smile. Ekman (1985) described some 18 different forms of smiling. He defined enjoyment smiles as those smiles associated with pleasure, relief, amusement, etc. Nonenjoyment smiles include masking smiles (in which the smile at least partially covers muscular movements associated with another emotion), false smiles (smiles intended to mislead another into believing enjoyment is felt when it is not), miserable smiles (grin and bear it smiles), and so on.

Although there has been some empirical support for each of the proposed markers that distinguish enjoyment from other smiling (e.g., Ekman, Friesen, & O'Sullivan, 1988, on other muscular differences; Ekman, J. C. Hager, & Friesen, 1981; J. C. Hager & Ekman, 1985, on symmetry; Hess & Kleck, 1990, on timing), the largest number of studies have examined Duchenne's observation. In all of these studies, the smile with contraction of the outer portion of the orbicularis oculi muscle (which in his honor Ekman called Duchenne's smile), is compared with other kinds of smiling which do not include that muscular action. Three types of evidence support Duchenne's distinction.

Social Context.   Ekman et al. (1988) found more Duchenne smiles when subjects truthfully described pleasant feelings than when they followed instructions to claim to be feeling pleasant when they were actually watching very gruesome surgical films. In another study (Ekman, R. J. Davidson, & Friesen, 1990) in which people were not asked to deceive but simply watched emotion-inducing films alone, there were more Duchenne smiles when they watched pleasant as compared to unpleasant films, but no difference in how often other kinds of smiling occurred. Ten-month-old infants showed more Duchenne smiles when approached by their mother and more of other kinds of smiling when approached by a stranger (N. A. Fox & R. J. Davidson, 1988). Five- to seven-year-old children showed more Duchenne smiles when they succeeded and more other kinds of smiling when they failed in a game (K. Schneider, 1987). Psychiatrically depressed patients showed more Duchenne smiles at time of discharge from a hospital as compared to time of admission, with no difference in other kinds of smiling (Matsumoto, 1987). Similarly, there was more Duchenne smiling in late as compared to early psychotherapy sessions, but only among patients who had improved (F. Steiner, 1986).

Persons.   Schizophrenic patients showed fewer Duchenne smiles than normal individuals but there was no difference between the groups in other kinds of smiling (Krause, Steimer, Sanger-Alt, & Wagner, 1989). Mothers who were referred to a clinic by the courts because they had abused their child showed less Duchenne smiles when interacting with a child than a control group of mothers who had evidenced no child abuse (Bugental, Blue, & J. Lewis, 1990). Levenson and Gottman found that happily married couples showed more Duchenne smiles than unhappily married couples, but there was no difference in other kinds of smiling (Levenson, 1989).

Other Emotional Responses.   Only the Duchenne smile correlated with self-reports of positive emotions after subjects had seen two films intended to induce positive affect, and only the Duchenne, not other kinds of smiling, predicted which of the positive films each subject reported liking best (Ekman et al., 1990). In that same study, different patterns of regional brain activity were found when the subjects showed the Duchenne as compared to other smiles. The study of 10-month-old infants (N. A. Fox & R. J. Davidson, 1988) also found differences in regional brain activity when the infants showed Duchenne as compared to non-Duchenne smiles. In Ekman's recent unpublished study with R. J. Davidson, different patterns of regional brain activity were found when subjects deliberately performed a Duchenne smile as compared to a nonDuchenne smile.

This is a remarkable convergence of evidence supporting the distinction between Duchenne and other kinds of smiling. No account should be taken of studies that claim to show smiles are unrelated to emotion (e.g., Fridlund, 1991), which continue to treat all smiles as a single category, not separating Duchenne from non Duchenne smiles.

Recent work has shown that the Duchenne smile is recognizable to observers who were able to distinguish enjoyment from nonenjoyment smiles when they viewed a series of smiles (M. G. Frank, Ekman, & Friesen, 1993). The Duchenne smile was not related to observers' attributions when this type of smiling was embedded within the usual context competing for attention with speech content, voice, and gesture (Ekman, O'Sullivan, Friesen, & Scherer, 1991).

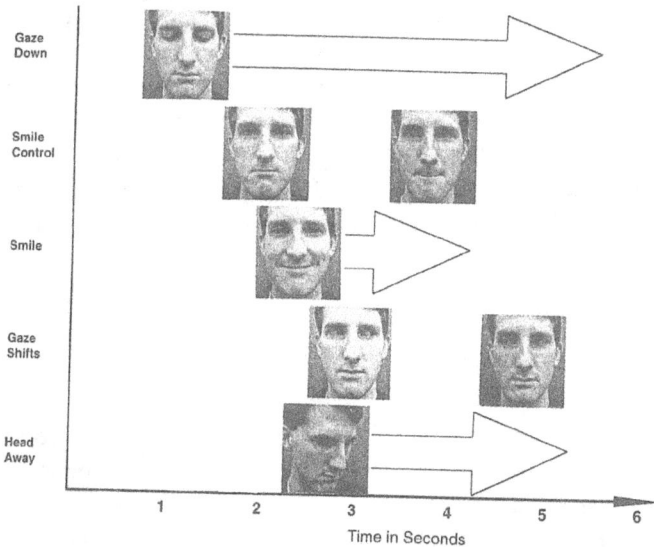

Fig. 2.2. Component actions of the expressions of embarrassment.

One of the questions remaining about smiles is whether the different positive emotions (e.g., amusement, contentment, relief, etc.) have distinctive forms of smiling or if the variety of positive emotions share one signal and can be inferred only from other behavioral or contextual cues. A similar question can be raised about whether various forms of nonenjoyment smiles (compliance, embarrassment, grin-and-bear-it, etc.) are marked in the smile itself. Recent research on the facial expression of embarrassment (Keltner, 1995) has found that when people report embarrassment, they show a consistent pattern of behavior distinct from that of amusement. The separate actions of this response are represented in Fig. 2.2.

When embarrassed, people look down with a latency of .7 seconds, then smile and simultaneously attempt to control the smile with facial actions that are antagonistic to the upward pull of the zygomatic muscle, and then turn their head away and touch their face. Follow-up studies have shown that observers are able to discriminate videotaped expressions of spontaneous embarrassment and amusement, and they are able to do so when the same facial actions are posed in still photographs. This suggests that an important part of the embarrassment signal is the sequential unfolding of its component actions.

The same emphasis on dynamic and morphological markers that was useful in differentiating different kinds of smiles should also be useful for distinguishing actual instances of each of the negative emotions from deliberate performances of those emotions. In each case, the actual negative emotional expression will include muscular elements that are difficult for most people to perform voluntarily. For example, most people cannot voluntarily contract the portion of the muscle in the lips that narrows the lip margin, and the absence of this muscular action should differentiate the deliberately performed from the actual expression of anger.

FACIAL MEASUREMENT

There are two different approaches for measuring facial expressions in muscular or anatomical terms. In one technique, human coders learn to recognize visually distinct facial actions that can singly or in combination account for all facial movement. The Facial Action Coding System (FACS; Ekman & Friesen, 1976, 1978) allows for the scoring of any observed facial movement. Izard (1979) developed a similar scoring system, but it includes only those facial movements that Izard believed relevant to emotion.

The other method is facial electromyography (EMG), in which surface electrodes placed over different regions of the face measure electrical discharge from contracting muscular tissue through the skin. The EMG signal lends itself to immediate recording, is not labor intensive, and is sensitive to slight muscular movements that may not be visible even to the trained eye. One drawback is that EMG is highly obtrusive; the application of surface electrodes makes subjects aware of the facial measurement. Another drawback is that the recording selectivity of facial EMG is not muscle specific, but rather regionally specific, and it is not yet certain whether EMG allows the differentiation of as many different emotions as can be done with measurement that relies on observer scoring of visible muscular actions. The first method—scoring observed facial movements in muscular terms—remedies these problems. It is precise, able to specify which muscles were active, and FACS allows measurement of any movement, not just an a priori set predetermined by the placement of EMG leads. The visible movement scoring techniques are also unobtrusive, performed from videotape records without intruding on the subject. The disadvantage of this approach is that it is labor intensive and insensitive to very slight changes in muscle tonus.

ACKNOWLEDGMENTS

Paul Ekman's work was supported by a Research Scientist Award from the National Institute of Mental Health (MH 06092).
Dacher Keltner's work was supported by a NIMH postdoctoral training grant (MH 18931).

REFERENCES

Birdwhistell, R. L. (1970). *Kinesics and context.* Philadelphia: University of Pennsylvania Press.

Bruner, J. S., & Tagiuri, R. (1954). The perception of people. In G. Lindzey (Ed.), *Handbook of social psychology* (Vol. 2, 634–654). Reading, MA: Addison Wesley.

Bugental, D. B., Blue, J., & Lewis, J. (1990). Caregiver cognitions as moderators of affective reactions to "difficult" children. *Developmental Psychology, 26,* 631–638.

Darwin, C. (1859). *On the origin of the species by means of natural selection.* London: Murray.

Darwin, C. (1872). *The expression of the emotions in man and animals.* New York: Philosophical Library.

Duchenne, G.-B. (1990). *The mechanism of human facial expression or an electrophysiological analysis of the expression of the emotions* (A. Cuthbertson, Trans.). New York: Cambridge University Press. (Original work published 1862)

Efron, D. (1941). *Gesture and environment.* Morningside Heights, NY: King's Crown Press.

Ekman, P. (1972). Universals and cultural differences in facial expressions of emotion. In J. Cole (Ed.), *Nebraska symposium on motivation* (pp. 207–283). Lincoln: University of Nebraska Press.

Ekman, P. (1979). About brows: Emotional and conversational signals. In M. von Cranach, K. Foppa, W. Lepenies, & D. Ploog (Eds.), *Human ethology* (pp. 169–248). Cambridge, UK: Cambridge University Press.

Ekman, P. (1984). Expression and the nature of emotion. In K. Scherer & P. Ekman (Eds.), *Approaches to emotion* (pp. 319–344). Hillsdale, NJ: Lawrence Erlbaum Associates.

Ekman, P. (1985). *Telling lies: Clues to deceit in the marketplace, marriage, and politics.* New York: Norton.

Ekman, P. (1992). An argument for basic emotions. *Cognition and Emotion, 6,* 169–200.

Ekman, P., Davidson, R. J., & Friesen, W. V. (1990). Emotional expression and brain physiology II: The Duchenne smile. *Journal of Personality and Social Psychology, 58,* 342–353.

Ekman, P., & Friesen, W. V. (1969). The repertoire of nonverbal behavior: Categories, origins, usage, and coding. *Semiotica, 1,* 49–98.

Ekman, P., & Friesen, W. V. (1971). Constants across cultures in the face and emotion. *Journal of Personality and Social Psychology, 17,* 124–129.

Ekman, P., & Friesen, W. V. (1976). Measuring facial movement. *Environmental Psychology and Nonverbal Behavior, 1,* 56–75.

Ekman, P., & Friesen, W. V. (1978). *Facial action coding system: A technique for the measurement of facial movement.* Palo Alto, CA: Consulting Psychologists Press.

Ekman, P., & Friesen, W. V. (1982). Felt, false and miserable smiles. *Journal of Nonverbal Behavior, 6,* 238–252.

Ekman, P., Friesen, W. V., & Ellsworth P. C. (1972). *Emotion in the human face: Guidelines for research in and an integration of finding.* New York: Pergamon.

Ekman, P., Friesen, W. V., & O'Sullivan, M. (1988). Smiles when lying. *Journal of Personality and Social Psychology, 54,* 414–420.

Ekman, P., Friesen, W. V., O'Sullivan, M., Chan, A., Diacoyanni-Tarlatzis, I., Krause, R., Heider, K., LeCompte, W. A., Pitcairn, T., Ricci-Bitti, P. E., Scherer, K. R., Tomita, M., & Tzavaras, A. (1987). Universals and cultural differences in the judgments of facial expressions of emotion. *Journal of Personality and Social Psychology, 53,* 712–717.

Ekman, P., Hager, J. C., & Friesen, W. V. (1981). The symmetry of emotional and deliberate facial actions. *Psychophysiology, 18,* 2, 101–106.

Ekman, P., Levenson, R. W., & Friesen, W. V. (1983). Autonomic nervous system activity distinguishes between emotions. *Science, 221,* 1208–1210.

Ekman, P., Roper, G., & Hager, J. C. (1980). Deliberate facial movement. *Child Development, 51,* 886–891.

Ekman, P., O'Sullivan, M., Friesen, W. V., & Scherer, K. R. (1991). Face, voice, and body in detecting deception. *Journal of Nonverbal Behavior, 15,* 125–135.

Ekman, P., Sorenson, R. E., & Friesen, W. V. (1969). Pan-cultural elements in facial displays of emotions. *Science, 164,* 86–88.

Fox, N. A., & Davidson, R. J. (1988). Patterns of brain electrical activity during facial signs of emotion in 10-month old infants. *Developmental Psychology, 24,* 230–236.

Frank, M. G., Ekman, P., & Friesen, W. V. (1993). Behavioral markers and recognizability of the smile of enjoyment. *Journal of Personality and Social Psychology, 64,* 83–93.

Fridlund, A. J. (1991). Sociality of solitary smiling: Potentiation by an implicit audience. *Journal of Personality and Social Psychology, 69,* 229–240.

Hager, J. C., & Ekman, P. (1985). The asymmetry of facial actions is inconsistent with models of hemispheric specialization. *Psychophysiology, 22,* 3, 307–318.

Hess, U., & Kleck, R. E. (1990). Differentiating emotion elicited and deliberate emotional facial expressions. *European Journal of Social Psychology, 20,* 369–395.

Hunt, W. A. (1941). Recent developments in the field of emotion. *Psychological Bulletin, 38,* 249–276.

Izard, C. E. (1971). *The face of emotion.* New York: Appleton-Century-Crofts.

Izard, C. E. (1979). *The maximally discriminative facial movement coding system* (MAX). Unpublished manuscript, Instructional Resources Center, University of Delaware, Newark.

Keltner, D. (1995). The signs of appeasement: Evidence for the distinct displays of embarrassment, amusement, and shame. *Journal of Personality and Social Psychology, 68,* 441–454.

Klineberg, O. (1940). Emotional expression in Chinese literature. *Journal of Abnormal and Social Psychology, 33,* 517–520.

Krause, R., Steimer, E., Sanger-Alt, C., & Wagner G. (1989). Facial expression of schizophrenic patients and their interaction partners. *Psychiatry, 52,* 1–12.

LaBarre, W. (1947). The cultural basis of emotions and gestures. *Journal of Personality, 16,* 49–68.

Landis, C. (1924). Studies of emotional reactions: II General behavior and facial expression. *Journal of Comparative Psychology, 4,* 447–509.

Levenson, R. W. (1989, April). *Social psychophysiology of marriage.* Paper presented at the meeting of the Western Psychological Association, Reno, NV.

Levenson, R. W. (1994). The search for autonomic specificity. In P. Ekman & R. Davidson (Eds.), *The nature of emotion* (pp. 252–257). New York: Oxford University Press.

Levenson, R. W., Carstensen, L. L., Friesen, W. V., & Ekman, P. (1991). Emotion at the end of the human lifespan. *Psychology and Aging, 6,* 28–35.

Levenson, R. W., Ekman, P., & Friesen, W. V. (1990). Voluntary facial expression generates emotion-specific nervous system activity. *Psychophysiology, 27,* 363–384.

Levenson, R. W., Ekman, P., Heider, K., & Friesen, W. V. (1992). Emotion and autonomic nervous system activity in the Minangkabau of west Sumatra. *Journal of Personality and Social Psychology, 62,* 972–988.

Lutz, C., & White, G. M. (1986). The anthropology of emotions. *Annual Review of Anthropology, 15,* 405–436.

Matsumoto, D. (1987). The role of facial response in the experience of emotion: More methodological problems and a meta-analysis. *Journal of Personality and Social Psychology, 52,* 769–774.

Matsumoto, D. (1990). Cultural similarities and differences in display rules. *Motivation and Emotion, 14,* 195–214.

Matsumoto, D. (1991). *Similarities and differences in American and Japanese attribution of emotional intensity* Unpublished manuscript.

Matsumoto, D., & Ekman, P. (1989). American-Japanese cultural differences in rating the intensity of facial expressions of emotion. *Motivation and Emotion, 13,* 143–157.

Ortony, A., & Turner, T. J. (1990). What's basic about basic emotions? *Psychological Review, 97,* 315–331.

O'Sullivan, M., Ekman, P., Friesen, W. V., & Scherer, K. (1991). *Judging honest and deceptive behavior.* Unpublished manuscript.

Plutchik, R. (1962). *The emotions: Facts, theories, and a new model.* New York: Random House.

Schneider, K. (1987). Achievement-related emotions in preschoolers. In F. Hahseh & J. Kuhl (Eds.), *Motivation, intention, and volition* (pp. 163–178). Berlin: Springer.

Steiner, F. (1986). Differentiating smiles. In E. Branniger-Huber & F. Steiner (Eds.), *FACS in psychotherapy research* (pp. 139–148). Zurich: University of Zurich, Department of Clinical Psychology.

Stemmler, G. (1989). The autonomic differentiation of emotions revisited: Convergent and discriminant validation. *Psychophysiology, 26*, 617–632.

Tomkins, S. S. (1962). *Affect, imagery, and consciousness: Vol. 1. The positive affects.* New York: Springer.

Tomkins, S. S. (1963). *Affect, imagery, and consciousness: Vol. 2. The negative affects.* New York: Springer.

3

PSYCHOPHYSIOLOGICAL REACTIONS TO FACIAL EXPRESSIONS

Ulf Dimberg
University of Uppsala

In this chapter I summarize experimental data collected in my laboratory that support the hypothesis that humans are biologically preprogrammed to react with different emotional responses to different facial expressions.

In a more general perspective, my interest is focused on the psychology and psychophysiology of emotion, and therefore I would like to begin by first, very briefly, describing the general background and the theoretical perspective that provide the basis for my research. Second, I present some of the specific questions I have focused on and describe the different experimental paradigms I have used to explore the questions at issue. Finally, I present results from a number of studies that are consistent with the proposition that humans are biologically prepared to react adaptively to facial expression stimuli.

FACIAL EXPRESSIONS AND EMOTION

The study of facial expression of emotions has a long tradition. Darwin (1872), for instance, proposed that emotions and emotional expressions have a biological basis. This proposition is incorporated in modern theories of emotion that propose that there are a number of fundamental emotions such as happiness, surprise, fear, anger, sadness and disgust. These emotions are further presumed to be distinctly manifested in different facial expressions (e.g., Ekman, 1972; Izard, 1977; Tomkins, 1962). Certainly, the expressive component of the emotional response system is a very important aspect. However, there are also other important levels such as the experiential and the physiological ones. This means that emotional activity may be reflected in all these components, that is, the cognitive/experiential, the behavioral/expressive and the physiological/autonomic system (for reviews cf. Izard, Kagan, & Zajonc, 1984). One central issue for research on emotion has been to determine whether these components are interrelated or if one of them is basic or more important than the others in the evocation of emotional reactions.

My theoretical position is based on the differential emotion theory (e.g., Izard, 1977), which states that emotional reactions are controlled by biologically given "affect programs" (Tomkins, 1962). These affect programs may further evoke activity in all three components of the emotional response system. In this chapter, I focus on the physiological reactions and the behavioral/expressive component, particularly the facial expressions of emotion.

FACIAL EXPRESSIONS, BIOLOGICAL BASIS, AND FUNCTION

There are several types of evidence suggesting that the facial expressions of emotion have a biological basis. First, indirect support is provided by the fact that a complex pattern of facial muscles has evolved, providing the basis for the display of different emotional expressions. Further pieces of evidence have been found in crosscultural studies (e.g., Ekman, 1972), infant studies (e.g., Izard, 1977), and studies on nonhuman primates (e.g., Andrew, 1963). All this research provides support for the proposition that human facial expressions are part of our biological inheritance.

There are at least two convincing attempts to explain why we have (or use) facial expressions. The first and most apparent function of facial expressions is, of course, that of social/nonverbal signals and emotional communication in face-to-face interactions. The second one, which I only briefly mention here, is that of facial feedback. The facial feedback hypothesis postulates that our facial muscles serve as a sensory feedback system for the intraindividual experience of emotion (for a review, see, e.g., Buck, 1980).

EMOTIONAL REACTIONS TO FACIAL EXPRESSIONS

In light of the present background, it seems clear that humans are biologically preprogrammed to display distinct facial expressions of emotion. From an evolutionary point of view, it is possible to argue that an overt expression would be of little value if members of the group failed to decode and respond appropriately to the display. It therefore seems reasonable to expect that we are biologically predisposed not only to display different facial expression and act like *senders,* but also to act as *receivers;* that is, to recognize and react adaptively to the facial display of others.

This ability or capacity to react to facial expressions has been a main focus of my research for several years (for reviews see Dimberg, 1983, 1988b, 1990). In a series of experimental studies I have tried to explore whether human subjects react with a response pattern that can be predicted from a biological preparedness perspective. Particularly, I have measured psychophysiological reactions when subjects have been exposed to different facial expression stimuli. More specifically, I have argued that an expression of threat and anger, for instance, is likely to induce components of a negative emotional reaction, such as fear. Conversely, a positive expression, such as the display of happiness, is more likely to evoke a positive emotional response pattern. Based on this logic, I have in most of my experiments restricted the task to specifically comparing the different effects of exposure to angry and happy faces.

Furthermore, I have used two different experimental paradigms to study this phenomenon. The first is the study of learning and Pavlovian conditioning of physiological responses in which pictures of facial expressions are used as conditioned stimuli. The second one is simply to expose subjects to facial expressions. This latter procedure makes it possible to study physiological responses that are spontaneously evoked.

AVERSIVE CONDITIONING TO FACIAL
EXPRESSION STIMULI

One way to approach the question of whether humans are predisposed for emotional reactions to facial expressions is to invoke the prepared learning theory formulated by Seligman (Seligman & J. E. Hager, 1972), for instance. According to this theory, and contrary to the expectations of traditional learning theory, stimulus situations differ in their associability with emotional responses, because a given species has an evolutionarily determined readiness to easily associate some events but not others. The preparedness theory has been useful in understanding important characteristics of phobic fear such as the genesis of snake fear.

In the present context, the theory would imply that fear responses to an angry face would be much more easily learned than responses to a happy one, whereas a happy face could even be expected to be contraprepared to be associated with aversive stimulation (e.g., Dimberg, 1983).

In one of the first studies (Öhman & Dimberg, 1978), three different groups of subjects were aversively conditioned to pictures of angry, happy, or neutral faces, while their skin conductance responses (SCR) from the hand were measured. To those not familiar with psychophysiology, it can be noticed that skin conductance activity is innervated by the sympathetic branch of the autonomic nervous system (e.g., Grings & Dawson, 1978), and has commonly been used as an indicator of emotional responses, particularly in the aversive Pavlovian conditioning paradigm.

In this experiment, as in all the reported studies, I used the slide viewing technique. Subjects are situated in a comfortable chair located in a sound-attenuated room. In front of the subjects is a screen onto which different slides of facial expressions are projected. Consequently, with this technique it is possible to present standardized stimulus pictures with high validity. It is also possible to manipulate not only the emotional display, but also other factors, such as eye contact and the direction of the face. Thus, with this procedure it is possible to mimic important aspects of a face-to-face interaction.

As noted earlier, there were three different groups exposed to angry, happy, or neutral faces. The duration of each exposure was 8 seconds and the pictures were repeatedly exposed with intertrial intervals of 20 to 40 seconds. SCRs were detected by help of electrodes and scored as short-term responses during the slide exposure. Furthermore, mild electric shocks to the fingers were used as the aversive unconditioned stimulus (UCS).

The experiment consisted of three different experimental stages: habituation, acquisition, and the extinction phase. Furthermore, in these experiments a differential conditioning paradigm was used. The essence of this conditioning paradigm is that the subjects are required to differentiate between two different stimulus faces, the CS+ and the CS-. During the acquisition phase, the CS+ but not the CS- is reinforced with the UCS, the electric shocks. During extinction, subjects are exposed to both stimuli, but nonreinforced. This conditioning procedure efficiently controls for extraneous effects such as sensitization or habituation. A pure measure of conditioning is obtained by calculating the difference in responding to the CS+ and the CS-.

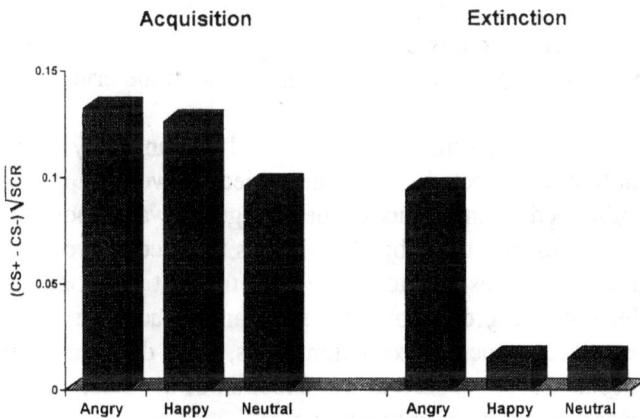

Fig. 3.1. Skin conductance responses expressed as conditioning effects for three groups conditioned to Angry, Happy, or Neutral faces, respectively, during the acquisition and the extinction phase. (The figure is a simplified version redrawn from Öhman & Dimberg, 1978.)

In summary, pictures of different facial expressions were used as the conditioned stimuli (CS), electric shock as the aversive UCS, and SCRs as the dependent measure. To simplify the interpretation of the results, data are presented in a figure in which the difference between CS+ and CS- is already calculated. Consequently, Fig. 3.1 illustrates the pure conditioning effects for the three different groups.

Only the group conditioned to angry faces showed resistance to extinction, whereas responses conditioned to happy or neutral faces extinguished immediately.

These data showed that autonomic responses conditioned to angry faces do not extinguish even when the aversive stimulation is withdrawn. The results suggest that angry facial expressions are particularly effective as conditioned stimuli in aversive conditioning and these results support the prepared learning theory.

These results have been replicated in a number of different studies (Dimberg, 1983, 1986a, 1987; for a review see Dimberg, 1988b), in which I have also explored other aspects of the question of whether subjects are predisposed to react to facial expressions.

For instance, in some of those experiments, I explored whether the direction of a face is critical in the present paradigm (Dimberg, 1983; Dimberg & Öhman, 1983). The orientations of head and eyes are important factors in social interactions, indicating to whom the attention is directed. Therefore, one would expect that the functional significance of an angry face should be critically dependent on the orientation of the face.

In one of the experiments, it was found that an angry face was effective only when directed toward the subjects. Two groups of subjects were conditioned to angry faces. The first group was exposed to angry faces directed toward the subjects, whereas the second group was conditioned to angry faces directed away from them. It was found that only the subjects in the group conditioned to angry faces directed toward them showed resistance to extinction. Thus, these data show that other important facial factors, such as the direction of the face, are also critical in order for conditioning to emerge.

In one further study, I measured not only SCR but also other indicators of autonomic activity, such as heart rate (Dimberg, 1987). The results from this study showed that the response conditioned to angry faces appeared as a heart rate acceleration. This effect was not apparent for happy facial stimuli. This suggests that angry faces induce a response pattern that in traditional terminology can be interpreted as a defense reaction (Grings & Dawson, 1978). This interpretation was further supported by emotion rating data. When the subjects were required to rate their own experience of emotion, it was found that the group conditioned to angry faces experienced more fear as compared to the group conditioned to happy faces (Dimberg, 1987). Thus, combining these results, the data support the preparedness perspective, in the sense that responses aversively conditioned to angry facial stimuli carry aspects of a negative emotional response pattern, which corresponds to a fear reaction.

FACIAL REACTIONS TO FACIAL EXPRESSIONS

A second way to approach the question of whether humans are predisposed for emotional reactions to facial expressions would be to study how people spontaneously react when exposed to different facial expressions. The studies I review in this section are concerned mainly with facial reactions to facial expressions, and they include particularly facial electromyographic (facial EMG) reactions to angry and happy facial stimuli. The facial-EMG technique is a psychophysiological technique that provides the detection of activity and tension in different facial muscles. These activities are measured with the help of electrodes, which are attached to the skin above different facial muscles. First, I give a short background to the studies and also briefly describe the facial EMG technique.

In a face-to-face situation, it is obvious that the face can serve either as a visual stimulus or as an emotional readout system for both the sender and the receiver. As we have seen, the receiver may be biologically prepared to react with diverse emotional response patterns to different facial expressions. If the face constitutes an emotional output system, one way to detect these different response patterns would be to measure the facial reactions of the receiver. Note that this question can be divided in at least two steps. One is whether the facial muscles function as a readout system in a social situation. The second one is whether facial muscle activity is a normal component of the emotional response and therefore constitutes one important factor in emotional activation and responding in general.

Although there has been much interest in both these questions (for a review see Dimberg, 1990), in this chapter, I only present data that throw light on the first question; that is, whether people spontaneously react with different facial reactions to nonverbal signals, such as facial expressions.

Let me first give a short comment on facial EMG. In previous research, it was found that it is possible to detect different facial electromyographic activities while subjects were imagining different emotions. For instance, Schwartz and coworkers (e.g., Schwartz, Fair, Salt,

Mandel, & Klerman, 1976) found that pleasant thoughts increased the activity in the zygomatic muscle (this is the muscle that normally elevates the cheeks to form a smile; Hjortsjö, 1970). The imagination of unpleasant thoughts, on the other hand, increased the activity in the corrugator muscle, which is the muscle used when frowning. These studies demonstrate that the facial EMG technique may be used to detect and differentiate between positive and negative emotional reactions.

A main reason for using the EMG technique is that it is easy to quantify and compare different intensities of the facial muscle reaction. A second advantage is that the EMG signal is instantanously detectable, which makes it possible to detect very rapid reactions of short duration. Particularly, the EMG technique allows for the detection of activity that is too small to be visible as an overt expression.

To approach the present question—whether people spontaneously react with different facial reactions when exposed to different facial expressions—I first performed one study in which subjects were exposed to angry and happy facial expressions while their own facial muscle activity was measured (Dimberg, 1982). The angry and happy stimuli were slides selected from Ekman and Friesen's (1976) *Pictures of facial affect.* The electrodes were attached over the corrugator and zygomatic muscle regions (e.g., Fridlund & Cacioppo, 1986). To conceal the registration of facial EMG activity a cover story was used. The subjects were told that their facial sweat gland activity was going to be measured. In other words, the subjects were not aware of that their facial muscle activity was measured. The predictions were as follows: Happy faces should elicit a positive facial muscle response pattern, as indicated by an increase in zygomatic activity. An angry face, on the other hand, should evoke a negative response as indicated by increased corrugator activity. The typical results from these studies are illustrated in Fig. 3.2.

As can be seen, happy and angry faces evoked quite different response patterns. Subjects exposed to happy faces reacted with increased activity in the zygomatic muscle. Angry faces, on the other hand, evoked increased activity in the corrugator muscle. Consequently, these data demonstrate that happy and angry facial stimuli spontaneously evoke facial EMG responses that are consistent with a positive and a negative emotional reaction, respectively. These results seem to be very consistent and have been replicated in a number of studies (Dimberg, 1988a; Dimberg & Christmanson, 1991; Dimberg & Lundquist, 1990; for a review see Dimberg, 1990).

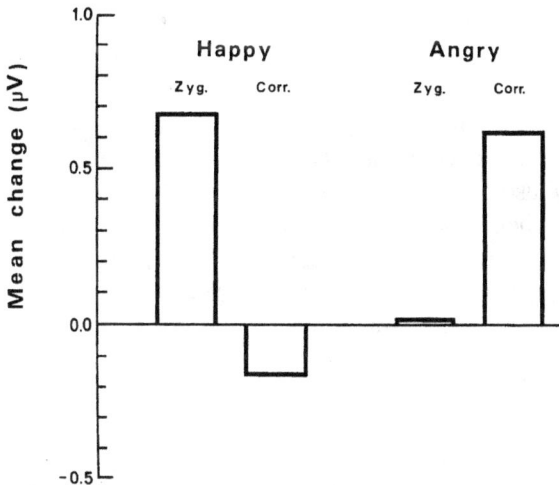

Fig. 3.2. The mean facial EMG response to happy and angry faces for zygomatic (Zyg.) and corrugator (Corr.) muscles. Data are expressed as change score from a prestimulus level. This implies that positive scores indicate increased activity and negative signs indicate decreased activity. (Copyright: The Society for Psychophysiological Research, 1982)

For instance, in one study we explored whether there are gender differences in facial EMG reactions to facial expressions (Dimberg & Lundquist, 1990). Previous research in nonverbal communication has demonstrated that females are more facially expressive than males. In the present paradigm and laboratory situation, it was convenient to study if females react with more intensive facial EMG responses. From a social interaction point of view, this paradigm also allows the evaluation of possible interaction effects between gender of subjects and gender of facial stimuli. Thus, the gender was manipulated in 2 x 2 factorial design by exposing males and females to slides of angry and happy facial expressions displayed by both sexes.

The results from this experiment showed that the gender difference was also detectable at the physiological level; that is, both males and females differed between angry and happy stimuli in a similar way as in my previous research: There was increased corrugator activity to angry faces and increased zygomatic activity to happy faces. Females, however, reacted with a significantly more pronounced reaction pattern as compared to males.

It is interesting to note, however, that gender of the stimulus faces did not influence the response patterns. Thus, if it is possible to gener-

alize these results, they demonstrate that females certainly are more expressive than males, but the facial expression of a woman is not more
effective than the facial expression of a man in inducing emotional responses.

These results have been interpreted as supporting the notion that facial EMG reflects emotional reactions. It can be argued that these reactions may also be interpreted as an effect of, or as carrying aspects of,
mimicking behavior. To more carefully explore whether facial EMG
reactions reflect emotional responses more generally, I performed a
series of studies in which subjects were exposed to different types of
negative and positive emotional stimuli such as pictures of snakes,
flowers, or preferred and nonpreferred landscape scenes (for a review
see Dimberg, 1990). Those studies showed that negative stimuli (e.g.,
pictures of snakes) evoke increased corrugator muscle activity, whereas
positive pictures (e.g., pictures of flowers) spontaneously evoke increased zygomatic activity (Dimberg, 1986b; Dimberg & Thell, 1988).
It seems therefore plausible to interpret the facial EMG reaction as
mainly reflecting emotional activity rather than mimicking behavior in
the present paradigm.

FACIAL REACTIONS TO FACIAL EXPRESSIONS: A CASE OF AUTOMATIC RESPONDING?

I would like to conclude this chapter by reporting the results from some
studies performed recently, which are very interesting in the present
context. In these experiments I have investigated the latency for the facial response, or in other words, how fast facial reactions are evoked
when subjects are exposed to facial expression stimuli.

The general reason for this research was to investigate basic questions related to emotion, such as how the different components of the
emotional response system are related, and whether emotional responses can be more or less automatically evoked.

Particularly, in the present context, it is possible to predict that if
the facial reactions are controlled by genetically given affect programs,
then the reactions should not only be spontaneously evoked, but also be
detectable after only a short duration of exposure.

One clear indication of how fast the facial response can be was
demonstrated in one experiment in which data were collected only
during the first second after stimulus onset. The data from this exper-

Angry   **Happy**

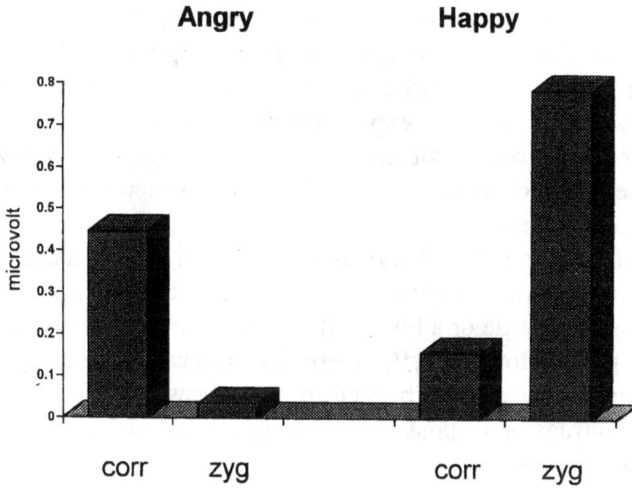

Fig. 3.3.   The mean facial EMG response during the first second of exposure to angry and happy faces for corrugator and zygomatic muscles.

iment are shown in Fig. 3.3. As can be seen in Fig. 3.3 the typical response pattern (similar to the one found in the previous studies) was already apparent after 1 second of exposure (i.e., increased corrugator activity to angry faces and increased zygomatic activity to happy faces).

CORRUGATOR

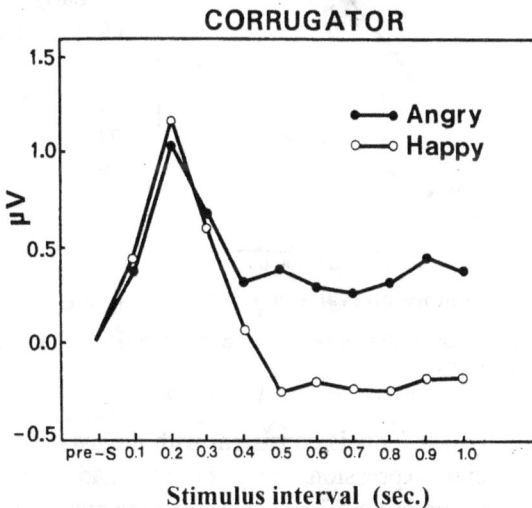

Stimulus interval (sec.)

Fig. 3.4.   The mean facial EMG response to angry and happy stimuli for the corrugator muscle, plotted in intervals of 100 msec during the first second of exposure.

To further elucidate how short the latency of the facial response may be, I performed one study in which it was possible to detect and score the facial muscle response in intervals of 100 msec (Dimberg, 1991). The results from this experiment are shown in Fig. 3.4. This figure illustrates the corrugator muscle reaction to angry and happy faces during the first second of exposure. Note that the activity is plotted in intervals of 100 msec.

As can be seen in Fig. 3.4, both the angry and happy faces evoked a quick increase during the first three 100-msec intervals. This response reminds us of a startle or a blink reflex or may be interpreted as an orienting response. However, after these first intervals, the corrugator response began to dissociate betwen the two faces, and already at 400 msec the corrugator response to angry faces was significantly larger than to happy faces.

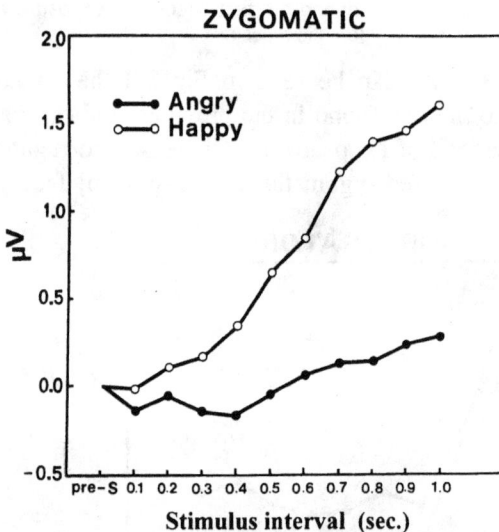

The results for the zygomatic muscle reaction are shown in Fig. 3.5. The zygomatic response, on the other hand, tended to increase to happy faces as early as 200 msec after stimulus onset, and the response was significantly larger to happy as compared to angry faces as early as 300 msec after stimulus onset.

These results demonstrate that the differential facial reactions to angry and happy faces can be evoked extremely fast. This is consistent with the hypothesis that facial reactions to facial expressions may be automatically evoked and controlled by fast operating affect programs. One may further speculate whether these facial reactions can occur prior to or independent of conscious cognitive processes.

Fig. 3.5. The mean facial EMG response to angry and happy stimuli for the zygomatic muscle, plotted in intervals of 100 msec during the first second of exposure.

SUMMARY AND CONCLUDING REMARKS

Let me conclude this chapter by summarizing the major findings and interpretation. These studies demonstrate that angry facial expressions, contrary to happy faces, appear to be particularly effective when used as conditioned stimuli in aversive conditioning. The conditioned psychophysiological response pattern to angry facial stimuli carries aspects of a fear reaction.

Furthermore, angry and happy facial stimuli, spontaneously, evoke different facial EMG response patterns, which correspond to a negative and a positive emotional response, respectively. These differential response patterns can be evoked extremely fast and they are detectable as early as 300 to 400 msec after stimulus onset.

I interpret these results as consistent with the proposition that humans have a preprogrammed capacity to react to facial expressions and that facial reactions are automatically evoked and controlled by fast operating facial affect programs.

ACKNOWLEDGMENT

The preparation of this chapter was supported by the Swedish Council for Research in Humanities and Social Sciences.

REFERENCES

Andrew, R. J. (1963). Evolution of facial expression. *Science, 142,* 1034–1041.

Buck, R. (1980). Nonverbal behavior and the theory of emotion: The facial feedback hypothesis. *Journal of Personality and Social Psychology, 38,* 811–824.

Darwin, C. (1872). *The expression of the emotions in man and animals.* London: Murray.

Dimberg, U. (1982). Facial reactions to facial expressions. *Psychophysiology, 19,* 643–664.

Dimberg, U. (1983). Emotional conditioning to facial stimuli: A psychobiological analysis. *Acta Universitatis Upsaliensis, Abstracts of Uppsala dissertations from the faculty of Social Sciences, 29.* Uppsala, Sweden: Almqvist & Wiksell.

Dimberg, U. (1986a). Facial expressions as excitatory and inhibitory stimuli for conditioned autonomic responses. *Biological Psychology, 22,* 37–57.

Dimberg, U. (1986b). Facial reactions to fear-relevant and fear-irrelevant stimuli. *Biological Psychology, 23,* 153–161.

Dimberg, U. (1987). Facial reactions, autonomic activity and experienced emotion: A three component model of emotional conditioning. *Biological Psychology, 24,* 105–122.

Dimberg, U. (1988a). Facial electromyography and the experience of emotion. *Journal of Psychophysiology, 3,* 277–282.

Dimberg, U. (1988b). Facial expressions and emotional reactions: A psychobiological analysis of human social behavior. In H. Wagner (Ed.), *Social psychophysiology: Theory and clinical practice* (pp. 131–150). New York: John Wiley.

Dimberg, U. (1990). Facial electromyography and emotional reactions. *Psychophysiology, 27,* 481–494.

Dimberg, U. (1991). Emotional reactions to facial expressions: A case of automatic responding? *Psychophysiology, 28S,* 19.

Dimberg, U., & Christmanson, L. (1991). Facial reactions to facial expressions in subjects high and low in public speaking fear. *Scandinavian Journal of Psychology, 32,* 246–253.

Dimberg, U., & Lundquist, O. (1990). Gender differences in facial reactions to facial expressions. *Biological Psychology, 30,* 151–159.

Dimberg, U., & Öhman, A. (1983). The effects of directional facial cues on electrodermal conditioning to facial stimuli. *Psychophysiology, 20,* 160–167.

Dimberg, U., & Thell, S. (1988). Facial electromyography, fear relevance and the experience of stimuli. *Journal of Psychophysiology, 2,* 213–219.

Ekman, P. (1972). Universals and cultural differences in facial expressions of emotion. In J. K. Cole (Ed.), *Nebraska Symposium on Motivation* (Vol. 19, pp. 207–283). Lincoln: University of Nebraska Press.

Ekman, P., & Friesen, W. (1976). *Pictures of facial affect.* Palo Alto, CA: Consulting Psychologists Press.

Grings, W. W., & Dawson, M. E. (1978). *Emotions and bodily responses: A psychophysiological approach.* New York: Academic Press.

Fridlund, A. J., & Cacioppo, J. T. (1986). Guidelines for human electromyographic research. *Psychophysiology, 23,* 567–589.

Hjortsjö, C. H. (1970). *Man's face and mimic language.* Malmö, Sweden: Nordens Boktryckeri.

Izard, C. E. (1977). *Human emotions.* New York: Plenum.

Izard, C. E., Kagan, J., & Zajonc, R. B. (Eds.). (1984). *Emotions, cognition and behavior.* New York: Cambridge University Press.

Öhman, A., & Dimberg, U. (1978). Facial expressions as conditioned stimuli for electrodermal responses: A case of "preparedness"? *Journal of Personality and Social Psychology, 36,* 1251–1258.

Schwartz, G. E., Fair, P. L., Salt, P., Mandel, M. R., & Klerman, G. L. (1976). Facial muscle patterning to affective imagery in depressed and nondepressed subjects. *Science, 192,* 489–491.

Seligman, M. E. P., & Hager, J. E. (1972). *Biological boundaries of learning.* New York: Appleton-Century-Crofts.

Tomkins, S. S. (1962). *Affect, imagery and consciousness: The positive affects.* New York: Springer-Verlag.

4

Universals in Interpersonal Interactions

Wulf Schiefenhövel

Max Planck Institute, Andechs

The question of human universals has preoccupied many schools of philosophers, and cultural and biological scientists as well. Since Darwin's ingenious usage of a questionnaire sent out to administrators, missionaries, farmers, and other addressees in order to find possible universal "expressions of emotions" (Darwin, 1872), cross-cultural research has increased in scope and depth and has been quite successful in discovering a large number of universal behavior patterns. Human ethology, the biology of human behavior (Eibl-Eibesfeldt, 1989), has made important contributions to the corpus of knowledge in this field. This discipline is particularly interested in describing human universals and analyzing their proximate mechanisms as well as in assessing their possible ultimate causation on the basis of evolutionary adaptedness. Human ethological fieldwork is also directed to documenting nonuniversals, culture-specific forms of behavior, especially when they seem to, or actually do, contradict expectations inspired by evolutionary biology.

Universals become more interesting the more detached they are from our mammalian machinery. However, even with our shared biology things are not so easy. Most people will agree that the drive to satisfy thirst and hunger as well as sexual desires are "natural" for women and men. However, it is not uncommon, and at certain levels of religious institutions even demanded, that groups of people stay chaste or near chaste during their life, and a few members of our species can step out of biology as far as voluntarily starving themselves to death. These examples may suffice to demonstrate how complicated it is to speak of "universals." In the context of this chapter, the criterion for a perception or a behavior to be classed as universal will simply be that it regularly occurs in the societies examined so far.

We will never know with certainty that specific behavior patterns were or are universal in a diachronic or synchronic sense, because we have only scanty knowledge of behavioral aspects of prehistoric Homo sapiens and because ethnographic records are far from complete. Therefore, we know little or nothing about the perceptions, thoughts, and behaviors of members of the manifold ethnic groups that are now either extinct or did not get sufficiently documented by anthropologists before they were subject to substantial acculturation.

On the other hand, the concept of universals as such is indeed a powerful tool for gaining insight into the intricate interaction between biology and culture, nature and nurture. For the last three decades, my own research has concentrated on cross-cultural field studies, examining behavior, concepts, and thoughts of indigenous peoples. Here I have been employing two kinds of anthropological approaches: emic (following indigenous conceptions) and etic (following Western conceptions).

The anthropologist George Peter Murdock (1968), initiator of the ethnographic thesaurus *Human Relations Area Files*, listed the following universals in the cultures contained in that large database:

> Age-grading, athletic sports, bodily adornment, calendar, cleanliness training, community organization, cooking, cooperative labour, cosmology, courtship, dancing, decorative art, divination, division of labour, dream interpretation, education, eschatology, ethics, ethnobotany, etiquette, faith healing, family, feasting, fire making, folklore, food taboos, funeral rites, games, gestures, gift giving, government, greetings, hair styles, hospitality, housing, hygiene, incest taboos, inheritance rules, joking, kin-groups, kinship nomenclature, language, law, luck, superstitions, magic, marriage, mealtimes, medicine, modesty concerning natural functions, mourning, music, mythology, numerals, obstetrics, penal sanctions, personal names, population policy, post-natal care, pregnancy usages, property rights, propitiation of supernatural beings, puberty customs, religious ritual, residence rules, sexual restrictions, soul concepts, status differentiation, surgery, tool making, trade, visiting, weaning, and weather control. (p. 232)

This list could easily be prolonged with entries like sexual jealousy, genital shame, the avoidance of sexual intercourse in public, mourning behaviors after the death of a close person, babytalk, superlatives involving expressions of fear (e.g., *terribly* nice, *frightfully* good, etc.; see Eibl-Eibesfeldt, 1989), a tendency to instantaneously and almost irreversibly learn to fear snakes and spiders (see E. O. Wilson, 1984), the concept of the obscene, swearing and the use of tabooed terms in such exclamations, the concept and consequences of ethnicity, and many others.

SILENT SMILE AND VOCAL LAUGHTER

Smiling and laughter are not specifically mentioned by Murdock but constitute an inherent part of his "joking" category. Both behaviors are indeed typical for humans and can be phylogenetically traced back to our animal ancestry. They seem to be very similar and are actually often mixed up in everyday language. Yet, as van Hooff (1971) and other authors have shown, the evolutionary origins of the two patterns are different. Human smiling has most probably developed from the silent bared-teeth display present in infrahuman primates, in which the corners of the mouth are pulled obliquely upward. It is connected to a fearful, submissive mood. In humans this movement is produced mainly through the action of the muscle *zygomaticus major,* action unit 12 (described later). The phylogenetically old "fear grin" still occurs in our species (particularly in slightly threatening or embarrassing situations), but the silent smile is usually a signal of friendliness and joy (Fig. 4.1). Indeed, it is a very typical human expression indicative of a prosocial mood, especially when accompanied by a contraction of the muscle *orbicularis oculi* (action unit 6, Fig. 4.2).

Fig. 4.1. Smiling young Trobriand woman. The corners of the mouth are pulled sideways and upward, giving the mouth a specific shape and exposing the white teeth. A universal sign of prosocial mood.
(Photo: W. Schiefenhövel)

Fig. 4.2.   Strong smile with activated ring muscles around the eyes resulting in crows feet. Acording to Ekman, this indicates "felt smile", whereas in a "nonfelt smile" this action unit is missing. (Photo: Renate Krell)

Laughter, on the other hand, is most likely to have its origin in the "open-mouth display" so common in young mammals and especially in those of primates. This pattern is related to playbiting and indicative of the corresponding mood of slightly aggressive but friendly rough-and-tumble play. These signals are understood across species borders (Fig. 4.3) and are often accompanied by spasmodical expiratory vocalizations (for the most recent research on the social function of "smile" and "laughter" in primate species, see Preuschoft and van Hooff, chap. 9, this volume).

Fig. 4.3.   The "open mouth display" or "play-face" is understood across species borders. It is seen as the phylogenetic origin of the human laughter. (Fig. from van Hooff, 1971).

Probably more than any other single behavior (e.g., yawning), laughter is infectious. This fact is used by producers of TV shows who pipe in "canned laughter" at points in their apparently unconvincing funny films where the viewers at home are supposed to laugh. Chapman (1976) found that, whereas the amount of laughter increases through this technoethological trick, the contents of the films are not evaluated to be more funny than without the artificial laughter boost.

Laughter is indeed a very social behavior in the sense that a group of individuals behave in the same expressive way. At least one of its specifically human characteristics is that this kind of group laughter can be directed toward one or more outsiders whose appearance, behavior, clumsiness, or mishap releases this type of slightly aggressive behavior.

It can thereby function as in-group bonding through the common reaction toward out-group members (Eibl-Eibesfeldt, 1989). The question of whether the infectiousness of laughter has its main root in this or in another functional field has to remain unanswered for the time being. The fact is that in all cultures, we like to laugh together.

NONUNIVERSALS RE-EXAMINED

In his recent book *Human Universals* Brown (1991) gave a useful account of the changing conceptions on this subject. In his first chapter, he examined six cases where the existence of universals was denied by authors famous at their time only to be later acknowledged by other researchers who re-examined the earlier claims in the light of new fieldwork or new theory: (a) "arbitrary" color classification, (b) "problem-free" Samoan adolescence, (c) "reversed" male and female roles among the Tchambuli (the inhabitants of the shore of lake Chambri near the Sepik river in Papua New Guinea), (d) "culture-specific" facial expressions, (e) "nonexistent" or "nonreconcilable" (with Western concepts) Hopi perceptions of time, and (f) the "redirected" Oedipus complex on the Trobriand islands. In the light of my 11 years of fieldwork among the Trobrianders, I am doubtful about the last case, but, of course, this does not challenge the general idea that universals exist. Brown took the same position. He illustrated the problems involved in conceptualizing, defining, and demonstrating universals, but argued that it is scientifically useful to further pursue this line of research.

The cross-cultural film documentation of unstaged social interactions, mainly carried out by Eibl-Eibesfeldt in a number of traditional cultures since the early 1970s, has clearly proven the existence of universal facial, proxemic, and, to a lesser extent, gestural behaviors as well as general principles structuring our perception and behavior. A number of quantitative analyses carried out by our group have corroborated these claims (e.g., Grammer, Schleidt, Lorenz, & Eibl-Eibesfeldt, 1988; Hold, 1976; Schiefenhövel, 1992; Schiefenhövel, Schleidt, & Grammer, 1985; Schleidt, 1988; Tramitz, 1990)

Influential work on universals in facial expression was done by Ekman and Friesen (1978) who based their Facial Action Coding System (FACS) on Hjortsjö's (1970) method of identifying the smallest neuromuscular units in our facial musculature (for an overview of the research of Ekman and his associates up to the present, see Ekman &

Keltner, chap. 2, this volume). Recent work, especially by Frank (1988, chap. 15, this volume), has demonstrated that communication most likely evolved on the grounds of basically true emotions and not as a mechanism of mere manipulation, as suggested by some sociobiologists (see Sommer, 1992).

WRINKLING THE NOSE AND LOWERING THE EYEBROWS

When an aversive smell is perceived, two facial muscles, *nasalis* and *levator labii superioris alaeque nasi* (action units 8 and 9 according to Hjortsjö, 1970) are activated, apparently in a reflex-type response, narrowing the nasal channels. In this way, the olfactory sensorium and the organism in general are protected from potentially harmful chemical substances. Eibl-Eibesfeldt filmed this response in semi-experimental

Fig. 4.4.   Reaction of an Eipo woman to the smell of toothpaste: The lids are lowered, the head is turned away, and the typical nose wrinkling occurs while the friendly smile is changed into a less prosocial expression.
(Stills from film of I. Eibl-Eibesfeldt)

settings, for instance among the Eipo, Mountain Papua in Western New Guinea. The villagers were confronted with olfactory stimuli like toothpaste, whiskey, and garlic, which were unknown to the members of this isolated group and perceived as aversive. They reacted by very briefly closing their eyelids and turning their heads away. Their smiles typically changed with the corners of the mouth often pulled sideways instead of upward and, for a very short period of time, they wrinkled their noses (see film stills, Fig. 4.4).

Another protective reflex-type reaction is the activation of the *corrugator supercilii* (action unit 4), which pulls the eyebrows together and down when one is suddenly confronted with bright light. The delicate, highly sensitive retina is primarily protected by the mechanism constricting the pupil. The bushy eyebrows are a secondary protection acting very much like a sunshade in front of a camera lens.

Like nose wrinkling, pulling the eyebrows down and together occurs much more often in situations where there is no appropriate physical stimulus. Rather, we observe these facial actions typically in interpersonal interactions, where they serve as social signals and are by no means reactions to aversive smell or glaring light. Nose wrinkling occurs most commonly in interactional situations that are of a basically friendly character (Schiefenhövel, 1992).

Fig. 4.5. As in other regions of the world, nose wrinkling is often part of flirtatious interactions on the Trobriand Islands. A young woman is complemented on her beauty by a man and reacts with signals combining approach and withdrawal, typical constituents of coyness behavior. (Photo: I. Eibl-Eibesfeldt)

Nose wrinkling is often seen in flirt situations where one interaction partner, usually the woman, shows facial expressions of approach, e.g., eye contact and smiling, and, at the same time, those of slight withdrawal, e.g., turning eyes and head away for short moments, and wrinkling the nose. A young Trobriand woman reacted in this way to a man who had complimented her on her beauty (Fig. 4.5). Nose wrinkling occurs in many other situations as well. Some years ago, a saleswoman at the fish market of Tokyo reacted by smiling plus nose wrinkling and

pressing her eyelids together to being hugged and kissed by Raisa
Gorbacheva: Approach and withdrawal were simultaneously activated.

Nosewrinkling - Social   context

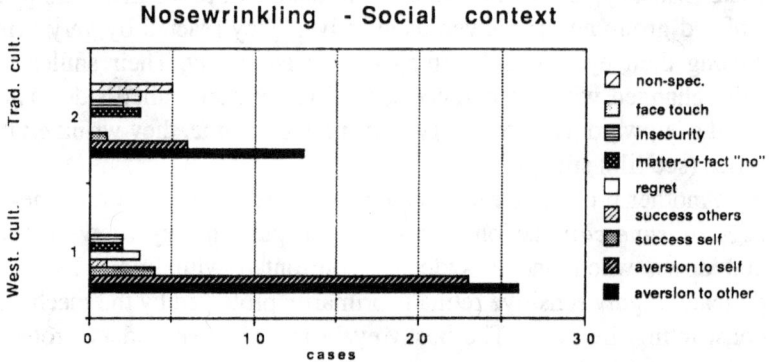

Fig. 4.6.   The categories of social context in which nose wrinkling occurs in Western cultures (examples taken from TV shows) and traditional cultures (16mm films
by I. Eibl-Eibesfeldt).   Aversion to another person and aversion to oneself were the
two most common reasons for wrinkling the nose.

Nose wrinkling in friendly encounters signals that there is something slightly aversive, a bit "smelly" in what the interaction partner has
been doing or saying, or in what one has done or said oneself (Fig. 4.6).
(The readers may observe this in their own daily social interactions.)
The woman at the Tokyo fish market reacted this way to what she must
have perceived as very non-Japanese seeking of body contact and
friendly intimacy in public. My suggestion is that an aversive stimulus
in this type of social communication is perceived and answered along
an old neurobiological pathway that is also present in other mammals:
that of protecting the self against an unwanted but not essentially dangerous olfactory perception.

The English terms *fishy* and *smelly* and the German *anrüchig*
(originally coming from *anrüchtig* and thereby signifying bad social
standing, but later assimilated to a form suggesting a connection to
smell) are good examples of how the wisdom of language expresses
particular shades of microcommunication. What makes us wrinkle the
nose in a primarily friendly interaction is a slightly to moderately aversive social act against which we, for only fractions of a second, signal
the intention to distance ourselves.

The semantic quality of the previously mentioned *corrugator
supercilii* action falls into the same category of other nonverbal signs
that are rooted in biology. In a similar way as we shield our retina

against the glare of excessive light, we use our eyebrows to shield ourselves against acts of partners that we disapprove of, that we shut out.

The specific semantic value of these communicative signs can thus be parsimoniously explained on the grounds of evolutionary biology. Once a genetically coded pathway was established to achieve a certain physiological function, the animal and human organism could utilize the existing machinery for other ends; in the examples given here to create unmistakable communicative signals. Of course, it would have been possible in principle to communicate a slight social distance by widening the nostrils (*dilatator naris*, unit 38) instead of closing them through units 8 and 9. However, nature did not take this course. Widening the nostrils occurs in situations where the intake of smell is fostered, for example, in sexual encounters. As is typical in animal organisms, existing anatomical, neurological, and neurochemical transmitter mechanisms are extended from the physiological realm into the semantics of social communication.

Ethology defines part of this process as *ritualisation*: A behavior normally occurring in the repertoire of a given species, but yet without specific communicative value, undergoes a process whereby it is made more conspicuous for the intended addressee, better distinguishable from the "white noise" of nondirected behaviors. This aim is usually achieved by enlarging the amplitude of the movement and/or by repeating it. The thus newly shaped behavior serves the basic function of unambiguous intraspecies communication.

Fig. 4.7. An Eipo woman exhibiting the "disgust face," the ritualized form of the act of vomiting. In contrast to wrinkling one's nose the disgust face is, understandably, a very aggressive signal. (Still from film of I. Eibl-Eibesfeldt

As comparative morphology shows, life has very conservative "engineering" principles. Organs necessary for new functions are built out of already existing structures. This principle seems to have been at work in constructing a number of our facial expressions as well, and that is precisely why these signs are cross-cultural universals.

A third example may be added: the "disgust" face. As can be seen from Fig. 4.7, the *levator labii superioris* (unit 10), a direct neighbor of the muscle mainly responsible for wrinkling the nose (unit 9), produces a facial configuration that turns the nasolabial furrow into a inverted U and exposes the upper teeth in a specific way. In their much debated experiment Ekman, Levenson, and Friesen (1983) showed that subjects who were technically instructed to move their faces in specific ways to produce (without relying on inner feelings) the expressions corresponding to the six basic emotions (joy, sadness, surprise, anger, fear, and disgust) reacted with lowered heart rates in the last case, whereas in the other five cases heart frequency was increased. The authors did not offer an interpretation for this phenomenon. However, it can easily be explained on physiological and neuroanatomic grounds.

If one assumes that the specific communicative sign is indeed a ritualized act of vomiting, and the facial action involved in producing the disgust face actually indicates this, the lowering of the heart rate comes as no surprise: The nerves *glossopharyngeus* and *vagus*, the main pathways for executing the protective act of getting rid of harmful or dangerous substances in the upper intestinal tract, belong to the parasympathicomimetic network and thereby decrease the frequency of the heart rate.

It is, therefore, no wonder that making the disgust face toward an interaction partner is a very strong signal, much different from the slight social distancing indicated by wrinkling the nose. The disgust face signals that what you have said or done is as repulsive to me as rotten food or another bad substance that makes me vomit. In German there is an aggressive saying: *"Du bist für mich zum Kotzen!"*, that carries precisely the semantics of the facial expression. To spit in front or even onto somebody can, I believe, be explained as another form of ritualized vomiting. All these behaviors are obviously strong insults.

SOCIAL GROOMING: A PHYLOGENETICALLY ROOTED, CULTURALLY REPRESSED BEHAVIOR

Social grooming is a behavior very common among mammals. It also occurs in various birds species and even among certain insects (see Wallis, 1962). Whereas the latter cases are probably analogous (i.e., functionally equivalent to the behavior "higher up" in the phylogenetic tree), social grooming among birds and mammals including the primates and Homo sapiens   seems to be phylogenetically linked, and thereby homologous. Social grooming or allogrooming is carried out by one or more groomers toward a groomee, whereas autogrooming is the act of taking care of one's own body surface.

A plausible hypothesis as to the evolution of social grooming is that those animals whose fur or skin was groomed had hygienic advantages over others who were not thus freed from parasites, foreign bodies, and so on, and that this was the driving motor of grooming behavior and motivation. In the course of phylogeny, this medical aspect of social grooming seems to have been increasingly replaced by a social aspect. In a number of animal species, when individuals are kept in captivity and thereby completely or almost free of parasites, grooming continues despite the absence of a hygienic function. In some species, behavioral elements of social grooming have become ritualized, for example, as greetings (Eibl-Eibesfeldt, 1987). Goodall (1971) said of chimpanzees that grooming is the most peaceful and friendly of all body contacts.

In recent years, some primatological and human ethological studies have dealt with the psychophysiological effects of touching in general and social grooming in particular, as well as with the relationships between hormones, especially beta-endorphin, and social grooming (see Strecke, 1991).

A. Social Grooming in Traditional Societies

Among the Eipo in the highlands of Western New Guinea, social grooming is a common activity, but carried out only between members of the same sex, at least in public. Children, adolescents, and adults engage in social grooming, sometimes forming chains of several individuals (Fig. 4.8).

In the society of the Trobriand islanders off the eastern tip of New Guinea, social

Fig. 4.8. Social grooming, in this case lousing, among a group of older and younger males of the Eipo language group in the highlands of West New Guinea. In this society, body contact in public is only permitted within the same sex. (Photo: W. Schiefenhövel).

grooming is equally common (Fig. 4.9). Yet, here the sex boundary is freely crossed and one may see spouses, lovers, friends, and siblings of the opposite sex show social grooming in public. No time budget studies have been carried out in these and other traditional societies, but it is quite obvious that social grooming occupies an important position in the spectrum of daily activities.

Fig. 4.9. Lousing between the sexes on the Trobriand Islands. (Photo: W. Schiefenhövel)

Among the first behaviors that a mother of a newborn infant carries out on the Trobriand islands is social grooming. She cleans the body surface of her child, picking off scales of skin, and so on. The mother will also gently massage and stroke the body of her newborn.

The most frequent behavior pattern in the complex of grooming activities is to free the groomee of lice in the hair of the head. This is done with precise hand movements that push aside tufts of hair, so that a good view of the scalp is revealed. Between the thumbnails, lice and nits are destroyed by a hard squeezing movement and then often put in the mouth and eaten. Through this surprisingly primatelike act, the parasites are destroyed effectively. Whether or not other benefits (e.g., protein intake) are connected to this behavior remains an open question. Grooming persons appear to be very concentrated and attentive, dedicated to carrying out their task efficiently.

Other activities seen frequently in Melanesia include cutting, shaving, combing, or decorating the hair; shaving or plucking the beard; and removing splinters or other foreign bodies and ectoparasites like sandfleas or mites from the skin. Heymer (1987) filmed Bayaka Pygmies in Central Africa and documented among other things a slightly aggressive competition between two groomers for the head of a groomee. Other instances also indicate that to be able to carry out social grooming is a favored position. It is therefore very likely that specific proximate and ultimate mechanisms bring about this preference.

Whereas social grooming bouts often seem to be initiated by the groomer, it is also common for would-be groomees to signal their intentions to a partner. This is done mostly nonverbally by presenting one's body in a posture whereby the social grooming can be done in an ergonomically easy way. These eliciting acts include lowering the body, presenting the part to be groomed, and generally moving close to the possible groomer. The facial expressions and body postures of the groomee signal the feelings of well-being and relaxation. Grooming generally occurs among individuals who know each other well, either because they are related or friends. It is linked to positive emotions in both the active and the receiving individual. These good feelings are most likely brought about by specific reward mechanisms in the central nervous system, of which beta-endorphin may be just one element.

B. Social Grooming in Germany

Recollection and introspection enable most Westerners to recall instances of social grooming carried out on or by themselves. Since 1979, various groups of students taking courses in medical psychology have talked about their own experiences with social grooming in the Balint-type group atmosphere of weekend courses in medical psychology.

Each time, the first students to speak about their biographical involvement in both active and passive social grooming were usually a bit shy and preferred to talk about "acceptable" behaviors like the pleasure of being combed or massaged or rubbing sun cream on somebody's skin, and so on. Once the ice was broken, other students, both female and male, eventually stated that they were, for example, "possessed by a strong urge" to carry out acts of social grooming, particularly squeezing out the pimples of a partner. Two individuals reported that when they were children, a parent or grandparent had bribed them with money to hold still, thereby allowing the adults to carry out acts of pimple squeezing on the apparently somewhat reluctant groomees.

From these reports it seems likely that in the industrialized German society of today social grooming is still occurring, and that at least for a number of persons, the motivation to carry out active grooming seems comparable to that in traditional cultures. Some people, who admit to enjoying acts of social grooming, rationalize their inclination by stating that "pimples must be squeezed out, otherwise they become infected" or by giving similar, quasi-medical, and often wrong explanations. The readiness to submit oneself to being groomed is, however, reduced vis-à-vis nonindustrialized societies.

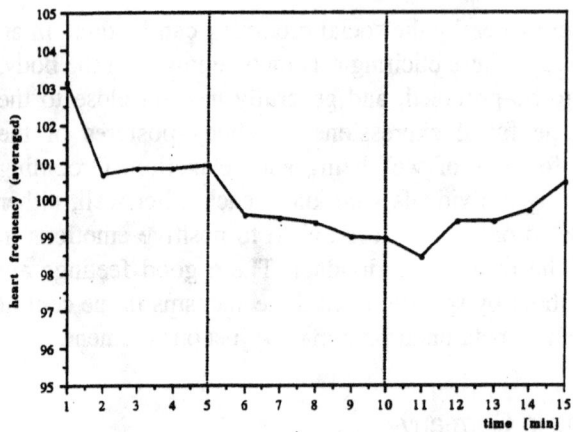

a)

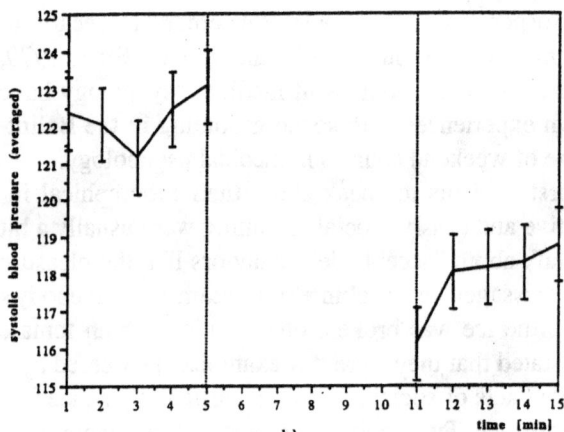

b)

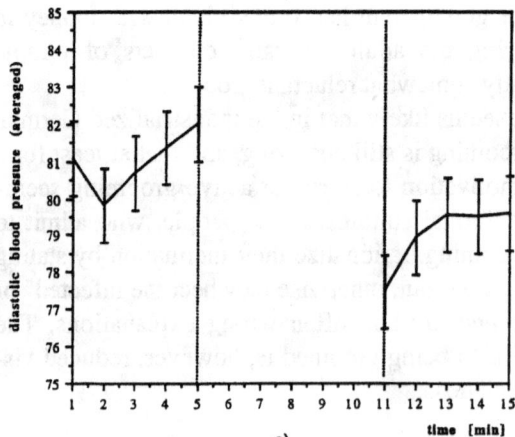

c)

Fig. 4.10. A 5-minute slight massage of the back of hospitalized patients produced a marked decrease in heart frequency (a) and systolic (b) as well as diastolic (c) blood pressure. During the massage, no blood pressure readings were taken. (After Strecke, 1991)

Enhuber (1989) analyzed the answers in 430 questionnaires, which were developed and used in courses on medical psychology, and found ambivalent reactions to allogrooming. Combing, applying oil, cream, and the like, or having fingers run through one's hair were on average classed as pleasant, but other behaviors, like squeezing out pimples and opening abscesses were considered unpleasant by the majority. The discrepancy between the questionnaire results and the self-reports suggests that questionnaires are a less valid method to collect data in this tabooed area of behavior.

Strecke (1991) carried out an experiment with 37 patients between 31 and 81 years of age who were recovering from operations or serious diseases in an intensive care unit, but who were not critically ill anymore. She found a significant decrease in heart rate and both systolic and diastolic blood pressure in the subjects who received a slight massage of their backs (Fig. 4.10).

C. Evolutionary Adaptations

Humans have an apparent predisposition for their role as groomees, with strong pleasurable feelings (e.g., a "shiver" along the back and the appearance of "goose pimples") resulting from being touched and cared for in ways typical for social grooming, although this is not found in all subjects in "modern" countries. The afferent sensory signals from the head and the back are likely to be perceived as more pleasurable than those from other parts of the body. If this is correct, it might be explained as a special adaptation to focus allogrooming on those parts where one cannot groom oneself, either because visual access is lacking or because those areas cannot be reached sufficiently with one's own hands. Studies in primates have found a correlation between these two variables: More social grooming is directed to areas that cannot be self-groomed. It seems likely that psychophysiological processes beyond the already mentioned role of beta-endorphin play an important part in the perceptual and behavioral regulation of social grooming.

From an evolutionary point of view, it needs to be explained why an individual would want to act as groomer, because the payoff for that role is much less obvious than that for the groomee. Active allogrooming entails investment of time and effort, perhaps even an increased risk for the groomer to become infested herself or himself. Hemelrijk and Ek (1991) stated: "A preliminary analysis of a large number of species indicates that reciprocity of grooming might be common in primates.

Perhaps this might reflect reciprocal altruism, but [it] is questionable whether grooming reduces the inclusive fitness of the actor and therefore it is altruistic at all" (p. 934). The two Dutch authors found a limited degree of interchangeability of social grooming and support in agonistic encounters among captive chimpanzees; one favor is "traded off" for another.

For animals and humans, parental grooming obviously enhances reproductive success as better groomed offspring have better chances to survive. In rat and human infants, even stereotyped, experimentally applied physical touching led to better growth and healthier condition (Barnes, 1988). One can easily imagine how much more effective the natural way of handling and grooming must be. In the case of nonparental grooming, the groomer benefits by establishing a strong social bond, which is likely to yield delayed favors in return for the investment into another individual's health and psychological well-being (Hemelrijk & Ek, 1991). From observations in traditional societies and from Western self-reports, there is the already mentioned striking "urge" to carry out allogrooming, a desire to be competent in the techniques involved and a high degree of attentiveness of the individual engaged in grooming.

Ethological observations of animals and the preliminary studies carried out so far in humans support the claim that social grooming is phylogenetically deeply rooted in our animal past and is based on a set of a motivational mechanisms, which only partly overlap with the motivations and behaviors of parental care and sexual behavior.

D. Cultural Repression of Social Grooming Through Professionalization

The German subjects seem to differ from members of traditional societies particularly with regard to three aspects:

1. German subjects often complained about the pain and discomfort entailed in the procedure and sometimes rejected the role of groomee altogether.

2. Some persons state that they are disgusted by the idea of carrying out social grooming activities like squeezing out pimples of others. However, the same individuals admit to doing these behaviors in (often intensive) autogrooming bouts, mostly in front of a mirror.

3. In industrialized societies various activities of the spectrum of social grooming have become professionalized.

Cutting, combing, or otherwise caring for the hair of family members or friends has become rare in Western-type societies. These functions have been taken over by the hairdresser, whom a number of the interviewed subjects visit spontaneously when they feel stressed. In these cases the relaxing effect of social grooming is quite obvious. It seems that the "figaro" establishes a close bond to his customers because the act of allogrooming creates a close social bond. Perhaps it is for this reason that the "figaro" represents, at least in some theatrical plots, someone who obtains many secrets from his customers.

Other elements of social grooming have been taken over by dermatologists, facialists, manicurists, pedicurists, masseurs, and masseuses, as well as by surgeons and other specialists. In industrialized countries these medically and socially important activities have shifted away from family and friends, where they are likely to have had their place since the appearance of Homo sapiens and still have in most societies, to the realm of professionalism.

Interconnected with this trend, a strong cultural bias must have acted on the cognitive and emotional perception of allogrooming. Although the process of professionalization is not unique to social grooming but rather a common historical phenomenon among industrialized societies, the apparent cultural repression of allogrooming is intriguing. Here, the powerful biopsychological disgust mechanism seems to be involved. As described in the first part of this chapter, the disgust reaction builds on a strong universal emotion. I believe that it is often involved in the evaluation of cultural traits uncommon in one's own group, particularly when it comes to "strange" food and customs.

The repression of social grooming may also have an admixture of cognitive assessments related to the conviction that members of "modern" societies do not ordinarily have lice, fleas, ticks, sandfleas, or mites in their skin. Therefore, the need for allogrooming is seen as a sign of "unhygienic" living conditions and rough origins. Thus, it seems likely that it was this novel definition of "healthy" as clean and parasite-free that brought about the often strongly negative emotional responses to active and passive allogrooming in industrialized countries. Western culture has thereby, in a coevolutionary process involving as yet unknown mechanisms, repressed an archaic and universal behavior and redirected human nature.

REFERENCES

Barnes, D. M. (1988). Meeting on the mind. *Science, 239,* 142–144.

Brown, D. E. (1991). *Human universals.* New York: McGraw-Hill.

Chapman, A. J. (1976). Social enhancement of laughter: An experimental analysis of some companion variables. *Journal of Experimental Child Psychology, 21,* 201–218.

Darwin, C. (1872). *The expression of emotions in men and animals.* London: Murray.

Eibl-Eibesfeldt, I. (1987). *Grundriß der vergleichenden Verhaltensforschung (Ethology. The biology of behavior).* 7th revised edition. Munich, Germany: Piper.

Eibl-Eibesfeldt, I. (1989). *Human ethology: The biology of human behavior.* New York: Aldine de Gruyter.

Ekman, P., & Friesen, W. (1978). *Facial action coding system.* Palo Alto, CA: Consulting Psychologists Press.

Ekman, P., Levenson, R. W., & Friesen, W. (1983). Autonomic nervous system activity distinguishes among emotions, *Science,* 221, 1208–1210.

Enhuber, C. (1989). *Soziale Hautpflege beim Menschen. Eine Fallstudie in einer modernen Industriegesellschaft (Social grooming in humans. A case study in a modern industrialized society).* Diploma. Technical University, Munich, Germany

Frank, R. (1988). *Passions within reason. The strategic role of the emotions.* New York: Norton.

Goodall, J. (1971). *In the shadow of man.* London: Collins.

Grammer, K., Schiefenhövel, W., Schleidt, M., Lorenz, B., & Eibl-Eibesfeldt, I. (1988). Patterns on the face: The eyebrow flash in crosscultural comparison. *Ethology, 77,* 279–299.

Hemelrijk, C., & Ek, A. (1991). Reciprocity and interchange of grooming and "support" in captive chimpanzees. *Animal Behaviour, 41,* 923–935.

Heymer, A. (1987). Bayaka-Pygmäen (Zentralafrika)—Soziales Lausen bei Frauen und Mädchen (Bayaka pygmies (Central Africa)—Social grooming among women and girls). *Encyclopaedia Cinematographica, Biologie 19/13, E 2989.* Göttingen, Germany: Institut für den wissenschaftlichen Film.

Hjortsjö, C. H. (1970). *Man's face and mimic language.* Lund, Sweden: Studentlitteratur.

Hold, B. (1976). Attention structure and rank specific behaviour in preschool children. In M. R. A. Chance & R. R. Larsen (Eds.), *The social structure of attention* (pp. 177–201). London: Wiley.

Hooff van, J. A. R. A. M. (1971). *Aspecten van het sociale gedrag en de communication bij humane en hogere niet-humane primaten (Aspects of social behavior and communication in human and other higher primates).* Rotterdam, The Netherlands: Bronder.

Murdock, G. P. (1968). The common denominator of cultures. In S. L. Washburn & P. Jay (Eds.), *Perspectives on human evolution* (pp. 230–57). New York: Holt, Rinehart & Winston.

Schiefenhövel, W. (1992). Signale zwischen Menschen. Formen nichtsprachlicher Kommunikation (Signals among people. Forms of nonverbal communication). *Funkkolleg, Studieneinheit 11, Der Mensch. Anthropologie heute.* Tübingen, Germany: Deutsches Institut für Fernstudien.

Schiefenhövel, W., Schleidt, M., & Grammer, K. (1985). Mimik und Emotion. Verhaltensbiologische Aspekte (Facial expression and emotion. Aspects of the biology of behavior). In V. Schubert (Ed.), *Der Mensch und seine Gefühle (Humans and their emotions)* (pp. 175–209). St. Ottilien, Germany: Eos.

Schleidt, M. (1988). A universal time constant operating in human short-term behavior repetitions. *Ethology, 77,* 289–290.

Sommer, V. (1992). *Lob der Lüge. Täuschung und Selbstbetrug bei Mensch und Tier (In praise of lying. Deception and self-deception in humans and animals)*. Munich, Germany: Beck.

Strecke, D. (1991). *Psychophysiologische Effekte der Körperberührung bei Patienten auf einer Intensivstation (Psychophysiological effects of touching the body of patients in an intensive care unit)*. Diploma. Munich: Technical University.

Tramitz, C. (1990). *Auf den ersten Blick (At first glance)*. Wiesbaden, Germany: Westdeutscher Verlag.

Wallis, D. I. (1962). Behavior patterns of the ant *Formica fusca*. *Animal Behaviour, 10,* 105–112.

Wilson, E. O. (1984). *Biophilia*. Cambridge, MA: Harvard University Press.

PART II

Development of Emotions in a Social and Cultural Context

The second part of this volume deals with the development of non-verbal communication skills and emotions. Although humans seem largely prewired for emotional communication (e.g., Ekman, 1982; Steiner, 1979), these emotions require a human interactional context to develop. What is the mechanism by which infants and children learn to communicate? There seems to be an agreement that the infant–mother bond is crucially important, and the proper establishment of this bond is basic for later normal social development (e.g., Bowlby, 1969; Harlow, 1959; Spitz, 1965). This bond is being formed almost immediately after birth through such mechanisms as preferential tracking of facelike stimuli (Johnson, Dziurawiec, Ellis, & Morton, 1991) and mimicking (e.g., Meltzoff, 1985; Meltzoff & Moore, 1977) and involves the mother's face, gaze, voice, and touch. It also seems to be this emotional attunement that forms the basis for the infant's later understanding of social rules and of language (e.g., Brazelton, Koslowski, & Main, 1974; H. Papoušek & M. Papoušek, chap. 5, this volume; Trevarthen, 1977).

In the first chapter, Hanus and Mechthild Papoušek present the results of the accumulating research from their laboratories in Amsterdam and Munich on children's preverbal development. Here they employ microanalytic, experimental, and comparative approaches. One of their most important achievements is establishing the ways in which competent parents facilitate and guide the infant's transition from a world of prevailing biological predispositions to a world of predominantly cultural influences. They introduce a framework of dynamic systems theory to emphasize the adaptive relevance of nonverbal communication for the evolution of language and the genesis of culture. (For other current research on preverbal development, see Velichkovsky & Rumbaugh, 1996; particularly Bornstein, 1996.)

Klaus Schneider, a leading representative of the invisible college of ethologically oriented psychologists, presents the results of several of his studies on emotions in infants and young children. He focuses on the development of positive emotions and how these are elicited in social as well as nonsocial situations. Schneider shows how a real expression of an internal state (in this case a feeling of achievement) in the presence of others turns into a mastered social signal. Such social signals may be instrumental for competence in social negotiations in general (see Hinde, 1987), and they tend to develop into behavioral dispositions; components of a developing achievement motivation system (Trudewind, Unzner, & Schneider, 1989).

Stephen Suomi, a worker in the tradition of Harlow, discusses results from both experimental and field studies showing the central importance of the mother–infant bond for the development of social competence in young infants—this time, in vervet monkeys. Although Harlow showed that sociality is in a sense "inborn" (through demonstrating that infant monkeys preferred a terrycloth "mother" to a milk-producing wire "mother"; Harlow, 1959), he also pointed to the need for an adequate social environment for the full development of social competence (monkeys raised in isolation developed aberrant social behavior). Suomi has gone a step further and demonstrated the overwhelmingly strong influence of the social environment on personality development. His studies show that congenitally shy monkeys, if guided by strong foster mothers, may become even more socially capable than normal monkeys. Considering the recent suggestion by one of Suomi's collaborators, child psychologist Jerome Kagan, that shyness in humans may be largely inborn (e.g., Kagan, Sniderman, Arcus, & Reznick, 1994), these findings could bring with them a lesson for child education, too. Suomi's research combines genetical, physiological, and behavioral aspects, and tests laboratory findings in the natural environment and vice versa. Here we may in fact have a good example of ecological relevance, Egon Brunswik's (1976) important requirement for any study of behavior.

REFERENCES

Bornstein, M. H. (1996). Origins of communication in infancy. In B. M. Velichkovsky & D. M. Rumbaugh (Eds.), *Communicating meaning: The evolution and development of language* (pp.139–172). Mahwah, NJ: Lawrence Erlbaum Associates.

Bowlby, J. (1969). *Attachment and loss*. New York: Basic Books.

Brazelton, T. B., Koslowski, B., & Main, M. (1974). The origins of reciprocity: The early mother–infant interaction. In M. Lewis & L. A. Rosenblum (Eds.), *Origins of behavior. Vol. I: The effect of the infant on its caregiver* (pp. 49–76). New York: Wiley.

Brunswik, E. (1956). *Perception and the representative design of psychological experiments*. Berkeley: University of California Press.

Ekman, P. (1982). *Emotions in the human face*. Cambridge: Cambridge University Press.

Harlow, H. (1959). Love in infant monkeys. *Scientific American, 20*, 2–8.

Kagan, J., Sniderman, N., Arcus, D., & Reznick, J. S. (1994). *Galen's prophecy: Temperament in human nature*. New York: Basic Books

Hinde, R. A. (1987). *Individuals, relationships and culture: Links between ethology and the social sciences*. Cambridge, UK: Cambridge University Press.

Johnson, M. H., Dziurawiec, S., Ellis, H., & Morton, J. (1991). Newborns' preferential tracking of face-like stimuli and its subsequent decline. *Cognition, 40*, 1–19.

Meltzoff, A. N. (1985). The roots of social and cognitive development: Models of man's original nature. In T. M. Field & N. Fox (Eds.), *Social perception in infants* (pp. 1-30). Norwood, NJ: Ablex.

Meltzoff, A. N., & Moore, M. K. (1977). Imitation of facial and manual gestures in human neonates. *Science, 198*, 75–78.

Spitz, R. (1965). *The first year of life: A study of normal and deviant development of object relations*. New York: International Universities Press.

Steiner, J. E. (1979). Human facial expressions in response to taste and smell stimulation. *Advances in Child Development and Behavior, 13*, 257–295.

Trevarthen, C. (1977). Descriptive analyses of infant communicative behavior. In H. R. Schaffer (Ed.), *Studies in mother-infant interaction* (pp.). London: Academic Press.

Trudewind, C., Unzner, L., & Schneider, K. (1989). Die Entwicklung der Leistungsmotivation (The development of the achievement motivation). In H. Keller (Ed.), *Handbuch der Klinikforschung* (pp. 491-524). Berlin: Springer.

Velichkovsky, B. M., & Rumbaugh, D. M. (1996). *Communicating meaning: The evolution and development of language.* Mahwah, NJ: Lawrence Erlbaum Associates.

5

PREVERBAL COMMUNICATION IN HUMANS AND THE GENESIS OF CULTURE

Hanuš Papoušek
University of Munich
Mechthild Papoušek
University of Munich

Research on communicative development in humans has recently profited from microanalytic, experimental, interdisciplinary, and comparative approaches to preverbal forms of communication and has provided new arguments for the interpretation of both phylogeny and ontogeny of human communication. We discuss them in relation to the contribution of dynamic systems theory and the adaptive relevance of human communication in the evolution of speech and in the genesis of culture.

The acquisition of the first language—the mother tongue—is an intriguing developmental process from both a biological and a psychological viewpoint. A newborn human being, incompetent in locomotion, foraging, and vocal production except for crying, enters culture and within 1 or 2 years, often in spite of unfavorable circumstances, masters the first words and sentences of communication, the complexity of which surpasses all other forms of animal communication. This achievement may seem to result from a mere cultural impact: The infant will always learn the language of the cultural niche. To acquire language is *sine qua non* for the infant's integration into culture. However, those whose language has been acquired are rarely able to explain how the cultural impact has been mediated to an individuum that to many looks more like an animal than like a human being. To what extent do certain biological predispositions play a part in this process, and are these specific for human language acquisition? Or are there perhaps common biological predispositions for both language and the genesis of culture, and the acquisition of speech and the genesis of culture?

THE HISTORY AND COURSE OF PREVERBAL COMMUNICATION

This very question calls for a closer look at the history and course of preverbal communication. Culture has too often been viewed as an antipole of nature, and this view inhibited attention to biological origins of culture. Language, with its unexplainable, almost mythical origin, has shared the position with culture. Humans have learned much about their past from fossil relics, but this is not the best form of documentation on the origin of software concerning language, self-consciousness, or culture. We may trace the beginnings of these phenomena to the use of fire or to the funeral rituals of our ancestors; however, we know that these pieces of evidence were perhaps the first products, but not the causes of those phenomena. We cannot exclude the possibility that the products resulted from integrative or communicative capacities of evolutionary origin. One way to begin solving the evolutionary puzzle, no matter how unconvincingly, is to study the proportions and the order of emergence of those pieces of software during early ontogeny.

It is seemingly easy, although doubtful, to separate cultural and biological determinants at the level of adult life. It is even more dubious, however, to do so in relation to early stages of life. To view culture as independent of nature would be as naive as the attempts of some behaviorists to declare all human behavior to be learned and disregard any innate predispositions for the capacity to learn, to learn at all, to learn only during some stages of development, or to learn with certain preferences, as Huxley (1965) pointed out.

Morphologically, the human organism is unique, for instance, in relation to preadaptedness for upright walking or the amount of space available for the growth of the neocortex in the brain. However, at the beginning of this century, scientific embryology revealed that during ontogeny this unique organism passes several stages of differentiation

—invertebrate, molluscan, mammalian—while developing into the primate organism with the largest brain, a differentiation that is largely determined by a robust genetic plan. Fetal functional differentiation into all the complex patterns of movements observable in newborns follows a similar plan, as recent real-time ultrasound records of fetal behavior have shown (de Vries, Visser, & Prechtl, 1982). Early postpartum development in humans has become hardly interpretable without a close cooperation between behavioral scientists and biologists. Infancy research has rapidly developed into an important discipline bringing about discoveries that have forced revisions of major speculative interpretations of early development; most of the discoveries have resulted from comparative, psychobiological approaches.

As a particularly complex process, the preverbal phase of language acquisition has long remained underresearched. Three aspects appear to be particularly difficult. First, communication is an *interactional process*. Every stimulus is a response, and every response functions as a stimulus. The standard psychological repertoire of methods and statistics for laboratory observation and evaluation of one-way responses in stimulus–response designs cannot help in analyses of interactional processes; at best, it can be used for verification of partial aspects.

Second, communication is a *multidimensional process* in which biological and cultural factors interact within and between two different, independently regulated human organisms—the parent and the infant; expressions of emotions interact with communicative intentions, each partner interacts with the situational context, and so on. Attempts to capture the dynamics of such complexity with the help of linear mathematical models, dominating the present psychology, often lead to dead ends.

Third, the common methodology in social sciences—the use of *interviews and questionnaires*—is also of little help in studies of preverbal communication. The infant obviously cannot report, and the parent gives misleading information inasmuch as most parents are unaware of what their communication with infants is based on, as we explain later. In order to overcome these and similar difficulties, infancy researchers have been compelled to try ethological ways, to sharpen observational methods, and to approach parent–infant dyads almost as members of an unknown species. We maintain that the approach has paid off: It has opened new perspectives and improved former interpretations. It has also brought about further difficult topics for future research. However, what we already know about the reciprocal interactions between biological and cultural factors paving the way toward language and about the integration of a newly born individuum into culture stimulates comparisons with general conceptions of the genesis of culture. Within such a general framework and with a certain preference for our own research topics, we wish to approach human communication from an evolutionary viewpoint and discuss its biological significance and early ontogeny. First, however, we wish to comment on one major conceptual problem facing psychology and biology, namely, the question of whether and how to apply the theory of highly dynamic systems.

SELF-REGULATION IN HIGHLY DYNAMIC SYSTEMS

The highest abstraction of a process, physical or biological, is a mathematical model. Attempts to reach this level of abstraction in behavioral sciences have mostly remained unfulfilled. Mathematicians are not primarily motivated to model complex biological behaviors, although they have been very helpful in applied statistics. Conversely, behavioral scientists have displayed high motivation as seen, for instance, in behavioristic attempts to capture learning processes in mathematical formulas during the 1950s. They did so, however, at the price of an overexaggerated simplification; they typically disregarded biological determinants of individual variability and allowed them to disappear in the wastepaper basket of *ceteris paribus*.

This situation changed in the 1980s when physicists detected an increasing number of physical or chemical systems in which highly dynamic changes indicated the existence of some type of self-regulation and/or communication among atoms or molecules, phenomena that used to be expected only in living systems and show no linearity. Exploiting the advantages of modern computer simulations, mathematicians have suggested various nonlinear models for similar phenomena and have successfully applied them in solutions of technical problems. However, in extrapolation of these models, physicists have come to the border between hard science and belief; some do believe that they may be close to detection of universal laws, common to all systems—from infinitely small dimensions in systems of elementary particles to infinitely large dimensions in cosmic systems. Although the criterion of truth is hard to imagine, the attractiveness of the idea that these laws may also be valid in living systems is easy to understand.

In fact, graphic displays of relatively simple mathematical formulas, repeated and at the same time slightly modified with random deviations in innumerable steps, simulate phenomena that are similar to the growth of snowflakes or plants. Other models simulate an infinite growth of complexity in a minimal amount of mass—principles that in living organisms may have regulated the evolution of light, but firm bone tissues or of enormously long chains of DNA molecules in chromosomes. Understandably, nonlinear models of systems that include several independent oscillators and easily tumble out of control due to omnipresent variations in individual components, but still return to a new, though unpredictable order due to self-regulation, promise attractive interpretations for some very complex phenomena in biological systems. Here, social interaction and communication in humans offer opportunities par excellence.

APPLICATION OF DYNAMIC MODELS
IN HUMAN INTERACTION

In spite of recommendations that have already been made, for instance by Fogel (1990), application of highly dynamic models in human interactions is not easy. Behavioral scientists should be advised to first reconsider two premises: the specificity of the system to be explored, and the degree of knowledge on regulatory functions involved in that system. Soon after the introduction of systems theory, Bertalanffy (1968) pointed out the special status of developing biological organisms in comparison with physical systems. Although, according to the second law of thermodynamics, complex systems and order in them should disintegrate, the flow of energy still keeps washing life and consciousness into nature. Genetic programs keep enforcing a specific direction in living systems that, at least temporarily, can accumulate energy for their own sake and under their own control. It is true that the universe is randomness and dissipation, but randomness with direction can produce surprising complexities.

For Ford (as quoted by Gleick, 1987), for instance, evolution is chaos with feedback. And feedback with rewards for successful problem solving as a direction given to a large population of interrelated computers has led to a hierarchic selection among them that seems to model evolutionary processes. Nature forms patterns, some orderly in space or in time and others fractal, exhibiting structures self-similar in scale (Gleick, 1987). It is often difficult to find out which of the many physical forces involved are important, and when a sensitive dependence on initial conditions serves to destroy or to create. Fractal mathematics shows that pattern formation resulting from the interdependence of stabilizing and destabilizing forces often depends on the tiniest, microscopic scales, leading finally to formation of physical patterns that are vividly reminiscent of biological patterns.

The tendency in biological systems to work against entropy brings about a parallel tendency to work against randomness and disorder, particularly in human social systems. The notion that systems including several oscillators may become unpredictable could be a nightmare to physicians, businessmen, traffic police or Japanese managers, although, conversely, it might fascinate creative artists. Learning as an attribute of life is based on processing of probabilities and predictions both in individuals and populations. The motivation is evident in human infants from the beginning of life: Newborns have been shown to be capable and motivated for detection of contingencies and to express pleasure on predictability (H. Papoušek, 1967). The later capacity of adults to introspect, to realize the risks of low predictability, and to reduce the risks wherever organizational and technological measures allow it, may have much in common with the general specificity of living systems.

The other premise—knowledge of the regulatory processes involved in the system to be observed—makes it somewhat doubtful whether dynamic nonlinear models can be applied in analyses of social interactions soon. Some regulatory processes can be described only metaphorically: Exact definitions or, more importantly, methods of quantification are not yet available or are too difficult. It often takes a long time merely to show that a regulation exists, such as the regulation of circadian rhythms in behaviors; yet, no measures allow a practical quantification of this regulation. In adults, its functioning can perhaps be neglected; in young infants, however, problems in the balance between serotonin and melanin in circadian regulation may cause colics during the first 2 or 3 months, and this circumstance can hardly be neglected. Otherwise, the infant's cry might be interpreted as a response to incidental behaviors in the caregiver or other events. Similar examples show that coincidences in space and time cannot explain causal relations unless all major factors are taken into consideration.

The first attempts to analyze cyclic motor activities, such as leg movements, and to find out whether relatively simple phenomena—in comparison with interactional and communicative behaviors—would allow dynamic modeling in behavioral development have met with serious difficulties. The knowledge of the state variables involved is not yet sufficient, it is difficult to search directly in the system's state space for the evidence of an attractor, and thus, caution is recommended (Robertson, A. H. Cohen, & Mayer-Kress, 1993). Those authors warn that there is a danger in the temptation to naively adopt a new terminology or set of metaphors to merely redescribe the phenomena psychologists have been studying for so long, and then to conclude that we have explained them. It is our impression that an intensive interdisciplinary cooperation with biologists, anthropologists, and neuroscientists is still necessary for preparing the ground for a successful application of highly dynamic nonlinear models.

ADAPTIVE RELEVANCE OF HUMAN COMMUNICATION

Although it is still questionable whether and how physical or chemical agents communicate in physical self-regulating systems, in living systems intercellular or interindividual forms of communication are evidently among the fundamental processes. All crucial life events, reproduction, foraging, care for progeny, and struggle for life depend on some form of communication. Its role and complexity has increased in individual species with the evolution of nervous systems. In humans, communication has reached a particularly high level of verbal communication and its evolution has been closely interconnected with the genesis of culture. MacLean (1973, 1990) has studied the evolution of the brain for several decades and summarized it in the concept of the *triune brain* with three levels of controlling circuits.

The first level is the *reptilian brain,* which corresponds to the corpus striatum in the human brain. It controls movements in forms of innate releasing mechanisms, fixed action patterns, and instinctive stereotypes. These movement patterns represent a great deal of behavioral repertoire, for instance, in lizards or birds, whereas in mammals they occur less frequently.

The second level of circuits, the *old mammalian brain,* dominates in mammals, such as rodents or rabbits. It corresponds to the limbic system, which mediates emotions. Some of the modules added to the reptilian brain concern three forms of behavior that characterize the evolutionary transition from reptiles to mammals and, at the same time, a new communicative system:

1. *Nursing and additional components of maternal care.* A new type of hormonal regulation controls not only the estrous cycle, ovarian implantation after conception, maintenance of pregnancy, and course of parturition, but also prelactational growth of mammary glands and at the onset and maintenance of lactation. Maternal behavior also involves retrieving and nest building.

2. *Vocal communication for maintaining contact between mothers and pups.* This was presumably important in the first mammals, small and nocturnal animals depending on audiovocal signals, such as "the separation cry" present in most mammal infants. Although fossilized relics cannot confirm the use of vocal communication, they do provide indirect evidence for its use in the change of small reptilian bones in the jaw—articulation into quadrate and articular bones in distinct mammals; such bones are believed to improve auditory perception.

3. *Playful behavior.* Although play has not been observed in reptiles, its role in mammals is prominent. Playfulness has presumably participated in the genesis of human culture; Huizinga (1955) suggested calling modern humans *Homo ludens* instead of *Homo sapiens*. However, play as a behavior that is difficult to define and measure has gained little attention in the neurosciences. Experimental lesions of the brain in rats (destruction of the cingulate cortex and the proximoseptal hippocampus underneath) lead to the loss of both maternal behaviors and playful activities (Slotnick, 1967; Stamm, 1955).

The third level of circuits, the *new mammalian brain*, corresponds to the neocortex. It is responsible for the higher mental faculties and culminates in humans in logical thoughts, verbal communication, and the emergence of culture.

The roles of the three levels in the triune brain were documented by M. R. Murphy, MacLean, and S. C. Hamilton (1981) in hamsters. Experimental removal of the neocortex at birth does not impair instinctual behaviors; however, further removal of the limbic structures disrupts maternal behavior and play. The reptile brain can obviously control instinctual behaviors, whereas maternal behavior and play are specific functions of the limbic system, the supracallosal cingulate cortex, and the proximoseptal hippocampus in particular. Unlike the reptilian hatchling, the mammalian infant critically depends on parental care; most often, a separation from the mother is fatal. Not surprisingly, various forms of attachment have evolved in mammals, and separation causes a serious stress. The separation call presumably started vocal communication 100 million years ago.

During the Fayum Oligocene, approximately 30 million years ago, a new species of small arboreal mammals, the Zeuxis, appeared on the scene. The first apelike changes of skull, teeth, and limbs differentiated a new group, the Australopithecus (Simon, 1967). The most striking feature was impressive forward-facing eyes, advantageous for movement on tree branches, due to a better depth perception. This shift in the body plan indicated a shift with far-reaching consequences in relation to communication—a shift from the dominance of chemical signals in mammals to the dominance of vision, characterizing primates. The olfactory apparatus began to shrink and the rear part of the brain enlarged. Depth vision, color vision, and eye–hand coordination improved.

The first deviation from apes into the protohuman direction occured either in the *Ramapithecus* or in the *Australopithecus afarensis*; this question is still open to discussion. *Ramapithecus* was adapted to life on the open savanna and to grazing or seed eating. Relatively small teeth and less prominent jaws differentiated *Ramapithecus* from other Miocene apelike forms: The face assumed humanlike features. Vulnerability to predation probably led to formation of social groups of substantial size and to some hierarchical ordering, similar perhaps to the order in present baboon groups.

The first evidence of fully upright walkers was discovered in fossilized footprints (Leakey & Hay, 1979) and in the most complete skeletal specimen of Australopithecus fossils dated in the early Pliocene, at 3.5 million years (Johanson & T. D. White, 1979). There is no evidence of tool making and tool use in this hominid species, although Australopithecus might have used wooden tools like the modern-day wild chimpanzees. That would, however, hardly explain the emergence of upright walking. The earliest recognized stone tools from the Olduvai Gorge are about 2 million years old. Consequently, the most commonly cited interpretation of the divergence in hominids due to tool use and material culture (Darwin, 1871) calls for a revision.

Anthropologists turned attention to a more probable type of biological pressure for divergence, namely, demographic propagation. Humans—and hominids, too, perhaps—have a higher rate of reproduction. The birth span is shorter than in apes (3 years in hunters and gatherers versus 6 or 7 years in wild chimpanzees) so that parents have to care for two or more dependent offspring simultaneously. Lovejoy

(1981) suggested that upright walking—an unusual and disadvanta-geous nonsaltatory form of walking—may have originally resulted from a mere variation in the genetic plan, and that it may then have been se-lected due to advantages related to carrying and intense parenting. Car-rying is one of the most distinctively human behaviors. Disadvantages in slower locomotion would also call for closer social cooperation, or-ganization, and communication.

Following the further history of the protohuman line, we may dis-regard Australopithecus africanus, Australopithecus robustus, and *Homo habilis* and mention *Homo erectus,* dominating the scene throughout the Old World a million years ago as the last ancestor of *Homo sapiens.* The size of the brain enlarged in *Homo erectus,* particu-larly in the frontal lobes, the parietal lobes, and the poles of the tem-poral lobes—areas related to human intellectual functions, memory, and language—and may have already caused risks in childbirth. The way of life was probably comparable to the nomadic life of gatherers and hunters.

The emergence of language is difficult to date from the fossils. Lieberman (1984) pointed out the structure of the upper vocal tract as one of the necessary conditions for speech and its lack in the Neander-thalian fossils 30,000 years ago. However, the most recent interpreta-tion—the so-called "Eve theory"—is based on independent, but congru-ent genetic and linguistic analyses by Cavalli-Sforza and Greenberg from Stanford University in Palo Alto, who have come to the conclu-sion that all present variants of *Homo sapiens sapiens* and modern lan-guages had a common African ancestor 200,000 years ago. From there, *Homo sapiens* gradually spread through all other continents during the last approximately 100,000 years. In genetic terms, racial differences in present populations are caused by negligible genetic differences in comparison to the major, presumably unique and enormously advanta-geous change that gave rise to the differentiation of *Homo sapiens* and brought about self-consciousness and language with a new culture. Ac-cording to this theory, Neanderthal people lived together with the new migrants, but disappeared rather quickly around 30,000 years ago and had no noticeable impact on present languages (see Cavalli-Sforza, Menozzi, & Piazza, 1995).

This short excursion into evolution shows that human language emerged perhaps suddenly in its novel form, but on a prepared ground. Comparative research confirms (see Marler & Evans, chap. 8, this vol-ume), that a minimal repertoire of words exists in the monkey world.

Apes can decode or signal rather complex messages; however, they cannot speak, sing, or learn new sounds by imitation, because they lack an appropriate vocal tract for fine modifications of vocal sounds and a direct connection between the primary motor cortex and the laryngeal motoneurons that, in humans, allows a direct voluntary control of vocal cords (Ploog, 1992). Apes cannot write, either; they lack the proper form of hand and the nervous circuits for coordination of finger movements that humans have. With human help, however, apes can learn how to communicate in American Sign Language (R. A. Gardner & B. T. Gardner, 1969), in other gestures (Patterson, 1978), or in visual-symbolic "Yerkish" (A. J. Premack & D. Premack, 1972; Rumbaugh & Savage-Rumbaugh, 1996; Savage-Rumbaugh, Rumbaugh, & Boysen, 1978). Obviously, they have biological predispositions that cannot be utilized if an impact of culture is missing. Elementary forms of cultural transmission have, thus far, been reported only in Japanese macaques (Kawai, 1963; see Suomi, chap. 7, this volume, for further discussion of cultural transmission).

Thus, both language and culture seem to have deeper roots in biological precursors that can be found in partial forms in various species. The unique position of humans among other primates is dependent on the coexistence of all crucial predispositions for verbal communication in this species. Humans can richly modify vocal sounds, due to a well-developed upper vocal tract, and use them in fast chains for coding information, due to a well-developed neocortex. Cerebral lateralization of representational capacities allows humans to mediate experience or intention both in the direction of logically structured verbal messages, and in the direction of overall impressions and feelings. Advanced coordination of hand and finger movements under visual control offers further possibilities of skilled tool making, tool use, writing, and creative activities. The presence of these capacities within a society is a necessary condition for the development of culture, and within the culture, the development of rituals, traditions, and institutions that, among other things, further increase exploitation of the given capacities. Here, we can see examples of interactional relations among self-regulating systems, such as individual—social environment—culture, that lead to new forms of self-regulation at higher levels. It is doubtful to speculate about some primacy among them or to try separating forces from products, once we are aware of the theory of highly dynamic systems. If we want to apply this theory, then we should know which forces are involved.

For instance, mother–infant attachment used to be explained as a selected solution of three problems in the dependent infant: nutrition, protection, and emotional need. It really might have been like that at the beginning of mammalian history. However, research on early integrative development revealed further needs in infants, such as the need to acquire knowledge of the environment and to communicate with it. Moreover, some further distant consequences have been discussed. For instance, Konner and Worthman (1980) explained that mother–infant bonding in Kalahari populations of hunter-gatherers is important for maintaing the birth span of 3 years between births without contraceptives, and thus, that it helps avoiding overpopulation. Carrying infants allows frequent nursing, and short intervals in nursing maintain a blood level of prolactin that is necessary for inhibition of ovulation. In the next part of this chapter, we are going to argue that bodily proximity between parents and infants during the first postpartum year is crucial for acquisition of language (H. Papoušek & M. Papoušek, 1992a).

The relevance of words is another example. Language is dependent on genetically determined biological predispositions. However, due to use in a culture, words continuously acquire new properties and can function with a force of their own. Take, for instance, the integrative power of words. Human capacity for abstract representation allows us to use words either as concrete names for individual objects or events or as abstract names for entire categories. Consequently, abstract names can be used for hierarchical classifications; their availability can increase the tendency to use them, as more people become aware of the advantages of these classifications and learn how to use them. Simple hierarchical classifications, such as finch–songbird–bird–vertebrate–animal have an impact on our ways of thinking, regarding, for instance, how far a classification can go in both directions. In one case, such thinking can occasionally lead to the idea of gods, in another, to the idea of atoms.

It is reasonable to assume that new human motivations emerged with the new ways of thinking, for instance the quest for knowledge or the gatherer's need to collect not only food, but also knowledge, status symbols, objects of arts, and so on. To detect the evolutionary scenario of motivations related to integrative capacities is of course hardly possible. It may be more important to realize that the increasing cultural impact on the significance of words does not diminish the role of words for biological adaptation. In the long run, the immense accumulation of knowledge across ages and cultural borders leads to technologies that help humans compensate for biological constraints. Humans become capable of moving, flying or diving so fast and effectively that no other species can compete. They can kill any animal (or eradicate entire species), survive in hostile environments, improve resistance against diseases, and propagate more successfully. Here again, a specific human motivation for imitating successful models -- human or animal -- and at the same time for competing and getting ahead of imitated subjects may play a special role. Nevertheless, verbal communication and culture appear to function as powerful means of biological adaptation. The adaptive potential of language and culture has interested us for a particular reason. In organisms, it holds true for the relevant means of adaptation that they are based upon innate predispositions, develop early during ontogeny, are rather universally distributed, and often have supportive counterparts in social environments. Exactly these aspects of verbal communication have long remained underresearched, if not unnoticed, and call for attention in studies on early ontogeny.

COEVOLUTION OF PREDISPOSITIONS

We have realized that our studies on integrative and communicative development—a seeming antipole to genetics—would strongly benefit from better knowledge of biological aspects of these psychological phenomena in humans. The gaps have become particularly evident on the level of overt behaviors involved in parent–infant interactions, where we have seen spontaneous patterns that are difficult to interpret without considering their potential adaptive significance in the evolutionary past of humans.

In laboratory studies, we have witnessed 3- or 4-month-old babies solving difficult learning tasks and cognitive problems with no other reward than the intrinsic pleasure of success (H. Papoušek, 1977). However, it has also been evident that at this age, the infant's competence is still far from what is necessary for coping with the fast and rich chains of information included in the speech of adults. We have been able to demonstrate that learning abilities quickly improve in the next months, due to both maturation and practice. We have also realized that the modifications of learning situations that facilitate learning could be applied in some teaching programs for babies and that they would correspond to didactic recommendations, familiar to educational psychologists (H. Papoušek & M. Papoušek, 1984). For instance, they would correspond to the principles (a) to begin the training with easy tasks, and (b) to learn how to learn in frequent repetitive learning situations.

Our search for home situations comparable to learning situations has detected a minimum of them in infant responses to the physical environment, and a maximum in social interchanges with parents or other caregivers. We have realized—and confirmed in microanalyses of parent–infant interactions (H. Papoušek & M. Papoušek, 1987)—that caregivers rather generally tend to modify interactive behaviors so as to make them slower, repetitive, and easier to conceptualize and predict for the infant. Correspondingly, we have seen that infants tend to respond with anticipation and to express pleasure in cases of correct anticipations. The interaction, often viewed as a mere expression of emotional bonding, obviously meant more—a sequence of episodes activating integrative processes in infants and eliciting emotional expressions in response to successful integration.

Our observations have called for new interpretations of early social interactions. The standard view of infants as mere recipients of parental stimulation and the notion that they simply have to adapt to the social environment cannot hold anymore. The social environment has evidently been selected to adapt first and compensate for the infants' constraints, whereas the infants do not only adapt, but also function as very sucessful and autonomous elicitors of the caregivers' adaptations. In fact, parent–infant dyads represent prototypes of didactic systems with polar differences between both sides in the amount of experience, with infants having predispositions for learning, and parents having predispositions for teaching. We have revealed an entire set of parental capacities and special behavioral patterns that are involved in interactions with infants and fit the concept of a didactic system (H. Papoušek & M. Papoušek, 1987). However, our interviews with parents have also made it evident that parents are unaware of their didactic competence and they are unable to report on it verbally. That explains why this competence has long been escaping scientific evidence, and why it is necessary to turn attention to the category of involuntary, subconscious behaviors in human caregivers. The fact that the acquisition of language in infants is the main target of *intuitive parental didactics*, as we prefer to call it, lends the studies on early interactions a particular importance.

In general, speech as a species-specific and highly effective means of human adaptation seems to be based on predispositions that concern not only infants, but also parents. These predispositions also seem to belong to innate abilities and to result from a coevolution of genetically mediated premises. Thus, one of our tasks is to examine their innateness (H. Papoušek & M. Papoušek, 1992b). Due to ethical reasons, this cannot be done in direct experimental ways, common in biology; we have to examine indirect evidence, such as the universality of distribution across gender, age, and cultures or species, neurophysiological criteria, the relation to conscious, rational regulation of behavior, and incidental clinical evidence that sometimes provides "experiments of nature" of crucial importance. Some aspects of vocal communication, such as some specific modifications of prosody in infant-directed speech, have already been demonstrated in comparative studies to be universal across gender, age, and the cultures thus far investigated (Fernald, 1992; Fernald et al., 1989; M. Papoušek, H. Papoušek, & Symmes, 1991).

The intuitive character of parental didactics is another indicator of innateness. In cases where a latency between a distinct eliciting stimulus and a distinct onset of the elicited response can be safely measured, latencies under 500 milliseconds confirm the absence of conscious, rational control, which requires a minimum of 500 to 600 ms of cortical activation. Latencies in intuitive parental responses were frequently shorter than 300 ms. Careful interviews support these findings. Our coworkers found that mothers unwillingly reduced their observational distance of 40 to 50 cm to 20 to 25 cm to facilitate newborns' visual perception, although the majority of mothers believed that newborns cannot yet see (Schoetzau & H. Papoušek, 1977). Similarly, they adequately responded to cue gestures in infant hands—the only variable in drawings of infants—but believed that they were responding to changes in facial expressions (Kestermann, 1982). It should be stressed that these intuitive patterns of behavior are not fixed action patterns. Intuitive behaviors represent transitions between innate reflexes or fixed action patterns and conscious behaviors; subjects can become aware of their intuitive behaviors and focus attention on them; however, even then, they find it difficult to consciously control them. Vice versa, consciously learned patterns may become automatized through long-term training to a degree of nonconscious performance, as typically occurs in sports or artistic activities. Their advantage is that they may be carried out quickly and economically. Conversely, however, they may be inhibited in stressful situations (H. Papoušek & M. Papoušek, 1992a).

Studies of deaf infants and deaf mothers throw additional light on the problem of innateness. Deaf infants cannot learn the language of their cultural environment without special help. However, the development of their preverbal vocalization is parallel to the development in hearing infants, although distinctly slower (Oller & Eilers, 1988). Obviously, vocal development depends on innate regulations during an early age; however, audiovocal experience is soon necessary for further progress. Deaf mothers cannot modify infant-directed speech in didactic ways and those modifications cannot support speech acquisition in deaf infants. However, if deaf mothers teach their deaf infants American Sign Language, they unknowingly modify signing according to the same didactic principles as hearing mothers do so in audiovocal modality (Erting, Prezioso, & Hynes, 1990). Deaf infants develop signing in steps that are similar to the steps in vocal development, including babbling in the manual mode (Petitto & Marentette, 1991).

Yet another experiment of nature has been studied by Bornstein (1985) in twins. In comparison with singletons, each twin is exposed to less than half of maternal didactic interventions, as measured at the age of 6 months. At the age of 15 months, twins are already significantly delayed in cognitive and verbal competencies. Thus, various findings help elucidate the evolution and the preverbal ontogeny of the infantile and parental predispositions related to the infant's acquisition of speech, the participation of both genetically transmitted programs and enviromental impacts, and the amodal character of innate predispositions.

It is sometimes astonishing to observe a perfect fit between expressions of predispositions that have coevolved in parents and infants. The specific modifications of infant-directed speech in parents (the so-called baby talk or motherese) provide interesting examples. Parents, and speaking humans in general, are the first to start a dialogue; they strongly tend to speak to newborns even if there is no special reason for it (Rheingold & Adams, 1980). Unlike crying, the quiet vocalization develops slowly; infants are not capable of prolonging breathing for the display of fundamental voicing (H. Papoušek & M. Papoušek, 1981) that still hardly resembles any vowel. While speaking to infants, parents strikingly prolong vowels at the time when infants learn to control and prolong expiration; they use special melodic contours in the prosody of utterances as their first, context-related, prototypical messages at a time when the modulation of pitch is the main expressive capacity in infants' presyllabic vocalizations (M. Papoušek, H. Papoušek, & Bornstein, 1985); they strikingly display distinct models for the production of syllables when infants start producing their first primitive syllables; and they start modeling the first words and naming familiar persons or objects when the first canonical syllables (Oller & Eilers, 1992) from infants announce the beginning of verbal competence (H. Papoušek & M. Papoušek, 1987).

CONCLUDING REMARKS

The increasing evidence that important communicative processes already take place during the preverbal period of parent–infant interactions, that they are to a considerable degree genetically determined, and that they mainly serve as a relevant, species-specific means of biological adaptation, offers an opportunity for reconsidering the biological significance of human infancy and bonding. Infants have often been viewed as dependent due to a delay in locomotion, altricial in biological terms. However, their altricity is seriously contradicted by the progress in communication that is unique in the animal world. In this sense, infants are precocious. At the end of infancy they can speak enough to be confronted with the stream of cultural impact that is going to render them competencies unattainable by other animals—not only in locomotion, but in many other respects.

Parents are biologically prepared to facilitate and guide their infants' transition from the world of prevailing biological predispositions into the world of prevailing cultural influences. This transition is fluent and proportional rather than sudden, although there are milestones along the way that elicit new strategies in parental interventions. The appearance of smiles, cooing, canonical syllables, or first words may serve as examples. To parents, these milestones are biologically more effective than the progress in chronological age; however, they are not aware of this and they teach the child to celebrate chronological milestones. If we are willing to once again consider the notion that ontogeny recapitulates phylogeny, and that therefore, a better knowledge of ontogeny may help us understand evolution, we reach some interesting conclusions. The scenario of preverbal communication during postpartum ontogeny starts with a cry, for which such basic nervous circuits are sufficient that even an anencephalic newborn will make it. The first quiet sounds that may become parts of dialogues come days or weeks later. However, facial expressions of affects or hedonic feelings function from the first day as well and mostly elicit attention or matching on the parental side. Most of the following vocal interchanges up to canonical syllables concern training of how to produce new vocal sounds, consonants, and syllables. Parental guidance is directed at procedural aspects and teaching "know-how." The language hemisphere is probably still inactive.

The situation changes around 8 or 7 months. Infants start producing a new type of syllables that can hardly escape parental attention: reduplicated or canonical syllables, the first potential protowords and, obviously, cue signals that elicit a new strategy in parental guidance. Parents start modeling words of canonical syllables and giving them meanings. From now on, parents care distinctly more for declarative aspects of communication and teach infants "to know what" (H. Papoušek & M. Papoušek, 1984). From now on, playfulness, too, appears more and more frequently in parent–infant interchanges. Biological predispositions open the path along which the object of intuitive didactics will follow in the direction toward the concrete culture into which infants are to be integrated.

In our view, the main relevance of bonding may well concern this particular, species-specific function. Nursing and attachment for protection of infants are the oldest and biologically most general reasons for bonding. In humans, the original plan has been utilized for further purposes, as mentioned earlier. More importantly, attachment and bodily proximity is a sine qua non for the guidance along the avenue of verbal communication and cultural interchanges. A delay in locomotion is only a small price for the acquisition of language and through it, access to culture.

Not very much fantasy is necessary for attempting to find an analogy between the early ontogeny of integrative and communicative capacities in human infants and the genesis of culture in human evolution; that is, to further investigate whether predispositions for speech acquisition in infants and speech-directed didactics in parents are not, at the same time, predispositions for the genesis of culture. The circumstance that the evolution of specifically human characteristics of the bodily plan finds an analogy in the prepartum embryological development encourages attempts to look for an analogy to the evolution of specifically human psychological phenomena in postpartum behavioral development. The authors must not go too far away from their database. However, there are no such restrictions for the reader.

REFERENCES

Bertalanffy, L. von. (1968). *General systems theory: Foundations, development, applications.* New York: Braziller.

Bornstein, M. H. (1985). How infant and mother jointly contribute to developing cognitive competence in the child. *Proceedings of the National Academy of Sciences, 82,* 7470–7473.

Cavalli-Sforza, L. L., Menozzi, P., & Piazza, A. (1995). *The history and geography of human genes.* Princeton, NJ: Princeton University Press.

Darwin, C. (1871). *The descent of man.* London: Murray.

Erting, C. J., Prezioso, C., & Hynes, M. O. (1990). The interactional context of deaf mother–infant communication. In V. Volterra & C. Erting (Eds.), *From gesture to language in hearing and deaf children* (pp. 97–106). Berlin: Springer Verlag.

Fernald, A. (1992). Meaningful melodies in mothers' speech to infants. In H. Papoušek, U. Jürgens, & M. Papoušek (Eds.), *Nonverbal vocal communication: Comparative and developmental approaches* (pp. 262–282). New York: Cambridge University Press.

Fernald, A., Taeschner, T., Dunn, J., Papoušek, M., Boysson-Bardies, B., & Fukui, I. (1989). A cross-language study of prosodic modifications in mothers' and fathers' speech to preverbal infants. *Journal of Child Language, 16,* 977–1001.

Fogel, A. (1990). The process of developmental change in infant communicative action: Using dynamic systems theory to study individual ontogenies. In J. Colombo & J. Fagen (Eds.), *Individual differences in infancy: Reliability, stability, prediction* (pp. 341–358). Hillsdale, NJ: Lawrence Erlbaum Associates.

Gardner, R. A., & Gardner, B. T. (1969). Teaching sign language to a chimpanzee. *Science, 165,* 664–672.

Gleick, J. (1987). *Chaos. Making a new science.* New York: Viking Penguin.

Huizinga, J. (1955). *Homo ludens.* Boston: Beacon.

Huxley, J. (1965). *Essays of a humanist.* New York: Harper & Row.

Johanson, D. C., &. White, T. D. (1979). A systematic assessment of early African hominids. *Science, 203,* 321–330.

Kawai, M. (1963). On the newly acquired behaviors of the natural troop of Japanese monkeys on Koshima Island. *Primates, 4,* 113–115.

Kestermann, G. (1982). *Gestik von Säuglingen: Ihre kommunikative Bedeutung für erfahrene und unerfahrene Bezugspersonen. (Infant gestures: Their communicative signifance for experienced and unexperienced caregivers.)* Doctoral dissertation, University of Bielefeld, Germany.

Konner, M., & Worthman, C. (1980). Nursing frequency, gonadal function, and birth spacing among Kung hunter-gatherers. *Science, 207,* 788–791.

Leakey, M. D., & Hay, R. L. (1979). Pliocene footprints in the Laetolil Beds at Laetolil, Northern Tanzania. *Nature, 278,* 308–312 .

Lieberman, P. (1984). *The biology and evolution of language.* Cambridge, MA: Harvard University Press.

Lovejoy, C. O. (1981). The origin of man. *Science, 211,* 341–350.

MacLean, P. D. (1973). *A triune concept of brain and behavior.* Toronto: University of Toronto Press.

MacLean, P. D. (1990). *The triune brain in evolution. Role in paleocerebral functions.* New York: Plenum.

Murphy, M. R., MacLean, P. D., & Hamilton, S. C. (1981). Species-typical behavior of hamsters deprived from birth of the neocortex. *Science, 213,* 459–461.

Oller, D. K., & Eilers, R. E. (1988). The role of audition in infant babbling. *Child Development, 59,* 441–449.

Oller, D. K., & Eilers, R. E. (1992). Development of vocal signaling in human infants: Toward a methodology for cross-species vocalization comparisons. In H. Papoušek, U. Jürgens, & M. Papoušek (Eds.), *Nonverbal vocal communication: Comparative and developmental approaches* (pp. 174–191). New York: Cambridge University Press.

Papoušek, H. (1967). Experimental studies of appetitional behavior in human newborns and infants. In H. W. Stevenson, E. H. Hess, & H. L. Rheingold (Eds.), *Early behavior: Comparative and developmental approaches* (pp. 249–277). New York: Wiley.

Papoušek, H. (1977). Entwicklung der Lernfähigkeit im Säuglingsalter (The development of learning ability in infancy). In G. Nissen (Ed.), *Intelligenz, Lernen und Lernstörungen. (Intelligence, learning, and learning disorders.)* (pp. 75–93). Berlin: Springer-Verlag.

Papoušek, M., & Papoušek, H. (1981). Musical elements in the infant's vocalizations: Their significance for communication, cognition, and creativity. In L. P. Lipsitt (Ed.), *Advances in infancy research* (pp. 163–224). Norwood, NJ: Ablex.

Papoušek, H., & Papoušek, M. (1984). Learning and cognition in the everyday life of human infants. In J. S. Rosenblatt (Ed.), *Advances in the study of behavior* (pp. 127–163). New York: Academic Press.

Papoušek, H., & Papoušek, M. (1987). Intuitive parenting: A dialectic counterpart to the infant's integrative competence. In J. D. Osofsky (Ed.), *Handbook of infant development* (pp. 669–720). New York: Wiley.

Papoušek, H., & Papoušek, M. (1992a). Beyond emotional bonding: The role of preverbal communication in mental growth and health. *Infant Mental Health Journal, 13,* 43–53.

Papoušek, H., & Papoušek, M. (1992b). Early integrative and communicative development: Pointers to humanity. In H. M. Emrich & M. Wiegand (Eds.), *Integrative biological psychiatry* (pp. 45–60). Berlin: Springer-Verlag.

Papoušek, M., Papoušek, H., & Bornstein, M. H. (1985). The naturalistic vocal environment of young infants: On the significance of homogeneity and variability in parental speech. In T. Field & N. Fox (Eds.), *Social perception in infant* (pp. 269–297). Norwood, NJ: Ablex.

Papoušek, M., Papoušek, H., & Symmes, D. (1991). The meanings of melodies in motherese in tone and stress languages. *Infant Behavior and Development, 14,* 414–440.

Patterson, F. G. (1978). The gestures of a gorilla: Language acquisition by another pongid. *Brain and Language, 12,* 72–97.

Petitto, L. A., & Marentette, P. F. (1991). Babbling in the manual mode: Evidence for the ontogeny of language. *Science, 251,* 1493–1496.

Ploog, D. (1992). Ethological foundations of biological psychiatry. In H. M. Emrich & M. Wiegand (Eds.), *Integrative biological psychiatry* (pp. 3–35). Berlin: Springer Verlag.

Premack, A. J., & Premack, D. (1972). Teaching language to an ape. *Scientific American, 227,* 92–99.

Rheingold, H. L., & Adams, J. L. (1980). The significance of speech to newborns. *Developmental Psychology, 16,* 397–403.

Robertson, S. S., Cohen, A. H., & Mayer-Kress, G. (1993). Behavioral chaos: Beyond the metaphor. In L. Smith & E. Thelen (Eds.), *A dynamic systems approach to development* (pp. 119–150). Cambridge, MA: A Bradford Book. MIT Press.

Rumbaugh, D. M., & Savage-Rumbaugh, E. S. (1996). Biobehavioral roots of language: Words, apes, and a child. In B. M. Velichkovsky & D. M. Rumbaugh (Eds.), *Communicating meaning: The evolution and development of language* (pp. 257–274). Mahwah, NJ: Lawrence Erlbaum Associates.

Savage-Rumbaugh, E. S., Rumbaugh, D. M., & Boysen, S. (1978). Symbolic communication between two chimpanzees *(Pan troglotydes). Science, 201,* 641–644.

Schoetzau, A., & Papoušek, H. (1977). Mütterliches Verhalten bei der Aufnahme von Blickkontakt mit dem Neugeborenen. (Maternal behavior during engagement in visual contact with the newborn.) *Zeitschrift für Entwicklungspsychologie und pädagogische Psychologie, 9,* 231–239.

Slotnick, B. M. (1967). Disturbance of maternal behavior in the rat following lesions of the cingulate cortex. *Behaviour, 24,* 204–236.

Simon, E. L. (1967). The earliest apes. *Scientific American, 217,* 28–35.

Stamm, J. S. (1955). The function of the median cerebral cortex in maternal behavior of rats. *Journal of Comparative and Physiological Psychology, 48,* 347–356.

de Vries, J. I. P., Visser, G. H. A., & Prechtl, H. F. R. (1982). The emergence of fetal behaviour. I: Qualitative aspects. *Early Human Development, 7,* 301–322.

6

DEVELOPMENT OF EMOTIONS AND THEIR EXPRESSION IN TASK-ORIENTED SITUATIONS IN INFANTS AND PRESCHOOL CHILDREN

Klaus Schneider
University of Bochum

THE INFANTS' SMILE IN SOCIAL AND NONSOCIAL SITUATIONS

Piaget (1936) described how his 2-month-old son Laurent happened to shake a rattle that was hanging over his bed and connected with a string to his arm. Smiling and cooing, Laurent repeated these movements several times and with shorter and shorter intervals: "Laurent naturally shook the balls by chance and looked at them at once (the rattle inside them made a noise). As the shaking was repeated more and more frequently Laurent arched himself, waved his arms and legs—in short, he revealed increasing pleasure and through this maintained the interesting result" (Piaget, 1977, p. 183).

Students of the development of competence and achievement motivation in children have interpreted the affective reactions to self-produced effects shown by little Laurent and many other infants in more controlled studies as an expression of positive emotional reactions, as an expression of contingency affects (see Lewis & Goldberg, 1969; Papoušek, 1967; Rovee & Rovee, 1969; Watson, 1972; Watson & Ramey, 1972). Following White (1959), many writers considered the contingency affects demonstrated by infants in such games as the proximate cause for the striving for mastery in young children and infants; this striving is assumed to be an evolved disposition due to its undeniable adaptation value. The adaptation value of such a striving to master the physical and social environment by acquiring knowledge and skills seems obvious, as parental tutoring could never provide all the necessary challenges for the cognitive, emotional, and motivational development of infants and children.

In this tradition of developmental theorizing, the smile has been interpreted as an expressive sign of a positive cognitive-emotional-motivational state (see Darwin, 1872). We know from developmental, comparative, and anthropological work, however, that a smile in older children and adults is also or even primarily a communicative tool, a gesture of affiliation or appeasement (Andrew, 1963; Bowlby, 1969; Darwin, 1872; Ekman, 1973; van Hooff, 1972). Especially in the attachment behavior of infants, the smile seems to have an important function for establishing and maintaining close proximity and secure relationships between the child and her or his caretaker (see Ainsworth, 1967; Bowlby, 1969). It has also been shown that the human face or parts of it are a potent releaser for the smile (Jones, 1926; Spitz & Wolf, 1946). In adults, we have learned that even in a social achievement situation the smile might be primarily a communicative act. Kraut and Johnston (1979), for example, observed members of a bowling party coming back from their turn, and found that a smile in this situation is a social smile; that it is only shown when the player turns around after a strike to look at her or his companions. Similar observations were made in a hockey game. Here, however, spectators also smiled when they were not engaged in social interaction and only their favorite team won.

However, in my view, this observation and some similar ones have been overstated in inferring that smiling in humans is exclusively socially determined. I believe that emotions have their nonsocial function for the regulation of behavior, including the regulation of inner states (specific emotional states and general arousal or activation), relating the specific situational and organismic givens to the distal goals of behavior. Such distal goals as, for example, finding a substitute for energy or fluid loss, or a mating partner, can be considered as evolutionary strategies that sometimes must be pursued socially but at other times can be pursued by dealing with the physical world alone. Therefore, emotions have a function in social as well as in nonsocial situations. I agree with other students of the development of emotions in humans that in the first 2 or 3 years the smiling reaction is becoming more and more social. However, there is enough proof that facial behavior and also the smile remains an index of internal behavior-regulating states over these years as well. In order to demonstrate this, I present some more examples from the literature and from my own work.

THE SMILE OF MASTERY IN INFANTS AND PRESCHOOL CHILDREN

Two- to three-month-old children demonstrate positive emotional reactions and they smile, not only to faces but also to the presentation of novel stimuli: visual figures, objects, and sounds (see McCall, 1972; Meili, 1957; Piaget, 1937; Shultz & Zigler, 1970; Zelazo, 1972; Zelazo & Komer, 1971). This has been interpreted as an expression of the assimilatory recognition (Piaget, 1936) or more general as an expression of a mastery of the perceptual input (Kagan, 1971; Meili, 1957; Piaget, 1945). Following Meili (1957; see also Meili-Dworetzki & Meili, 1972), we can assume that the processing of such a perceptual input is a task for infants that is more or less difficult, so that infants can succeed or fail in this task. This depends on the complexity of the percept and the cognitive abilities of the infants (depending on their cognitive development and interindividual differences).

Meili (1957) and many other proponents of the mastery hypothesis of the smile have shown that during the confrontation with a new figural pattern the smile is shown at the end of a period where the infant seems to perceive and process the informational input attentively. At this point the smile goes together with a general behavioral agitation, whereas in the phase before infants seem to be motorically inhibited.

The experiential states through which infants 3 to 4 months old go in such a task-oriented situation was described by Meili (1957) as the building up of tension in the phase where infants try to assimilate the percept, ended by a solution and the reduction of tension when infants finally succeed. Building up of tension followed by a solution seems to be a basic characteristic of emotional processes identified by Wundt (1896) as one of his three basic dimensions. The dimensions were the traditional pleasant–unpleasant, the excited–quiet and the tense–relaxed dimension. Using some more neurophysiological theorizing, Sroufe and Waters (1976) assumed that the smile marks the end of a sympathetic activation increase–decrease cycle (tension–release), becoming manifest in heartrate changes and, additionally, in general motility.

If a smile marks the end of a successful information processing episode in infants, it should take longer for the appearance of the smile the more difficult the percepts are. This was demonstrated by Shultz and Zigler (1970) and Kaufmann-Hayoz (1981). Shultz and Zigler (1970) confronted infants between 8 and 18 weeks old with a 10 inch brightly colored terrycloth clown, either stationary or moving (swung from one side to the other). The assumption was that the moving stimulus was harder to assimilate and that, therefore, it should take longer before a smile became manifest at all. Except for one, all infants smiled in this situation associated with vocalization. As predicted, the latency of the first smile was approximately 4 times longer in respect to the moving clown than to the stationary one (7.2 +/-4.4 vs. 1.7 +/-1.8 min). Thus, even these young infants smiled at such a complex nonsocial stimulus as a terrycloth clown when it was presented long enough. The necessary time for the presentation could not be measured in seconds but had to be measured in minutes. The typical sequence of the reaction of the infants was described by Shultz and Zigler (1970) as follows: "A typical infant studied the stimulus very quietly and seriously for several minutes. Then his eyes brightened, his arms and legs began to move excitedly, and he began smiling and vocalizing to the stimulus. All this activity gradually peaked and then dropped off. As he quieted, the infant began to look away from the stimulus, usually toward the experimenter" (p. 399).

The importance of the time of presentation of such percepts as well as of the general conditions of infant testing and the security provided by the situation was nicely demonstrated in a series of studies by Kaufmann-Hayoz and associates (Kaufmann-Hayoz, 1981, 1991; Kaufmann-Hayoz, Kaufmann, & Lang, 1978). These investigators presented to infants in the first trimester of life facelike abstract stimuli, which were presumably more or less easily to process due to deviations from symmetry and a decreasing similarity to the structure of a human face (see Fig. 6.1). These stimuli were presented to the infants either on a TV screen in the laboratory where infants were hooked to electrodes or on cardbords over their cribs in the infants' homes (Kaufmann-Hayoz, 1981, 1991). Whereas in the first study very few smiles were observed, presumably due to the strange environment (see Kaufmann-Hayoz,

1991), all infants from the age of 9 weeks on smiled at least once to the different stimuli in the more familiar environment of the home. Fig. 6.1 shows the averaged latencies of the first smile to the three stimuli for the 9-, 12-, and 16-week-olds. The latency increases with increasing difficulty of the stimuli, corroborating Meili's assumption that the smile indicates the successful termination of a perceptual assimilation.

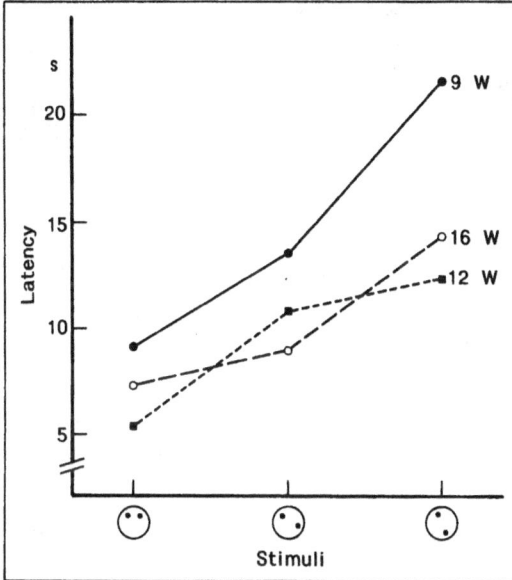

Fig. 6.1: Mean latencies of the first smile in three age groups of infants to three visual stimuli of increasing assimilation difficulty. The stimuli are presented below (from Kaufmann-Hayoz, 1981).

In a recent study, Kaufmann-Hayoz (1991) experimentally manipulated the behavioral arousal level of the infants by presenting them a prestimulus for 10 seconds (Stimulus B from the former study) either stationary at a distance of 40 cm or as a looming stimulus, brought forward to the child from a distance of approximately 100 cm to 15 cm. It was predicted and found that due to the increase of arousal caused by the looming stimulus that infants would smile less in this condition and, if they did, with longer latencies. The main results confirm these predictions.

Zelazo and Komer (1971) deduced from the mastery hypothesis for the indicator value of a smile (Piaget, 1945) that a novel stimulus, with repeated presentations, should elicit first more and more smiles, as the new schema is formed, and then lose its potency for eliciting smiles. Finally, the novel stimulus has become familiar and the smiling reaction will habituate. To test this hypothesis Zelazo and Komer (1971) confronted their subjects, 20 white home-reared male infants between 12 and 15 weeks old, with three complexity levels of visual (static) and auditory (dynamic) stimuli. Infants were tested in two 7-min blocks for 2 consecutive days. In each block each visual and each auditory stimulus was presented for 8 seconds, the sequence being randomized completely. The results of this study show the predicted curvilinear relationship between trials (time of exposure to the new stimuli) and amount of smiling for the auditory stimuli, but not for the visual ones. For the stimuli of this modality, smiling declined already on the very first day from the first to the second block of presentations (see Fig. 6.2).

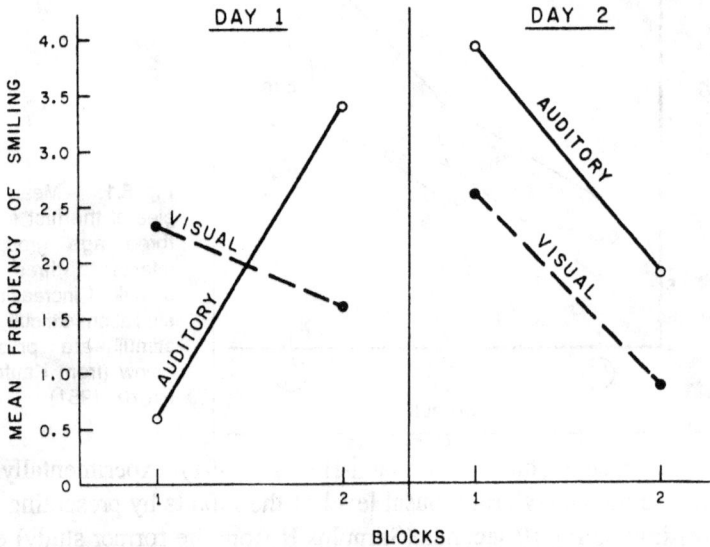

Fig. 6.2:   Mean frequencies of smiles as a function of the amount of exposure to different visual and auditory stimuli (from Zelazo & Komer, 1971; reprinted from *Child Development* (1971); by permission of the SRCD, The University of Michigan, Ann Arbor).

However, in a subsequent study Zelazo and Kagan (see Zelazo, 1972) presented in analogy to the dynamic (sequential) auditory stimuli a sequential visual stimulus to 100 infants from 5.5 to 11.5 months old. Three bulbs mounted on a box could be touched sequentially by a movable rod and were then lighted. The standard procedure, the movement of the rod and the sequential lightening of the bulbs touched by the rod, was presented 8 to 10 times to the children. After that some variations were presented. The younger children, the 5- to 7-month-olds, demonstrated the predicted curvilinear relationship between trials and the incidence of smiling but not the older children, 9 to 11 months old (see Fig. 6.3). On the first trial no younger child smiled whereas older children smiled in approximately half of all trials. This can be understood by assuming that the complexity level of this sequential stimulus is still high and demands assimilation effort for the 5 to 6 months olds but is low already for the 9 to 11 months olds.

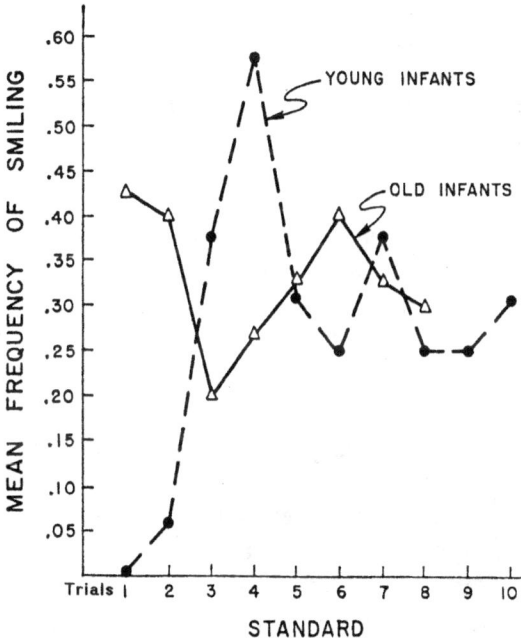

Fig. 6.3: Mean frequency of smiling to the first 10 presentations of the sequential visual stimulus shown in Fig. 6.5 in two age groups of infants: young infants (5–7 months old) and old infants (9–11 months old). Only for those infants who smiled at least once (N = 46) reactions are reported (reprinted from *Merrill-Palmer Quarterly, Vol. 18*, No. 4 (1972), p. 358; by Philip R. Zelazo. By permission of the Wayne State University Press).

The time taken by the assumed categorization and information processing, the end of which is marked by a smile, depends not only on the general cognitive development but also on interindividual differences in the rate of information processing. Therefore, the frequency of smiling in such task-oriented situations should also depend on interindividual differences in the rate of information processing. Kagan, McCall and their associates (see McCall & Kagan, 1970) could show that those infants who either habituated fast to a visual stimulus array (three objects) or looked at it very shortly in the first trial, did (a) inspect a changed stimulus longer—the more so the greater the change was—and (b) smile (at least some of them) while looking at this visual pattern. The percentages of smiling children were 0% (slow habituators), 19% (fast habituators), and 27% (short fixators).

The general conclusion from these observations is, as Kagan (1971) aptly stated, that the smile serves many masters in infants and children. It is part of the social behavioral system, attachment or bonding, and at the same time it is the expression of the solution of successful task-oriented behavior in a nonsocial situation, be it the perceptual assimilation of a stimulus or the contingent production of interesting effects in the physical world surrounding the infant.

Unfortunately, earlier students of infants' emotional expression argued that the only potent stimulus for the eliciting of a smile in infants is the human face (see Bühler, 1927), a hypothesis eagerly embraced by workers with a psychoanalytical and ethological background.

Presenting a wide variety of visual and auditory stimuli to 145 infants between 2 and 6 months old, Spitz and Wolf (1946) could not elicit one single smile in their subjects. This observation fits nicely with Spitz's supposition that psychology is not a science of psychic functions and structure but is essentially the science of interaction. Spitz and Wolf, however, presented their stimuli apparently for a short time and only once. Two other early students of infants' smiling reactions followed the same procedure: Hetzer and Tudor-Hart (1927), who had presented 15 different sounds and noises to infants between 1 day and 4 months old, found expressive signs of positive emotional reactions (smiling, sounds and expression of comfort, crying and sounds of discomfort when the presentation stopped) nearly exclusively in respect to human sounds (singing, friendly and angry addressing of the infant, and general conversation). Although it is true that exogenous smiles can be released most easily by the human voice in the first weeks of life, other sounds like a bell, a whistle, and a rattle also trigger smiles, although less effective ones (Wolff, 1963).

As mentioned, based on observations of smiling in mother–child interactions Ainsworth (1967) and Bowlby (1969) assumed that smiling evolved in humans as an instinctual behavior due to its adaptive value in fostering mutual rewarding interactions between mother and child and maintaining proximity between mother and child.

Even if we accept such a construction for the phylogeny of the smile reaction, this functional analysis cannot substitute for the causal mechanisms, the proximate causes of the release of the infants' smile. Although there is no one-to-one relation between expressive movements and emotional states, the functional analysis of emotional states and expressions started by Darwin (1872) made it clear that there must be some correspondence between emotional states and the related behavioral intention and expressive movements most of the time. Otherwise expressive behaviors could not have been of great value for the cooperative activities in hominid groups, which were for the good of all interactants. Therefore, an infant might show a smile when she or he feels like it, no matter whether there is an alter ego present or not.

The position I favor here is the so-called classical ethological position that contrasts with the modern "selfish gene" point of view (see Krebs & Dawkins, 1978; but see Krebs & Dawkins, 1984). At least in socially living animals the veridical expression of an emotional/motivational state and the correct understanding of this message by group members must have an advantage for both the sender and the receiver. The corresponding mechanisms should have evolved, therefore, by coevolution (Blest, 1961; Leyhausen, 1968).

CHILDREN'S SMILE IN ACHIEVEMENT-ORIENTED SITUATIONS

Students of achievement motivation consider the kind of mastery-oriented behavior in infants described earlier as a precursor system of the achievement motivation system of the older preschool child. According to Heckhausen and associates (see Heckhausen, 1972, 1982; Trudewind, 1976, 1982; Trudewind, Unzner, & Schneider, 1989), achievement motivation proper demands a self-referential standard of excellence for task outcomes and includes self-referential emotions like pride and shame or embarrassment. Not until children have such standards for their own performance and are willing and able to evaluate their task outcome according to such a standard can we assume that the working motivation in task performance is a mature achievement motivation. Somewhere between 2 and 3 years of age such a standard-oriented achievement motivation seems to develop out of the more unspecific and general striving for mastery, where children seem to be content with being effective; that is, with experiencing the "feeling of efficacy" (White, 1959; see Geppert & Küster, 1983; Stipek, 1983). A necessary cognitive prerequisite for the differentiation of achievement

motivation out of the less mature mastery motivation is the development of a "categorial" self-concept; that is, the child's structured knowledge of its own performance-related abilities (see Lewis & Brooks-
Gunn, 1979). Only in respect to self image can self-referential emotions
like pride, shame, and embarrassment develop (see Lewis & Michalson,
1983; Lewis, Sullivan, & Michalson, 1984; Lewis, Sullivan, Stanger, &
Weiss, 1989).

Developmental studies of preschoolers' emotional reactions and
their expression in achievement-oriented situations were started by
Heckhausen and associates in the early 1960s (see Heckhausen, 1984).
Lately, such studies have been taken up again by Geppert (1986), Lütkenhaus (1984), and myself in cooperation with Unzner and Josephs
(Schneider, 1987; Schneider & Josephs, 1991; Schneider & Unzner,
1989, 1992; Unzner & Schneider, 1990). The early studies by Heckhausen and associates were pioneering studies full of phenomenological
insights, but done in the tradition of German *Ausdruckspsychologie*
and, therefore, not differentiating clearly between the descriptive or
morphological features of facial and gestural behaviors and their inferred meaning. In addition, no normative data are given. Thus, we
really don't know how many children demonstrated the different facial
and postural features referred to in the secondary literature in the
achievement situations studied. Quite generally, however, it was observed that children between 3.5 and 4.5 years old demonstrated behavioral signs of positive emotions—of contentment, joy, and pride—
when they succeeded in a competitive ring stacking (tower building)
game against a female adult competitor. In trials where children finished the tower earlier than the adult, they (some children in some trials) raised their eyes from the tower, looked triumphantly at the experimenter, smiled, sat up straight, raised their head, and threw their
arms up in the air. However, if the experimenter won, they did not look
up from their work, their body collapsed, their head was lowered, and
they also often smiled in an—as the authors said—"ashamed" way
(Heckhausen & Roelofsen, 1962).

However, such a competitive game is a multi-incentive situation,
which may have instigated not only positive and avoidant achievement
motivation but also dominance and submissive behavior. In addition,
affiliation motivation and a mere tendency to please the adult experimenter is probably instigated in such a situation (e.g., Geppert, 1986).
Therefore, the meaning of the facial and postural reactions to winning
and losing in this competitive game is not clear. Most of the behavioral

expressions became manifest only when the child and the experimenter had finished the task and the experimenter asked the child who, the child or the experimenter, had won the game. At this moment the asymmetric social relationship must have become even more salient than before.

In these studies, older children, the 4.5- to 6.5-year-olds, already demonstrated signs of controlled expression, even of positive emotions in cases where children won the competition. The social asymmetric relation between the adult experimenter and the child in this situation may have motivated the child to dampen the triumph.

In our own studies we, therefore, created a game situation in which social interaction, not to mention competition, between child and experimenter was downplayed. In the first study (see Schneider, 1987) children played a psychomotor achievement game in the presence of an adult female without interacting with her. In this game, where children tried to hit gates of different width at the end of the playing table with a marble, the outcome of each could be assessed by the children themselves and was additionally signaled by the apparatus (light effects and discriminating sounds). The same physical game was used in two different settings: The first one was the aforementioned achievement situation, and the second one was a mere effect-producing game. The study was a longitudinal study with four age groups (3.5-, 4, 4.5-, and 5-year-olds) playing this achievement game and (with 1-day interval) the effect game in which children could produce interesting light and sound effects without heading for a goal. They were observed at time intervals of 6 months. (The 5-year-olds were observed only once.) For the effect game we removed the gate; the children were asked to roll the marble, which then triggered an unpredictable light and sound effect. For comparison, the experimenter played this game also. Facial reactions in this and all following studies were coded with the help of the Facial Action Coding System (FACS; Ekman & Friesen, 1978).

Even in this noncompetitive situation, where children were obviously attracted by this impressive apparatus and the game itself, children smiled in failure trials, although less intensively so (Fig. 6.4). However, at least the 5-year-olds showed the complete Duchenne smile—the simultanous appearance of the zygomaticus reaction and the orbicularis oculi reaction—longer in success than in failure trials (Fig. 6.5). Therefore, the emotional reaction to a success feedback seems at least more of a true joy than the one manifested to a failure feedback. Success smiles were also more intensive and more often combined with an open mouth than failure smiles.

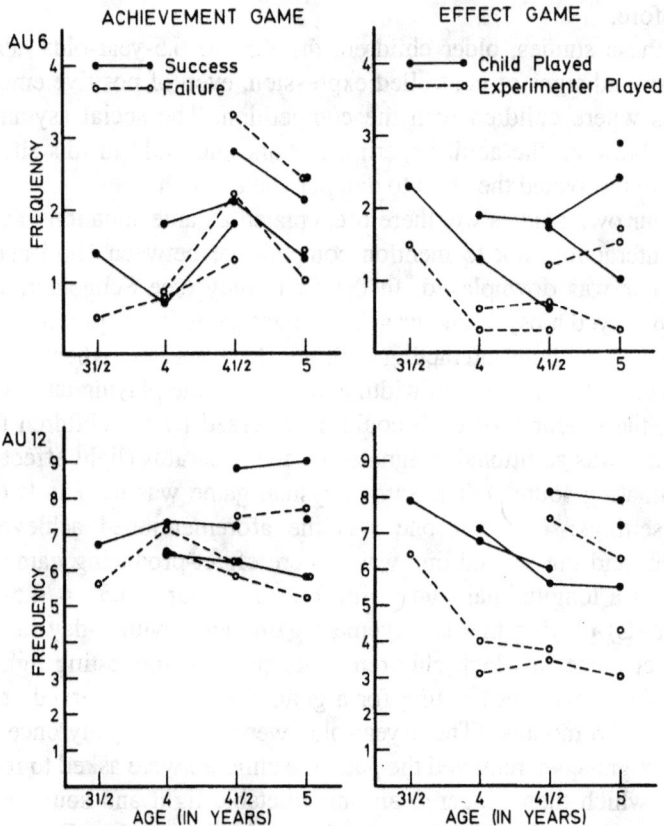

Fig. 6.4:   Mean frequency of the orbicularis oculi reaction (AU6) and the zygomaticus reaction (AU12) in the achievement game and the effect game for four cohorts (age 3½ – 5 years) (from Schneider & Unzner, 1989).

The assumption that our situation was predominantly a nonsocial situation is confirmed by the modal sequence of behavior of the children. The children's eyes followed in nearly all trials the rolling marble until it either hit the gate or did not; then they looked at the signal lamps above the table and smiled. Only later did they turn their head to the experimenter sitting at their left side.

It was found that on average the nonsocial smile (looking at the feedback signals) was five to six times longer than the social smile (looking at the experimenter). In addition, we never observed combinations of smiles with the dramatic head and postural movements described by Heckhausen and Roelofsen (1962) and Geppert and associates (see Geppert, 1986), confirming the assumption that these strong emotional reactions are not the expressions of achievement emotions proper but expressions of emotions related to submission and dominance.

The Duchenne smile also differentiates between the 5-year-olds' success trials in the achievement game and their own trials in the effect game. However, already at an age of 4 years does the functional looking behavior, the look toward the signal lights over the playing table, discriminate significantly between the two games. In the achievement game, 4-year-olds and all older children looked more often and also longer toward the signal lights, which announced success and failure, than in the effect game where the lights only presented contingently produced random effects. The emotional differentiation between mere effects in the effect game, which could not be evaluated according to a standard of excellence, and achievement-dependent outcomes, was also reflected in the pronounced habituation of the smiling reaction to the signals in the effect game in the first two cohorts (see Fig. 6.5).

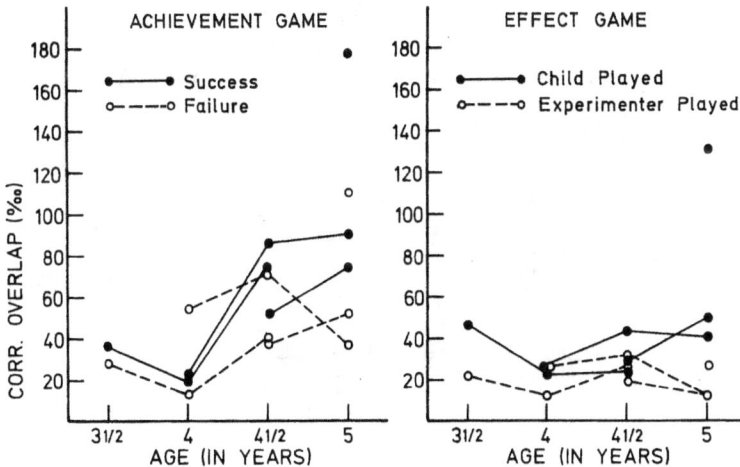

Fig. 6.5: Mean corrected overlap scores for the orbicularis oculi reaction (AU6) with the zygomaticus reaction (AU12) in the achievement game and the effect game for four cohorts (age 3½ – 5 years) (from Schneider & Unzner, 1989).

We concluded from these observations that preschool children smile as an expression of their contentment and joy in task behavior. They may also communicate this to other persons present; however, this does not seem to be their primary goal—at least not in this situation. Yet, a subsequent study with a different task, a game in which children had to snap plastic frogs into a pond on a table, taught us differently (Schneider & Josephs, 1991). Here, children always turned immediately smilingly to the experimenter. They also smiled more often and longer in failure trials, where the frog missed the pond, than in success trials where the frog hit the pond. Subjects in this study were 19 preschoolers, from 3 years 11 months to 6 years six months old. The experimenter sat next to the child and passed the frogs one after the other to the child.

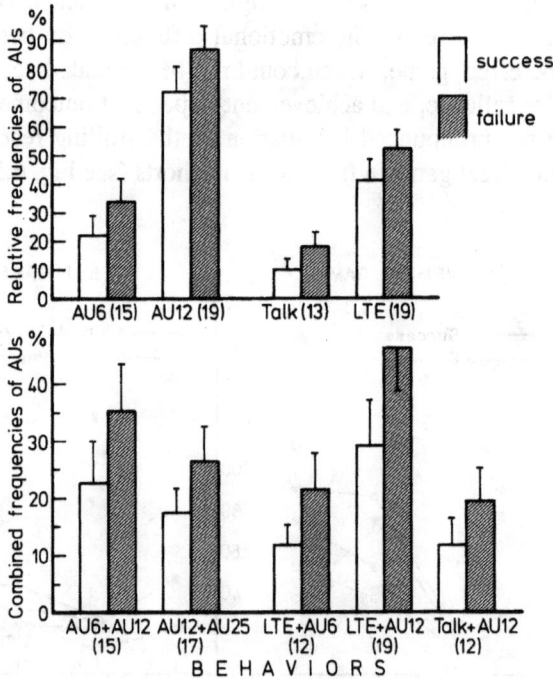

Fig. 6.6:   Mean relative frequencies (in %) of Lip Corner Pull (AU12), Cheek Raise (AU6), Talking (TALK), and Looking (LTE) to the Experimenter (Upper Part) and (Lower Part) of the combined appearance of two units (AU25 = Lips Part) after success and failure. The number of children showing the behaviors is given in parentheses (from Schneider & Josephs, 1991).

For 3 seconds after the frogs' jump the experimenter kept a neutral face. The next figure shows the mean frequencies of the components of the smile, the zygomaticus reaction (AU12) and the orbicularis oculi reaction (AU6), as well as talking and looking at the experimenter (Fig. 6.6). In addition, the lower part of the figure demonstrates the frequency of combinations of these movements, the Duchenne smile (i.e., the combination of the zygomaticus and the orbicularis oculi reaction) and the combinations of the smiling components with talking and looking at the experimenter.

Compared to success trials, children not only demonstrate more smiling in failure trials, they also show the "true" smile, the Duchenne smile, more often in failure than in success trials. In addition, they address the experimenter more often in combination with smiling. Compared to the former study, the marble-rolling task, children in the frog task smiled twice as long while they looked at the experimenter.

We concluded from these observations that in this task, snipping the frog and watching where it lands is the only attention-demanding part of the task. Communicative functions of the smile will, therefore, dominate. Children looked at the experimenter, they smiled more often in failure than in success trials, and they showed the Duchenne smile more often even then. We interpreted this behavior of the children as a kind of social referencing behavior: Being uncertain what it all means, the child might ask for an interpretation by looking smilingly to the experimenter or might offer an excuse for the misfortune of missing the pond. This interpretation is supported by the fact that in failure trials the smile (AU12) is more often associated with a look toward the experimenter than in success trials. In failure trials children look also faster toward the experimenter than in success trials ($\underline{M} = 1.5$, $\underline{SD} = .26$, and $\underline{M} = 1.76$, $\underline{SD} = .57$, $\underline{p} < .05$). Presumably due to this, the zygomaticus reaction, the smile in failure trials, precedes the look at the experimenter only by $^1/_{10}$ of a second, whereas in success trials the temporal gap between the beginning of the smile and the look at the experimenter is $^4/_{10}$ of a second. Although these time variables confirm the hypothesis that the smile in failure trials in this game is a deliberate (intentional) presentation of a happy face, the failure smiles in this situation are as often Duchenne smiles as in success trials. Therefore, it is questionable whether the Duchenne smile is a valid marker for the differentiation between true versus false or miserable smiles (see Ekman & Friesen, 1982; Ekman & Keltner, chap. 2, this volume).

In order to examine this hypothesis in more detail we loosened the contact between experimenter and child in the next study. In one condition the experimenter sat next to the child in the usual way; in the second condition the experimenter sat at a different table facing the wall and pretending to do some necessary work. In this nonsocial condition all facial behaviors were reduced. Children exhibited especially less expression of joy or contentment manifested in the zygomaticus and orbicularis oculi reaction. However, they did not demonstrate significantly more smiles after failure in the social condition as they had done in the study before, nor did they demonstrate more smiles after success in the nonsocial condition, as we had predicted (Fig. 6.7). The reason for this may be that children in this study were confronted with a strange environment: They had come with their parents to the institute and were welcomed there by an unfamiliar experimenter. In the aforementioned study, the experimenter had participated in normal activities of the nursery group for several days and the experiment was run in the nursery school itself. It might well be that the kind of social referencing or appeasing behavior we have assumed to stand behind children's smiles in failure trails before needs a familiar adult as an appropriate target.

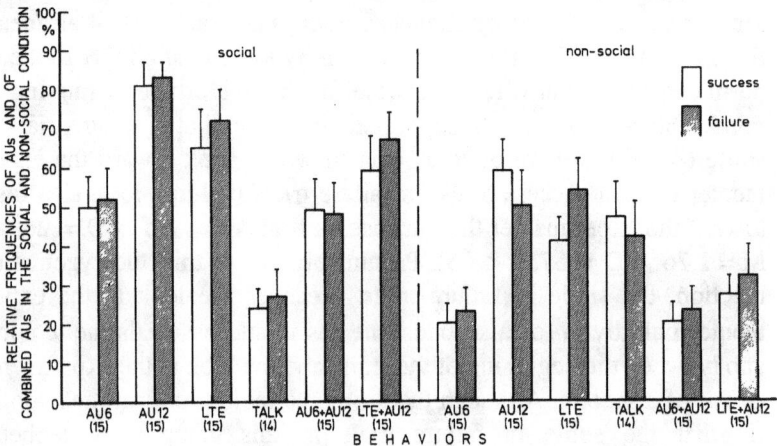

Fig. 6.7: Mean relative frequencies (in %) of Lip Corner Pull (AU12), Cheek Raise (AU6), Talking (TALK), and Looking (LTE) to the experimenter and the combined appearance of two units after success and failure in the social and nonsocial situation. The number of children showing the behaviors is given in parentheses (from Schneider & Josephs, 1991).

Taken together, we conclude from our studies that preschoolers' smiling in task behavior may have many functions. When the task is demanding and attracting the child's attention, the smile might very well be a valid indicator of the child's emotional reaction, joy, contentment, or pride. In case the task does not attract the attention of the child any longer after an effect was produced and a familiar person is present, the social communicative function might dominate. Preschoolers may use the smile as a tool in their social interaction: negotiating with the other person about what it all means (Hinde, 1985), belittling the failure, or asking for a comment. Whether this will happen or not depends not only on the task but also on the quality of the social relation between the child and the other persons present. This is, of course, a post hoc explanation that needs to be tested in a new study in which the quality of the social relation should be varied experimentally.

The interpretation offered here demands that preschoolers are able and willing to control their facial behaviors—be that intentionally or unintentionally. This has been shown by Cole (1986) and Saarni (1984) for children 4 years and older and recently by Josephs (1987) even for children between 3 and 4 years old.

Infants and children smile to social as well as to nonsocial stimuli. As both kinds of reactions to stimuli appear ontogenetically at about the same time, one cannot trace back one reaction to the other. In a nonsocial situation, the smile of infants and preschoolers seems to indicate a positive emotional evaluation of an accomplishment or of the mastery of a task. In such a situation the smile is an expression, the outward manifestation of a state. However, if there is somebody present, even the expression of an outcome-related emotion might become a social signal for mutual joy, or for a kind of negotiation on the meaning of the situation with the other person.

Our own results in the first study with the attention-demanding task show that this comes after the solitary emotional evaluation and expression of this evaluation of the task outcome: Only after some concentration on the task itself, especially on the signal lights, do our preschoolers turn around and look at the experimenter with a smile. Here, too, they smile after misses but they did more so in the not so demanding frog snapping task used in the following studies. There, children also turned faster to the experimenter when they failed than when they succeeded. Presumably, in a failure trial, where there was no inducement to enjoy the outcome, children stayed shorter with the task and started the kind of assumed negotiation with the experimenter earlier.

Such negotiations with other persons, especially with authorities, are sometimes necessary, as the evaluation of the outcome of task oriented behaviors is often not unequivocal. Children need reassurance or at least an interpretation of what it all means. If a person does not pay attention spontaneously, children try to catch attention by talking to the person. This might be an example of Hinde's (1985) social negotiation that is of special importance in achievement-oriented situations when the child fails. Successes are more easily taken for granted, whereas failures need to be explained in a way that is favorable for one's own self-esteem.

In infants and preschool children, achievement situations are very often social situations. Therefore, we have to assume that most of the time the social function of the smile dominates over the expressive one. However, it should not be forgotten that children also play alone, for example, when the caretakers are busy with routine activities. In addition, as we and others have shown, even in a social situation there are episodes where children's attention is primarily directed to the task and the task outcome and not to other persons. Therefore, by using additional behavioral indices of children's attention, the whole situation can be subdivided into those segments with a primarily social character and in those where children are task-oriented.

There can be no doubt that even preschoolers do spontaneously control their facial behaviors in accordance with the social demands of the situations. The preliminary results of the study by Josephs supported this conclusion based on the results of the experiments of Saarni and Cole for 3-year-olds.

In a social situation, therefore, the value of the smiling reaction as an indicator or behavioral marker of a positive emotional state is obviously doubtful. The child communicates often via his or her smiling reactions what might be an excuse or an appeasement or, at least, a request for some interpretational help of the situation from other persons. This might especially be the case when the other persons are authority figures and the child fails. In this case the emotional expression might also change as a reaction to the facial displays shown by the interactant, as the child takes over his or her interpretation. We can assume (see, e.g., Lütkenhaus, 1984) that this kind of mutual evaluation of a task and task outcome in the child–caretaker interaction helps the child to acquire standards for evaluation of his or her achievement. In this way, children's tentative evaluations are becoming stabilized. That means they are becoming behavioral dispositions and can be considered components of the developing system for achievement motive action (see Trudewind, Unzner, & Schneider, 1989).

REFERENCES

Ainsworth, M. (1967). *Infancy in Uganda: Infant care and the growth of love.* Baltimore: Johns Hopkins University Press.

Andrew, R. J. (1963). Evolution of facial expression. *Science, 142,* 1034–1041.

Blest, A. D. (1961). The concept of ritualization. In W. H. Thorpe & O. L. Zangwill (Eds.), *Current problems in animal behaviour* (pp. 102–124). London: Cambridge University Press.

Bowlby, J. (1969). *Attachment and loss: Vol. I. Attachment.* New York: Basic Books.

Bühler, C. (1927). *Kindheit und Jugend (Childhood and youth).* Leipzig, Germany: Hirzel.

Cole, P. M. (1986). Children's spontaneous control of facial expression. *Child Development, 57,* 1309–1321.

Darwin, Ch. (1872). *The expression of the emotions in man and animals.* London: Murray.

Ekman, P. (1973). *Darwin and facial expression: A century of research in review.* New York: Academic Press.

Ekman, P., & Friesen, W. V. (1978). *The facial action coding system. Manual for the measurement of facial movements.* Palo Alto, CA: The Consulting Psychologists' Press.

Ekman, P., & Friesen, W. V. (1982). Felt, false, and miserable smiles. *Journal of Nonverbal Behavior, 6,* 238–252.

Geppert, U. (1986). *A coding-system for analyzing behavioral expressions of self-evaluative emotions.* Unpublished manuscript, Max-Planck-Institute for Psychological Research, Munich.

Geppert, U., & Küster, U. (1983). The emergence of "Wanting to do it oneself": A precursor of achievement motivation. *International Journal of Behavioral Development, 6,* 355–369.

Heckhausen, H. (1972). Die Interaktion der Sozialisationsvariablen in der Genese des Leistungsmotivs (The interaction of socializing variables in the emergence of achievement motivation). In C. F. Graumann (Ed.), *Handbuch der Psychologie, Bd. 7* (pp. 955–1019). Göttingen, Germany: Hogrefe.

Heckhausen, H. (1982). The development of achievement motivation. In W. W. Hartup (Ed.), *Review of child development research* (Vol. 6, pp. 600–668). Chicago: University of Chicago Press.

Heckhausen, H. (1984). Emergent achievement behavior: Some early developments. In J. G. Nicholls (Ed.), *Advances in motivation and achievement: Vol. 3. The development of achievement motivation* (pp. 1–32). Greenwich: JAI Press.

Heckhausen, H., & Roelofsen, I. (1962). Anfänge und Entwicklung der Leistungsmotivation: (I.) Im Wetteifer des Kleinkindes (Beginnings and development of achievement motivation: (I.) The competing child). *Psychologische Forschung, 26,* 313–397.

Hetzer, H., & Tudor-Hart, B. (1927). Die früheste Reaktion auf die menschliche Stimme (The earliest reaction to the human voice). *Quellen und Studien zur Jugendkunde, Bd. 5.*

Hinde, R. A. (1985). Expression and negotiation. In G. Zivin (Ed.), *The development of expressive behavior. Biology-environment interactions* (pp. 103–116). New York: Academic Press.

Hooff, van, J. A. R. A. M. (1972). A comparative approach to the phylogeny of laughter and smiling. In R. A. Hinde (Ed.), *Non-verbal communication* pp. 209–241). Cambridge: Cambridge University Press.

Jones, M. C. (1926). The development of early behavior patterns in young children. *Pedagogical Seminary, 33,* 537–585.

Josephs, I. (1987). *Über den kindlichen Ausdruck bei Erfolg und Mißerfolg in einer leistungsthematischen Situation (On infantile expression at success and failure in an achievement focused situation).* A study with FACS, Bochum, Department of Psychology, (unpublished doctoral dissertation).

Kagan, J. (1971). *Change and continuity in infancy.* New York: Wiley.

Kaufmann-Hayoz, R. (1981). Das Lächeln des Säuglings als Ausdruck früher Kategorisierungsprozesse (The infant's smile as an indicator of early processes of categorization). In K. Foppa & R. Groner (Eds.), *Kognitive Strukturen und ihre Entwicklung* (pp. 35–49). Bern: Huber.

Kaufmann-Hayoz, R. (1991). *Kognition und Emotion in der frühkindlichen Entwicklung (Cognition and emotion in the development of young children).* Berlin: Springer.

Kaufmann-Hayoz, R., Kaufmann, F., & Lang, A. (1978). Der Einfluss von Reiz und Zustand auf den Wahrnehmungsprozess bei Säuglingen (The influence of stimulus and state on the infant's perception). *Schweizerische Zeitschrift für Psychologie und ihre Anwendungen, 37,* 1–21.

Kraut, R., & Johnston, R. E. (1979). Social and emotional messages of smiling: An ethological approach. *Journal of Personality and Social Psychology, 37,* 1539–1553.

Krebs, J. R., & Dawkins, R. (1978). Animal signals: Mind-reading and manipulation. In J. R. Krebs & N. B. Davies (Eds.), *Behavioural ecology: An evolutionary approach* (pp. 282–309). Oxford: Blackwell.

Krebs, J. R., & Dawkins, R. (1984). Animal signals: Mind-reading and manipulation. In J. R. Krebs & N. B. Davies (Eds.), *Behavioural ecology: An evolutionary approach* (pp. 380–402). Oxford: Blackwell.

Lewis, M., & Brooks-Gunn, J. (1979). *Social cognition and the acquisition of self.* New York: Plenum.

Lewis, M., & Goldberg, S. (1969). Perceptual-cognitive development in infancy: A generalized expectancy model as a function of the mother-infant interaction. *Merrill-Palmer Quarterly, 15,* 81–100.

Lewis, M., & Michalson, L. (1983). *Children's emotions and moods.* New York: Plenum.

Lewis, M., Sullivan, M. W., & Michalson, L. (1984). The cognitive-emotional fugue. In C. E. Izard, J. Kagan, & R. B. Zajonc (Eds.), *Emotions, cognition and behavior* (pp. 264–288). Cambridge: Cambridge University Press.

Lewis, M., Sullivan, M. W., Stanger, C., & Weiss, M. (1989). Self-development and self-conscious emotions. *Child Development, 60,* 146–156.

Leyhausen, P. (1968). Biologie von Ausdruck und Eindruck (Biology of expression and impression). *Psychologische Forschung, 31,* 113–176.

Lütkenhaus, P. (1984). Pleasure derived from mastery in three-year-olds: Its function for persistence and the influence of maternal behavior. *International Journal of Behavioral Development, 7,* 343-358.

McCall, R. (1972). Smiling and vocalization in infants as indices of perceptual-cognitive processes. *Merrill-Palmer Quarterly, 18,* 341-347.

McCall, R., & Kagan, J. (1970). Individual differences in the infant's distribution of attention to stimulus discrepancy. *Developmental Psychology, 2,* 90-98.

Meili, R. (1957). *Anfänge der Charakterentwicklung (The beginning of character development).* Bern: Huber.

Meili-Dworetzki, G., & Meili, R. (1972). *Grundlagen individueller Persönlichkeitsunterschiede (Foundations of individual differences in personality).* Bern: Huber.

Papoušek, H. (1967). Experimental studies of appetitional behavior in human newborns and infants. In H. W. Stevenson, E. H. Hess, & H. L. Rheingold (Eds.), *Early behavior. Comparative and developmental approaches* (pp. 249–277). New York: Wiley.

Piaget, J. (1936). *La naissance de l'intelligence chez l'enfant (The origin of intelligence in the child).* Neuchâtel, Switzerland: Delachaux & Niestlé.

Piaget, J. (1937). *La construction du réel chez l'enfant (The construction of reality in the child).* Neuchâtel, Switzerland: Delachaux & Niestlé.

Piaget, J. (1945). *La formation du symbole chez l'enfant (The formation of the symbolic in the child).* Neuchâtel, Switzerland: Delachaux & Niestlé.

Piaget, J. (1977). *The origin of intelligence in the child.* Harmondsworth, UK: Penguin.

Rovee, C. K., & Rovee, D. T. (1969). Conjugate reinforcement of infant exploratory behavior. *Journal of Experimental Child Psychology, 8,* 33–39.

Saarni, C. (1984). An observational study of children's attempts to monitor their expressive behavior. *Child Development, 55,* 1504–1513.

Schneider, K. (1987). Achievement-related emotions in preschoolers. In F. Halisch & J. Kuhl (Eds.), *Motivation, intention, and volition* (pp. 163–177). Berlin: Springer.

Schneider, K., & Josephs, I. (1991). The expressive and communicative function of preschool children's smiles in an achievement-situation. *Journal of Nonverbal Behavior, 15,* 185–198.

Schneider, K., & Unzner, L. (1989). Achievement-related cognitions and emotions in preschoolers. In F. Halisch & J. van den Bercken (Eds.), *International perspectives on achievement and task motivation* (pp. 87–111). Amsterdam: Swets & Zeitlinger.

Schneider, K., & Unzner, L. (1992). Preschoolers' attention and emotion in an achievement and an effect game: A longitudinal study. *Cognition and Emotion, 6,* 37–63.

Shultz, T. R., & Zigler, E. (1970). Emotional concomitants of visual mastery in infants: The effects of stimulus movement on smiling and vocalizing. *Journal of Experimental Child Psychology, 10,* 390–402.

Spitz, R. A., & Wolf, K. M. (1946). The smiling response: A contribution to the ontogenesis of social relations. *Genetic Psychology Monographs, 34,* 57–125.

Sroufe, L. A., & Waters, E. (1976). The ontogenesis of smiling and laughter: A perspective on the organization of development in infancy. *Psychological Review, 83,* 173–189.

Stipek, D. J. (1983). A developmental analysis of pride and shame. *Human Development, 26,* 42–54.

Trudewind, C. (1976). Die Entwicklung des Leistungsmotivs (The development of achievement motivation). In H. D. Schmalt & W. U. Meyer (Eds.), *Leistungsmotivation und Verhalten* (pp. 193–219). Stuttgart: Klett.

Trudewind, C. (1982). The development of achievement motivation and individual differences: Ecological determinants. In W. W. Hartup (Ed.), *Review of child development research* (Vol. 6, pp. 669–705). Chicago, ILL: University of Chicago Press.

Trudewind, C., Unzner, L., & Schneider, K. (1989). Die Entwicklung der Leistungsmotivation (The development of achievement motivation). In H. Keller (Ed.), *Handbuch der Kleinkindforschung* (pp. 491–524). Berlin: Springer.

Unzner, L., & Schneider, K. (1990). Facial reactions in preschoolers: A descriptive study. *Journal of Nonverbal Behavior, 14,* 19–31.

Watson, J. S. (1972). Smiling, cooing, and "the Game". *Merrill-Palmer Quarterly, 18,* 323–339.

Watson, J. S., & Ramey, C. (1972). Reactions to response-contingent stimulation in early infancy. *Merrill-Palmer Quarterly, 18,* 219–277.

White, R. W. (1959). Motivation reconsidered: The concept of competence. *Psychological Review, 66,* 297–333.

Wolff, P. (1963). Observations of the early development of smiling. In B. M. Foss (Ed.), *Determinants of infant behavior II.* London: Methuen.

Wundt, W. (1896). *Grundriß der Psychologie (Synopsis of psychology)*. Leipzig, Germany: Engelmann.

Zelazo, P. R. (1972). Smiling and vocalizing: A cognitive emphasis. *Merrill-Palmer Quarterly, 18,* 349–365.

Zelazo, P. R., & Komer, M. J. (1971). Infants' smiling to nonsocial stimuli and the recognition hypothesis. *Child Development, 42,* 1327–1339.

7

NONVERBAL COMMUNICATION IN NONHUMAN PRIMATES: IMPLICATIONS FOR THE EMERGENCE OF CULTURE

Stephen J. Suomi
*National Institute of Child Health and
Human Development, Bethesda, Maryland*

A fundamental feature of virtually all primate species is their inherent sociality. Members of these species typically spend most if not all of their lives residing in large, well-defined social groups characterized by complex kinship and dominance relationships. Extensive interaction with familiar conspecifics is an essential part of an individual's daily life within these primate social groups, and elaborate patterns of communication have evolved to facilitate such interaction. Although no living nonhuman primate species has developed a humanlike language to date, all species clearly possess the capacity to communicate a broad spectrum of information across multiple sensory modalities. Indeed, many aspects of human nonverbal communication appear to be largely homologous with the rich postural and facial communicative repertoires of most monkeys and apes (see van Hooff, 1967).

Consider the case of rhesus monkeys *(Macaca mulatta)*. Members of this highly successful species of Old World monkeys live in large social groups (termed troops) that range in size from several dozen to more than 100 individuals. Each troop consists of several multigenerational matrilines of females and prepubertal males, as well as adult males born outside of their resident troop (see Fig. 7.1). This form of social group organization derives from the fact that females remain in their natal troop throughout their entire lifetimes, whereas males typically emigrate from their natal troop around puberty and eventually join other established troops (see Berard, 1989).

Fig. 7.1. Typical matriline within a rhesus monkey troop. The mother and her new infant are surrounded by the maternal grandmother and the mother's maternal half-siblings.

Each of these troops represents a distinctive social entity, with its own unique history and blend of matrilines and immigrant males. Although different rhesus monkey troops may have overlapping ranges and even daily exposure to one another, an individual monkey's specific troop membership at any given point in time is clear cut, readily obvious to human observers and presumably known to every other member of that troop. Rhesus monkey troops are cohesive social units that can become remarkably tight-knit when challenged, such that a stranger's presence near or within a troop is immediately recognized by all, often eliciting xenophobic reactions by resident troop members (see Lindburg, 1971).

Within each matrilinearly organized troop all the monkeys are not equal. To the contrary, troop members clearly differ in their relative social status, and these differences are multidimensional. Each rhesus monkey troop is characterized by several distinct dominance hierarchies. For example, there is a clear-cut linear hierarchy among the troop's different matrilines, such that all members of the highest ranking matriline (including infants) outrank all members of the second-ranked matriline (including adults), who in turn outrank all members of the third-ranked matriline, and so on. There is also a clear-cut hierarchy among females within each matriline, following the general rule that younger sisters outrank older sisters. In addition, there is a separate hierarchy for the immigrant adult males (roughly related to relative tenure in their resident troop), as well as a hierarchy among like-aged infants born in the troop (precisely paralleling the relative rankings of their respective mothers; see Sade, 1967).

These multiple dominance hierarchies, as well as the relative position of each individual within each hierarchy, are also readily apparent to human observers and presumably well known to all troop members. Indeed, it seems clear that knowledge of every other member's specific kinship and dominance status within the troop is essential for any one rhesus monkey to survive, let alone thrive, in this complex social environment. How is such information communicated within the troop and how do individuals come to acquire the communicative skills necessary to both process and contribute to the troop's knowledge base? One way to address these questions is to examine the development of such communicative capabilities in young rhesus monkeys.

ONTOGENY OF RHESUS MONKEY COMMUNICATIVE REPERTOIRES

Rhesus monkey infants are born with most of their sensory systems fully functional. Unlike many nonprimate mammals (e.g., rodents and carnivores), rhesus monkey infants can see and hear much of the world around them within hours, if not minutes, of birth. They are not at all like the proverbial Lockeian *tabula rasa* that passively absorbs sensory information from its immediate environment. To the contrary, we now know that rhesus monkey infants enter their world with strong behavioral propensities, clear-cut perceptual biases, and a host of physical and social features that make them highly attractive to most conspecifics. These features help ensure that a newborn infant monkey becomes a major focus of attention within its extended family. At the same time, the infant's behavioral predispositions and preferences serve to channel virtually all of its attention and effort toward its mother, providing the basis for the establishment of a strong attachment relationship (Harlow & Harlow, 1965).

For example, rhesus monkey neonates possess numerous physical features that clearly distinguish them from older conspecifics and appear to serve as releasing stimuli for potential caregivers (see Fig. 7.2). These neonates share many of the same "babylike" physical and physiognomic characteristics that contribute to the distinctive appearance of human neonates, including a large head in proportion to the body, a

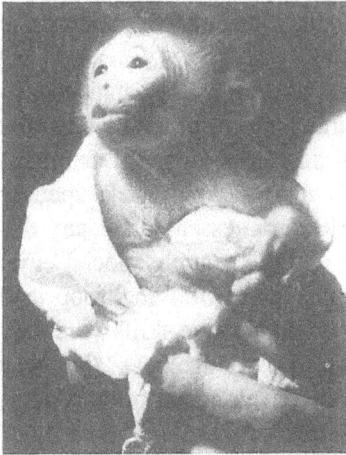

Fig. 7.2. Rhesus monkey neonate emitting "coo" vocalization. Note the babylike features described in text.

protruding large forehead in proportion to the rest of the face, and large eyes that are seated below the midline of the head (Alley, 1981; Brooks & Hochberg, 1960; Sternglanz, Gray, & Murakami, 1977). In addition, rhesus monkeys are born with an unusually dark pelage and bright red facial coloration, features that begin to fade around the time of weaning. Higley, Hopkins, Hirsch, Marra, and Suomi (1987) demonstrated that juvenile-aged monkeys whose fur was experimentally dyed and whose faces were reddened with rouge to match the neonatal coloration were perceived as more attractive by conspecifics than were like-aged individuals with normal fur and facial color or with novel coloration that did not match that of neonates.

Rhesus monkey infants are also born with behavioral propensities that serve to promote essential physical contact with their mother or other caregivers. Within minutes of delivery they are able to sustain ventral contact with their mother without support via powerful grasping and clasping reflexes and to locate and suckle from their mother's nipples via rooting and sucking reflexes (e.g., Mowbray & Cadell, 1962; M. L. Schneider & Suomi, 1992). In addition to maximizing the opportunity to obtain nourishment, such reflexive propensities enable rhesus monkey neonates to maintain continuous access to an external heat source (newborn infants require such a heat source until 2 weeks of age, when their thermoregulation system becomes more fully functional, see Harlow & Suomi, 1970). These neonatal reflexes also serve to ensure prolonged tactile stimulation from the mother via ventral-ventral contact, providing what Harlow (1958) deemed *contact comfort* and what subsequent research has linked to stimulation of growth hormone (Champoux, Coe, Shanberg, Kuhn, & Suomi 1989). Such extensive tactile communication between mother and infant helps cement the emerging attachment relationship between the pair.

In addition to having these reflexive propensities involving tactile modes of communication, rhesus monkey infants are born with visual and auditory preferences for stimuli associated with their most likely caregiver, their mother. They prefer female to male adult conspecifics, and they prefer conspecific females to females of different species within the genus (Sackett. 1970; Suomi, Sackett, & Harlow, 1970). To what extent such preferences might be based on differentially solicitous behavior on the part of the female conspecific stimulus monkeys is presently not known, but it is clear that very little previous experience with conspecific stimuli is required to generate such preferences, leading some to postulate that they represent "unlearned" response patterns (e.g., Sackett, 1970).

Finally, newborn rhesus monkeys are blessed with facial, vocal, and postural expressions that not only denote distinctive emotional states

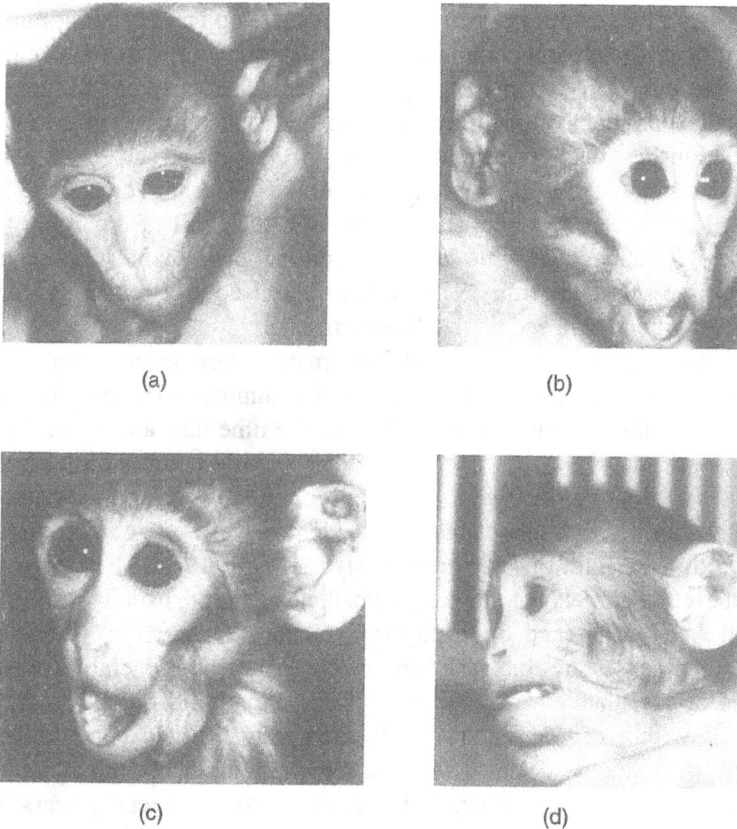

(a)   (b)

(c)   (d)

Fig. 7.3.   Facial expressions of infant rhesus monkeys expressing (a) interest, (b) surprise, (c) anger, and (d) fear, respectively (from Aaron, 1984).

but also serve as powerfully salient communicative agents for con-specifics within sight and sound. Darwin (1872) was among the first to argue that humans do not have a monopoly on emotional expressions, if not emotional states. There are compelling parallels between specific facial expressions universally displayed by rhesus monkey infants and those expressed by human infants and young children and universally interpreted as indicative of basic emotional states (see Suomi, 1984). Human subjects who have never seen a rhesus monkey infant can match pictures of specific infant monkey facial expressions to verbal descriptions of the situations that elicited those facial expressions with consid-erable accuracy, equivalent to their ability to match pictures of human infant faces to verbal descriptions of the eliciting situation (Aaron, 1984). Examples of such pictures are presented in Fig. 7.3.

As monkey infants grow older they develop an expanding range of physical, social, and communicative skills, many of which are acquired in the course of extensive play with peers. The early pre-eminence of tactile communication in establishing and sustaining long-term social relationships declines somewhat during the juvenile years, most notably in the greatly reduced incidence and duration of ventral contact with the mother. However, tactile stimulation is at the heart of emerging basic social interaction patterns such as grooming, play, sexual, and even ag-gressive bouts (Suomi, 1979). Even ventral contact reappears for fe-males when they become mothers themselves.

Nevertheless, as young monkeys mature they become increasingly reliant on visual and auditory modes of communication to order and to organize their day-to-day activities. By the time they are 6 months old, they spend only a tiny fraction of their waking hours within physical reach of their mother, yet they remain in virtually constant communica-tion with her throughout the day, seldom out of her sight. Youngsters that do lose sight of their mother typically emit a "coo" type of vocali-zation that attracts the mother's immediate attention, usually resulting in renewed visual (and often physical) contact. Conversely, whenever a mother senses trouble, she can display a specific facial expression and/or vocalization that will bring her 6-month-old quickly scurrying back within her protective reach. One result of this communicative system is that the young monkey is able to spend increasing amounts of time interacting with others in its social network, especially peers. Play with peers becomes a predominant social activity for rhesus monkeys during their juvenile years, and much of play behavior is initiated, modulated, and elaborated through a multitude of facial, postural, and vocal signals exchanged among the participants. Young rhesus monkeys communicate an intent to engage in social play by exhibiting a distinctive "play face," a particular gait, and any one of a characteristic set of play vocalizations (Biben & Suomi, 1992; see Fig. 7.4). Although certain types of social play are intensely physical (e.g., rough-and-tumble play), the patterns of visual and vocal interchanges characteristic of most complex play bouts suggest an elaborate communicative system that permits a participant to know not only who its partners are (and remember how they played in the past) but also what their current emotional states are, and how they might (differentially) respond to a particular action or reaction. It is in the context of play that young rhesus monkeys develop, practice, and perfect most of the physical movements and coordinated activities that will characterize their adult behavioral repertoires, but they also learn basic social information about dominance, alliances, aggression, and reconciliation—not only in their own interactions but also in observing the interactions of others (Suomi, 1979).

Fig. 7.4.   Peer play among rhesus monkey juveniles.

Moreover, visual and auditory signals emitted by peers and other group members convey crucial information to the young monkeys about their immediate environment that goes beyond specific characteristics of those emitting the signals. Mineka and her colleagues (Mineka, Davidson, Cook, & Keir, 1984), in a series of elegant laboratory experiments, demonstrated that rhesus monkey mothers can teach their offspring to avoid potentially dangerous features of their immediate environment (e.g., snakes) by exhibiting intensely fearful responses to such stimuli in the presence of their offspring. Young monkeys develop an immediate and essentially permanent aversion to snakes when they observe their mother's reaction to the appearance of a snake; when exposed to snakes in the absence of an experienced conspecific, young naive monkeys display scant evidence of fearfulness (Mineka et al., 1984). This form of nonverbal communication represents an extremely efficient means (essentially one-trial permanent conditioning) of passing highly adaptive response tendencies (e.g., avoidance of snakes) to successive generations of rhesus monkeys.

In summary, as they grow up, rhesus monkeys learn the essentials of a complex social life that requires a communicative system capable of providing relevant information about each troop member's identity, activity, affect, intent, and immediate knowledge of salient stimuli (e.g., the presence of food, friends, rivals, or predators). Monkeys that cannot master such a system will clearly not thrive, and probably not even survive, in a troop setting (see Higley, Linnoila, & Suomi, 1994).

CAPABILITIES AND LIMITATIONS OF MONKEY NONVERBAL COMMUNICATION

How sophisticated (i.e., humanlike) are the communication systems developed by nonhuman primate species such as rhesus monkeys? Over the past 25 years, numerous researchers working with a variety of primate species in both field and laboratory settings have described a dizzying array of communicative capabilities and competencies that monkeys and apes exhibit as part of their day-to-day social life (see Cheney & Seyfarth, 1990). For example, field research has disclosed that vervet monkeys warn their fellow troop members of the presence of predators via distinctive vocalizations that specify the general class of predator (e.g., birds, snakes, or felines), eliciting predator-specific avoidance responses (Marler & Evans, chap. 8, this volume; Seyfarth, Cheney, & Marler, 1980). Hamadryas baboon troops split up into well-defined subgroups each morning to spend the day foraging in different regions many miles from one another, yet every night they return to a common area to interact as a closely knit social unit (Kummer, 1971). Rhesus monkeys facing an aggressive encounter use highly specific vocalizations to recruit support from family and friends. Their vocalizations convey specific information about their opponent, in terms of whether the opponent is kin or nonkin, and higher ranking or lower ranking than themselves; the recipients use this information to decide whether or not to intervene (S. Gouzoules, H. Gouzoules, & Marler, 1984). These examples, taken from a rapidly expanding empirical literature, testify to the sophistication and complexity of nonhuman primate communicative capabilities. Although a comprehensive (or even cursory) review of this literature is beyond the present scope, it should be noted that it is difficult to read this literature without generating some feeling of anthropomorphism, because many of the parallels with well-established aspects of human nonverbal communication seem so very compelling.

On the other hand, carefully conceived studies have repeatedly demonstrated that for some basic cognitive and communicative capabilities, monkeys are clearly not the equivalent of furry little humans with tails. Monkeys generally fail to exhibit such basic human characteristics as self-recognition (Gallup, 1977), the ability to take perspective of another (Povinelli, Parks, & Novak, 1992), or a "rational" understanding of causality (Visalberghi & Trinca, 1989). These cognitive limitations affect the range and specificity of information conveyed in communication between members of monkey social groups, which in turn serve to limit the type of information (knowledge) that can be passed across generations or between social groups—a seeming prerequisite for the emergence of humanlike culture.

An example of such limitations can be found in the tool-using behavior of capuchin monkeys *(Cebus apella)*. These highly successful South American monkeys display a remarkable range of spontaneous manufacture and use of tools, as was first reported by E. Darwin (1794). More recently, captive capuchin monkeys have been observed modifying sticks, bamboo shoots, and bones for use as probing tools (Visalberghi, 1990; Westergaard & Fragaszy, 1987; Westergaard & Suomi, 1994b), modifying stones and pieces of bamboo for use as cutting tools (Westergaard & Suomi, 1994a, 1994b), cracking stones in order to produce flakes for use as scrapers to deflesh bones (Westergaard & Suomi, 1994c), and even throwing stones at moving targets in order to obtain highly desired food items (Westergaard & Suomi, 1994d). Some of these tasks required sequential combinations of different tools, whereas other involved simultaneous use of multiple tools. Some of the tools produced by these monkeys are highly similar to those utilized by prehistoric hominids, as are the direct products of their actions (e.g., the patterns of scrape marks left on bones defleshed by stone flakes). It should be noted that none of these well-documented instances of tool use by capuchin monkeys involved any direct or indirect training or modeling by humans or other monkeys; instead in every case the tool use (and/or manufacture) appeared to be spontaneous (e.g., Fragaszy & Visalberghi, 1989). These findings, along with other recent reports of spontaneous tool use by chimpanzees (e.g., C. Boesch & H. Boesch, 1990), are in direct conflict with the theory that the manufacture and use of tools is an exclusively human (or hominid) invention that provided an important basis for the development of human culture (see Westergaard & Suomi, 1994a).

However, there are some important differences between instances of tool use demonstrated by capuchin monkeys and those displayed by humans (and presumably by their hominid ancestors). First, it appears that although some capuchin monkeys clearly utilize tools in a goal-directed fashion, they do so with a complete lack of understanding of how the tool actually works. Elegant studies by Visalberghi and her colleagues (e.g., Visalberghi & Limongelli, 1994; Visalberghi & Trinca, 1989) have provided convincing evidence that even the most successful tool-using capuchin monkeys fail to distinguish causal relationships involving tools and goals from relationships that are "merely" correlated in time and space. These monkeys continue to repeat actions that represent "errors" from a causal perspective but are consistent with a correlative view, even long after the monkeys have clearly mastered and utilized the tools in hand. Perhaps more importantly, a successful tool-user cannot teach another capuchin how to use the tool, and other capuchins cannot learn how to use the tool via observation of successful tool-using episodes, even when they occur several times each day. Instead, each monkey must acquire the skill independently via trial and error and occasional insight. As Visalberghi and Fragaszy (1990) noted, "[capuchin] monkeys can not ape" (p. 269), at least not in terms of tool use acquisition (see Fig. 7.5).

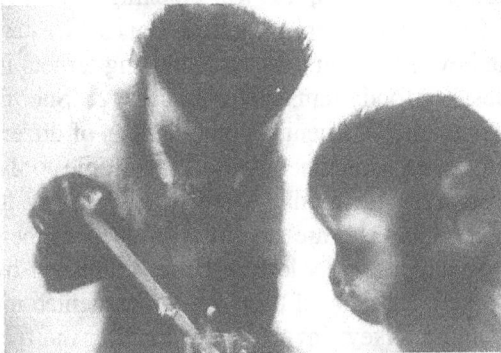

Fig. 7.5.   Capuchin monkey using probing tool to obtain syrup. Monkey on right observes, but cannot learn, this tool-using task (Courtesy of E. Visalberghi, Istituto di Psicologia, CNR).

The inability to communicate crucial information about the use of a tool, either by instruction or by example, severely limits the long-term benefits for a social group that can accrue from one individual's discovery. If the inventiveness of individuals cannot be shared with others in the group, then there can be no accumulated knowledge of such inventions over time and generations and no "culture" as we humans know it. For capuchin monkeys, the raw materials for a tool-using culture are clearly present, in that a few individuals readily acquire tool-using skills, albeit on an idiosyncratic basis (e.g., Fragaszy & Visalberghi, 1989). What they lack is the capacity to transmit these skills, to communicate their individual discoveries, to others. This is why capuchin monkeys and all other nonhuman primates (except possibly chimpanzees) do not have a true tool-using culture, whereas virtually every known *Homo sapiens* group clearly does.

On the other hand, monkeys and apes are obviously capable of transmitting a wealth of information about their immediate environment and about themselves to others in their social group, and at least some of this information is transmitted to the next generation, if not beyond. As was previously discussed, much of this information has considerable emotional content and much of it generates emotional reactions on the part of the recipients; for example, the reactions of young rhesus monkeys witnessing the fearful responses of their mothers to a snake stimulus (Mineka et al., 1984). Emotional expressions and responses are at the heart of the communicative repertoires of most nonhuman primates.

INDIVIDUAL DIFFERENCES IN EMOTIONALITY IN RHESUS MONKEYS AND OTHER PRIMATES

Given the central role of emotional expression, body postures, facial expressions, and specific vocal patterns in rhesus monkey communication, it is worth noting that there are major differences among rhesus monkeys in their basic emotional reactivity. The same environmental stimulus can elicit dramatically different emotional reactions in different monkeys of the same age and gender; conversely, rhesus monkeys of the same age and gender can have markedly different thresholds for activating comparable behavioral and physiological responses. Ultimately, it means that different members of a rhesus monkey troop are likely to communicate different sorts of information about the same environmental events or conditions.

For example, recent studies carried out in both laboratory and field settings have found that approximately 20% of rhesus monkeys at any age consistently exhibit significant behavioral disruption, physiological arousal, and negative affectivity when confronted with novel or mildly challenging situations. These monkeys typically display fearful emotions and avoidant responses in the face of stimuli that elicit emotional interest and exploratory behavior from most of their peers (see Fig. 7.6).

Fig. 7.6. Differential response to novel setting by high-reactive (on left) and low reactive (on right) rhesus monkey juveniles.

These differences in prototypical response to environmental novelty and challenge appear early in infancy (Suomi, 1983), and in the absence of major environmental alterations, appear to be remarkably stable throughout the life span (Suomi, 1991a). They are associated with distinctive physiological profiles: The monkeys who exhibit the most extreme behavioral and emotional reactions to challenge are also most likely to show the greatest adrenocortical response, psychophysiological activation, and monoamine turnover (Suomi, 1991b), and these differentiated physiological response patterns are also quite stable throughout development (Higley, Suomi, & Linnoila, 1992). The different response patterns appear to be highly heritable (Higley et al., 1993; Suomi, 1983), but it is also clear that any individual's response threshold can be modified substantially by early experiences, particularly those involving attachment objects (e.g., Suomi, 1987, 1991a).

Laboratory and field studies have also demonstrated that these differences in rhesus monkey reactivity to novelty and challenge can be of considerable significance with respect to long-term adaptation and perhaps reproductive success. For example, high-reactive pubertal males tend to leave their natal troops later chronologically, spend relatively less time in all-male gangs, and follow a different behavioral strategy for entering a new troop than their less-reactive male peers (Rasmussen & Suomi, 1989; Suomi, Rasmussen, & Higley, 1992). High-reactive females appear to be at greater risk for neglecting or abusing their first-born offspring, especially when social support is minimal (Suomi & Ripp, 1983). On the other hand, high-reactive rhesus monkeys are at lower risk for accidental injury or wounding under benign environmental conditions, although relative reactivity can become a significant risk factor for injury under high-stress conditions (Boyce, O'Neill-Wagner, Price, Haines, & Suomi, in press). Furthermore, high-reactive infants reared by unusually nurturant attachment figures are remarkably precocious socially and typically rise to the top of their group's dominance hierarchy (Suomi, 1994).

The implications of these and other possible differences in emotional thresholds among individuals for a troop of rhesus monkeys' communicative patterns are considerable. To begin, the development of any one monkey's communicative propensities and patterns will surely be affected by its specific early experiences, especially those observational learning episodes involving its mother's emotional responses to particular features of its world (e.g., snakes). There is considerable evidence supporting the cross-generational transmission of differences in reactivity threshold, some of it clearly via nongenetic mechanisms (Suomi, 1994). Thus, different patterns of reactivity and their emotional communicative consequences tend to run in families, passed on through generation after matrilineal generation. Second, with each rhesus monkey troop consisting of several different matrilines, that troop is virtually guaranteed a considerable range of responses to any environmental change or challenge and a corresponding range of communicative diversity, at least with respect to emotionality. The cross-generational transmission of these tendencies helps ensure that such diversity will become a tradition in the history of each troop. Thus, for rhesus monkeys, the development of "culture" does not encompass the emergence of a material technology. Rather, it is social in content and emotional in its expression.

To what degree does the diversity of differences in response patterns, clearly evident in rhesus monkeys, generalize to other primate species? To summarize a rapidly expanding literature, comparable diversity of emotional reactivity has been found in virtually every primate species studied to date, including prosimians, Old and New World monkeys, and apes, as well as in several nonprimate mammalian and even nonmammalian vertebrate species (see Kagan, Sniderman, Arcus, & Reznick, 1994). Most notably, it clearly exists in virtually every human sample studied to date. Diversity in emotional reactivity is at least as widespread in humans as it is in rhesus monkeys. Furthermore, Kagan and his colleagues have demonstrated that it shows comparable physiological concomitants, heritability, and sensitivity to early attachment relationships and experiences in humans as in rhesus monkeys (Kagan et al., 1994).

In summary, reactivity diversity in monkeys is reflected in patterns of nonverbal communication via differential emotional expressiveness and, it has been argued, may provide the basis for a monkey troop's emotional "traditions" and social "culture." A similar role for reactivity diversity may exist in human groups, societies, and cultures. It may also, in humans, contribute to the development of artistic traditions, technological advances, and other accumulated knowledge that clearly differentiate human culture from anything seen in any other primate species. In these respects culture is uniquely human.

REFERENCES

Aaron, N. (1984). *Recognition of human and rhesus monkey facial expression.* Undergraduate honors thesis. University of Wisconsin, Madison.

Alley, R. (1981). Head shape and perception of cuteness. *Developmental Psychology, 17,* 650–654.

Berard, J. (1989). Male life histories. *Puerto Rico Health Sciences Journal, 8,* 47–58.

Biben, M., & Suomi, S. J. (1992). Lessons from primate play. In K. MacDonald (Ed.), *Play and culture* (pp. 185–195). Albany: SUNY Press.

Boesch, C., & Boesch, H. (1990). Tool use and tool making in wild chimpanzees. *Folia Primatologica, 54,* 86–99.

Boyce, W. T., O'Neill-Wagner, P. L., Price, C. S., Haines, M., & Suomi, S. J. (in press). Stress reactivity and violent injuries in free-ranging rhesus monkeys. *Psychosomatic Medicine.*

Brooks, V., & Hochberg, J. (1960). A psychophysical study of "cuteness." *Perceptual and Motor Skills, 11,* 205–210.

Champoux, M., Coe, C. L., Shanberg, S., Kuhn, C., Suomi, S. J. (1989). Hormonal effects of early rearing conditions in the infant rhesus monkey. *American Journal of Primatology, 19,* 111–117.

Cheney, D. L., & Seyfarth, R. M. (1990). *How monkeys see the world.* Chicago: University of Chicago Press.

Darwin, C. (1872). *The expression of emotions in man and animals.* New York: D. Appleton.

Darwin, E. (1794). *Zoonomia, or the laws of organic life, Vol. 1.* London: Johnson.

Fragaszy, D. M., & Visalberghi, E. (1989). Social influences on the acquisition of tool-using behaviors in tufted capuchin monkeys *(Cebus apella). Journal of Comparative Psychology, 103,* 159–170.

Gallup, G. G. (1977). Self-recognition in primates: A comparative approach to the bidirectional properties of consciousness. *American Psychologist, 32,* 329–338.

Gouzoules, S., Gouzoules, H., & Marler, P. (1984). Rhesus monkey *(Macaca mulatta)* screams: Representational signalling in the recruitment of agonistic aid. *Animal Behaviour, 32,* 182–193.

Harlow, H. F. (1958). The nature of love. *American Psychologist, 13,* 673–685.

Harlow, H. F., & Harlow, M. K. (1965). The affectional systems. In A. M. Schrier, H. F. Harlow, & F. Stollnitz (Eds.), *Behavior of nonhuman primates* (Vol. 2, pp. 287–334). New York: Academic Press.

Harlow, H. F., & Suomi, S. J. (1970). The nature of love—simplified. *American Psychologist, 25,* 161–168.

Higley, J. D., Hopkins, W. D., Hirsch, R. M., Marra, L. M., & Suomi, S. J. (1987). Preferences of female rhesus monkeys *(Macaca mulatta)* for infantile coloration. *Developmental Psychobiology, 20,* 7–18.

Higley, J. D., Linnoila, M., & Suomi, S. J. (1994). Ethological contributions. In R. T. Ammerman (Ed.), *Handbook of aggressive and destructive behavior in psychiatric patients* (pp. 17–32). New York: Raven Press.

Higley, J. D., Suomi, S. J., & Linnoila, M. (1992). A longitudinal assessment of CSF monoamine metabolite and plasma cortisol concentrations in young rhesus monkeys. *Biological Psychiatry, 32,* 127–145.

Higley, J. D., Thompson, W. T., Champoux, M., Goldman, D., Hasert, M. F., Kraemer, G. W., Scanlan, J. M., Suomi, S. J., & Linnoila, M. (1993). Paternal and maternal genetic and environmental contributions to CSF monoamine metabolites in rhesus monkeys *(Macaca mulatta). Archives of General Psychiatry, 50,* 615–623.

Kagan, J., Snideman, N., Arcus, D., & Reznick, J. S. (1994). *Galen's prophecy: Temperament in human nature,* New York: Basic Books.

Kummer, H. (1971). *Primate societies: Group techniques of ecological adaptation.* Chicago: Aldine.

Lindburg, D. G. (1971). The rhesus monkey in North India: An ecological and behavioral study. In L. A. Rosenblum (Ed.), *Primate behavior: Developments in field and laboratory research* (Vol. 2, pp. 1–106). New York: Academic Press.

Mineka, S., Davidson, M., Cook, M., & Keir, R. (1984). Observational conditioning of snake fear in rhesus monkeys. *Journal of Abnormal Psychology, 93,* 355–372.

Mowbray, J. B., & Cadell, T. E. (1962). Early behavior patterns in rhesus monkeys. *Journal of Comparative and Physiological Psychology, 55,* 350–357.

Povinelli, D. J., Parks, K. A., & Novak, M. A. (1992). Role reversal by rhesus monkeys, but no evidence of empathy. *Animal Behavior, 44,* 269–281.

Rasmussen, K. L. R., & Suomi, S. J. (1989). Heart rate and endocrine repones to stress in adolescent male rhesus monkeys on Cayo Santiago. *Puerto Rican Health Sciences Journal, 8,* 65–71.

Sackett, G. P. (1970). Unlearned responses, differential rearing experiences, and the development of social attachments by rhesus monkeys. In L. A. Rosenblum (Ed.), *Primate behavior: Developments in field and laboratory research* (Vol. 1, pp. 112–140). New York: Academic Press.

Sade, D. S. (1967). Determinants of social dominance in a group of free-ranging rhesus monkeys. In S. A. Altmann (Ed.), *Social communication among primates* (pp. 99–114). Chicago: University of Chicago Press.

Schneider, M. L., & Suomi, S. J. (1992). Neurobehavioral assessment in rhesus monkey neonates *(Macaca mulatta):* Developmental changes, behavioral stability, and early experience. *Infant Behavior and Development, 15,* 155–177.

Seyfarth, R. M., Cheney, D. L., & Marler, P. (1980). Monkey responses to three different alarm calls: Evidence for predator classification and semantic communication, *Science, 210,* 801–803.

Sternglanz, S. H., Gray, J. L., & Murakami, M. (1977). Adult preferences for infantile facial features: An ethological approach. *Animal Behaviour, 25,* 108–115.

Suomi, S. J. (1979). Peers, play, and primary prevention of psychopathology. In M. Kent & J. Rolf (Eds.), *Primary prevention of psychopathology* (Vol. 3, pp. 127–149). Hanover, NH: New England Universities Press.

Suomi, S. J. (1983). Social development in rhesus monkeys: Consideration of individual differences. In A. Oliverio & M. Zappella (Eds.), *The behavior of human infants* (pp. 71–92). New York: Plenum.

Suomi, S. J. (1984). The development of affect in rhesus monkeys. In N. A. Fox & R. J. Davidson (Eds.), *The psychobiology of affective development* (pp. 119–160). Hillsdale, NJ: Lawrence Elbaum Associates.

Suomi, S. J. (1987). Genetic and maternal contributions to individual differences in rhesus monkey biobehavioral development. In N. Krasnagor, E. Blass, M. Hofer, & W. Smotherman (Eds.), *Perinatal development: A psychobiological perspective* (pp. 397–420). New York: Academic Press.

Suomi, S. J. (1991a). Early stress and adult emotional reactivity in rhesus monkeys. In D. Barker (Ed.), *The childhood environment and adult disease* (CIBA Foundation Symposium 156, pp. 171–188). Chichester, UK: Wiley.

Suomi, S. J. (1991b). Primate separation models of affective disorders. In J. Madden (Ed.), *Neurobiology of learning, emotion, and affect* (pp. 195–214). New York: Raven.

Suomi, S. J. (1994). Social and biological pathways that contribute to variation in health status: Evidence from primate studies. *Proceedings of the Honda Foundation Symposium on Prosperity, Health, and Well-Being* (pp. 105–112). Toronto: Canadian Institute for Advanced Research.

Suomi, S. J., Rasmussen, K. L. R., & Higley, J. D. (1992). Primate models of behavioral and physiological change in adolescence. In E. R. McAnarney, R. E. Kriepe, D. P. Orr, & G. D. Comerci (Eds.), *Textbook of adolescent medicine* (pp. 135–139). Philadelphia: Saunders.

Suomi, S. J., & Ripp, C. (1983). A history of motherless mother monkey mothering at the University of Wisconsin Primate Laboratory. In M. Reite & N. Caine (Eds.), *Child abuse: The nonhuman primate data* (pp. 49–77). New York: Liss.

Suomi, S. J., Sackett, G. P., & Harlow, H. F. (1970). Development of sex preference in rhesus monkeys. *Developmental Psychology, 3,* 326–334.

van Hooff, J .A. R. A. M. (1967). The facial displays of the Catarrhine monkeys and apes. In D. Morris (Ed.), *Primate ethology* (pp. 7–68). London: Weidenfield & Nicholson.

Visalberghi, E. (1990). Tool use in *Cebus. Folia Primatologica, 54,* 146–154.

Visalberghi, E., & Fragaszy, D. M. (1990). Do monkeys ape?. In S. Parker & K. Gibson (Eds.), *Language and intelligence in monkeys and apes* (pp. 247–273). Cambridge, UK: Cambridge University Press.

Visalberghi, E., & Limongelli, L. (1994). Lack of comprehension of cause-effect relations in tool-using capuchin monkeys *(Cebus apella). Journal of Comparative Psychology, 108,* 15–22.

Visalberghi, E., & Trinca, L. (1989). Tool-use in capuchin monkeys: Distinguishing between performance and understanding. *Primates, 30,* 511–521.

Westergaard, G. C., & Fragaszy, D. M. (1987). The manufacture and use of tools by capuchin monkeys *(Cebus apella). Journal of Comparative Psychology, 101,* 159–168.

Westergaard, G. C., & Suomi, S. J. (1994a), A simple stone-tool technology in monkeys. *Journal of Human Evolution, 27,* 399–404.

Westergaard, G. C., & Suomi, S. J. (1994b). The use and modification of bone tools by capuchin monkeys. *Current Anthropology, 35,* 75–77.

Westergaard, G. C., & Suomi, S. J. (1994c). Stone-tool bone modification by monkeys. *Current Anthropology, 35,* 468–470.

Westergaard, G. C., & Suomi, S. J. (1994d). Aimed throwing of stones by tufted capuchin monkeys *(Cebus apella). Human Evolution, 9,* 323–329.

Westergaard, G. C., & Suomi, S. J. (1995). The manufacture and use of bamboo tools by monkeys: Possible implications for the development of material culture among east Asian hominids. *Journal of Archeological Science, 22,* 667–681.

PART III

The Social Role of Nonverbal
Communication and Emotions:
Evolutionary Inferences

In the third part of this volume we turn to evolutionary explanations of the social role of nonverbal communication and emotions. In fact, the chapters in this part occasionally require the reader to put on the hat of the evolutionary biologist who is trying to explain from a phylogenetic standpoint just why a certain social behavior may have developed. What is perhaps most interesting in the following four chapters is that the traditional division of labor between evolutionary biologists and social scientists is here being blurred. Here it is in fact the biologically trained researchers who turn out to be interested in intentions and voluntary actions, whereas sociologists try their hands at evolutionary scenarios. Thus, ethologists Peter Marler and Christopher Evans argue for the existence of intentional communication in animals, and comparative psychologists Signe Preuschoft and J.A.R.A.M. van Hooff discuss strategical smiling and laughter in primates, whereas sociologists Alexandra Maryanski and Jonathan Turner explain the development of spoken language and emotions as evolutionary adaptations of early hominids.

The main message of Marler and Evans' chapter is that animal signals can be used for both emotional and referential purposes, and also, that this varies with the predator and the social situation of the signaller. They review the earlier discovery of Marler and his associates that vervet monkeys have three discrete types of alarm calls, each elicited by a particular class of predators (eagle, leopard, and snake). Staging an ingenious field test of recorded and played back alarm calls in Amboseli National Park, Kenya, they were able to establish a surprisingly specific linkage between predator stimulus, vocal reaction, and elicited response—the authors here introduce the tentative concept of proto-words. Other studies show that animals, including chicken, can withhold or emit signals at will. The ontogenic trajectories for these calls are already present at birth, but there is significant developmental plasticity. Thus, in many respects, animal communication is remarkably similar to that of humans.

Preuschoft and van Hooff argue that even though phylogenetically human smile and laughter can be seen as modifications of the primate "bared-teeth" and "open-mouth" displays (see van Hooff, 1972), primates may use smiles and laughter instrumentally or for appeasement; this varies with species, societies, and contexts. Their tentative power asymmetry hypothesis states that the social organization of the society determines the particular forms these evolutionarily "emancipated" displays will take: Despotic societies depend on a clear distinction between displays for submission and friendliness; in egalitarian societies the distinction is blurred.

Maryanski looks at both nonverbal and language communication as evolutionary adaptations to changing ecological conditions. She sees spoken language as the end result of a series of changes of primate sensory modalities that evolved first in an arboreal zone and were later modified in an open-country zone. For our tree-living ancestors, vision and touch were already under cortical control, but vocal expressions were involuntary and controlled by the emotion-regulating limbic system. Maryanski argues that the most obvious pathway for evolution was to also place vocal responses under cortical control, making voluntary sounds possible. These were later connected up with a cultural convention about the meaning of symbols.

Turner explains how the evolution of emotions represented a selective advantage for the ancestors of Homo sapiens who he sees as individualistic, loosely structured hominids (Maryanski & Turner, 1992). Strong emotionality brought the following benefits for group living: attunement, i.e., the capacity for empathic interaction with other group members; adult–infant attunement, facilitating learning; and the emergence of a moral code, promoting solidarity.

REFERENCES

Hooff van, J. A. R. A. M. (1972). A comparative approach to the phylogeny of laughter and smiling. In R. A. Hinde (Ed.), *Nonverbal communication* (pp. 209–241). Cambridge, UK: Cambridge University Press.

Maryanski, A. R., & Turner, J. H. (1992). *The social cage: Human nature and the evolution of society.* Stanford, CA: Stanford University Press.

8

COMMUNICATION SIGNALS OF ANIMALS: CONTRIBUTIONS OF EMOTION AND REFERENCE

Peter Marler
University of California, Davis

Christopher S. Evans
Macquarie University, Sydney, Australia

Most students of human communication, whether verbally or nonverbally mediated, agree that a distinction must be made between signals that are symbolic in nature and signals based on emotion. Language is, of course, the paradigmatic illustration of symbolic communication. It is at least potentially free of emotional content, although it is perhaps unrealistic to assume that this ever occurs in the course of natural usage. The communicative potency of emotion-purged speech is significantly diminished, but the presumed contrast with animal signals is nevertheless clear.

EMOTION AND ANIMAL SIGNALS

Until recently, it was a virtually universal view that the natural communication signals of animals, both visual and vocal, fall into the emotion-based category, and never qualify as symbols. This judgment seems to have been based primarily on experience with birds and mammals, especially primates, and focused on their natural behavior. Although the empirical basis for judgments about the affective nature of natural animal signals has rarely been made explicit, we believe that two properties of animal communication are relevant. The first is what we may call *input specificity;* that is, the relationship between signal morphology and the eliciting event. The second is the *behavioral context* of signals; this refers to the relationship between a signal and the other behavior accompanying production. In this survey we focus especially on signals such as alarm and food calls because they are experimentally tractable in the sense that they are associated with identifiable objects or stimuli in the environment. We identify these objects (predators or foods), as *referents* for signals associated with them.

Consider input specificity. It is undoubtedly the case that many animal signals are given in response to a wide range of stimuli, much as we may produce signs of anger or fear in many different situations. It has been presumed that this lack of specificity is general in animal signals, thus suggesting parallels with our own emotional behavior.

How about behavioral context? Just as our cries of fear or bellows of rage each have their own obligatory accompaniments of facial, postural and physiological responses to the same eliciting stimulus, many animal signals seem to be accompanied, in an obligatory fashion, by a range of other behavioral and physiological responses appropriate to the referent. This is another parallel with our own expressive behavior, lending weight to the argument that human emotional displays and animal signals are closely allied.

The aim of this chapter is to suggest that neither of these views is strictly correct and that the inaccuracies have seriously distorted our interpretation of animal signals. The issue of input specificity is discussed first. We describe examples of animal signals for which the stimulus or referent is so specific that it strains credibility to think of them as simple emotional displays. Other animal signals possess great breadth of reference. We suggest that animal signals range through the full spectrum, with the degree of input specificity varying according to the functional demands of the particular communicative situation.

In the second part of the chapter, we address the issue of behavioral context. We will present evidence that some animal signals are not inextricably bound to a suite of emotional responses. In certain situations, animals have the ability to control the production of a signal, such as a vocalization, independently of other concomitant responses to the referent. We make the case that signal production is determined not only by stimulus characteristics, but also by the social circumstances of the signaler. Certain signals are produced when communication is socially appropriate, and withheld when it is not. Both kinds of evidence argue against a comprehensive application of an emotional interpretation of animal signaling. Although expressive displays like our own undoubtedly occur, we can begin to discern the same kind of mixtures of affective and symbolic content in animal signals that are characteristic of our own natural speech behavior. Again, the balance between these components probably shifts according to functional demands.

A. Input Specificity 1: The Alarm Call System of the Vervet Monkey

Despite the great theoretical interest in alarm calling behavior as a possible case of altruism (e.g., Sherman, 1985), there has, until recently, been remarkably little systematic study of the specificity of the relationship between the production of alarm calls and the identity and behavior of the predator eliciting them. One of the first cases to be investigated was the unusually complex alarm call system of an east African monkey, the vervet, *Ceropithecus aethiops*.

About 25 years ago, primatologist Thomas Struhsaker (1967b, 1967c) conducted a pioneering study of vervet behavior and ecology, including a descriptive catalog of their large repertoire of vocalizations (1967a). Unlike most of its close relatives, which dwell deep in the rain forest, the highly social vervet monkey lives on the forest edge, and often ventures out onto the savanna. Like all plains-living animals, it is highly vulnerable to predation, and it has a correspondingly large repertoire of distinct alarm calls for different kinds of danger. Some are generalized, but three calls in particular are used by adult vervets in highly specific situations; each of these calls is evoked by one class of predator (leopards, eagles, and snakes). The three call types are distinct and do not intergrade.

The dangers presented by leopards, eagles and snakes are very different (Cheney & Seyfarth, 1981). If a prey animal lives in a complex environment, with many alternative refuges, then the best escape from one predator may be quite different from the optimal response to another. When we first realized the potential advantages to animals possessing signals that elicit specific adaptive responses, rather than generalized fear responses, we were led to reflect on the general relationship between alarm calls and emotion and on the difficulty of communicating about such different types of predation hazard by means of solely emotional displays (Marler, 1977, 1978).

Like many raptors, the martial eagle hunts by swooping down rapidly from a great height and seizing infant vervets in its talons. Monkeys are potentially vulnerable to such an attack when they are in the open; the appropriate escape strategy is to rush into the nearest bush. Vervets are also attacked by eagles when they are in the topmost branches of trees and in this case they leap down from the canopy into the heart of the tree. Thus, with eagles, the best strategy is to rush for cover.

Now consider leopards. They lie still for long periods, using their camouflage to hunt by ambush, typically waiting in dense cover until a vervet comes close enough for them to pounce. The best escape strategy with leopards is exactly the opposite from that for evading eagles. It is to run not into cover, but away from it, out onto the savanna or, preferably, up into the topmost branches of a tree, which are too weak to support a leopard's weight. Responses to both eagles and leopards are undoubtedly associated with fear, but a simple display of emotion seems inadequate to convey the specific needs of vervet monkeys in these two situations, with optimal responses that are virtually antithetical.

Convinced of the inadequacy of a simple emotional view of these alarm calls, Cheney, Seyfarth, and Marler decided to reinvestigate the fascinating problem opened up by Struhsaker's field studies, with new observational studies and a series of field experiments. Recordings of alarm calls uttered by known individuals were played back to free-ranging vervet monkeys at Struhsaker's original research site in Amboseli National Park in Kenya. The results confirmed Struhsaker's general findings, and demonstrated convincingly that playback of a single phrase of each of three alarm calls from a hidden loudspeaker, in the absence of any predator, elicited reliably different responses. Eagle alarm calls caused animals to rush into cover, and look up into the sky. When leopard alarm calls were played, the vervets rushed away from cover and up into the tree tops. Monkeys responded to snake alarm calls by standing bipedally and searching the grass around them, just as when a snake is discovered. The linkage between predator stimuli, vocal reaction, and the responses elicited in others by signal playback was so specific that it was tempting to think of the calls as proto-words (Seyfarth, Cheney, & Marler, 1980a, 1980b, reviewed in Cheney & Seyfarth, 1990).

In the jargon of semiotics, the function of these alarm calls can be viewed as prescriptive, identifying, or both (Marler, 1961, 1992). Lacking a shared communication system that can be used for interrogation, we must rely on the relationship between call type and eliciting event and on the responses elicited by playback for drawing inferences about meaning. It is clear that there is a high degree of input specificity, although we cannot determine whether it is more appropriate to view calls as labels for the eliciting stimulus or as commands to perform the specific response that the signal elicits, equivalent to an imperative verb (Cheney & Seyfarth, 1990). In either case, a simple emotional model simply does not fit the facts.

Nevertheless, it is likely that few, if any, monkey calls are entirely free of emotional content. Eisenberg (1976) and Green (1975), for example, presented cogent evidence that variations in the quality and degree of arousal associated with different monkey calls correlate well with certain acoustic features. Both authors make a case that entire repertoires can be ordered into a meaningful classification on the basis of such arousal related properties. The burden of this chapter is not to counter such interpretations but rather to complement them. It seems clear that affective components are there, and that they are important. However, we urge serious consideration of the likelihood that there is a symbolic component in monkey calls as well, designed to work in harmony with the affective component, as in our own speech behavior.

B. The Role of Cognition: Development of Alarm Calling

The alarm call data invite cognitive interpretations. On hearing a tape-recorded alarm call, vervets react as though the experience is associated with an internal representation of the predator class that is a referent for the call. Other interpretations are possible, however. We could imagine links between stimulus and signal, and between signal and response, that are reflexive and involuntary, and also highly specific, in which case rich cognitive interpretations would be inappropriate. Studies of the development of alarm calling should throw light on whether a reflexive model is appropriate, and preliminary field observations suggest that something more complicated is taking place during ontogeny than the simple maturation of a reflex.

In adulthood, the link between each of the three vervet alarm calls and predator type is highly specific. The martial eagle is the major stimulus for eagle calling, which is appropriate given that it is the principal

aerial predator for vervets. With infant monkeys, however, martial
eagles are only one of several stimuli that elicit eagle alarms. In infancy, the eagle alarm call is given to virtually any overhead moving
stimulus, including raptors, innocuous birds such as storks and bee-eat-
ers, and even a falling leaf (Seyfarth & Cheney, 1986). Hence, the data
from 1-month-old monkeys present a completely different picture from
the behavior of adults (Seyfarth & Cheney, 1980). A striking increase in
input specificity takes place during individual development that is not
what we would anticipate with a simple reflexive behavior.

Despite the clear evidence of developmental plasticity, the vervet
infants do not behave as though they were beginning with a *tabula
rasa*. They do not respond similarly to all predators; rather, they seem
from the outset to be making broad categorical distinctions between different predator types. The many different stimuli that evoke eagle calling in infants do, in fact, have something in common—they are all objects moving above the caller in free space. Infant monkeys never give
eagle calls to prototypical members of another predator class, such as a
leopard. Similarly, infants produce leopard alarms in response to a
broader array of stimuli than adults, including lions (*Panthera leo*),
hyenas (*Crocuta crocuta*), and even an antelope, but these calls are
never evoked by aerial objects. There is also a certain specificity in the
large class of stimuli evoking snake calls.

Young vervets thus behave as though they already possess an elementary set of rules for the perceptual analysis and classification of
predatory animals. These rules are sufficient to divide predators into
three lumped classes, although the divisions are too gross for the diag-
nostic classification of particular species. This result is consonant with
the findings of ethologists in other perceptual domains. Numerous cases
have been discovered of unspecific, generalized innate release mechanisms that do not produce automatic behavior, but rather, guide the perceptual development of the young toward certain species-specific trajectories, while preserving considerable flexibility (Gould & Marler,
1987; Marler, Dooling, & Zoloth, 1980; Marler, Zoloth, & Dooling,
1981). General ontogenetic trajectories are thus shared with other
members of the species and are individualized as a result of adjustments
and refinements in the face of personal experience.

During the development of eagle calls, for example, the monkeys
behave as though they start with a generalized responsiveness to moving aerial stimuli, which is sharpened by experience to a very small
subset (just one eagle species out of many). This is reminiscent of the

process by which word meaning becomes more sharply focused in the course of semantic development in children.

C. Behavioral Context: Vervet Alarm Calls

Approaching animal signaling from a different but not unrelated, viewpoint, one may ask whether vervet alarm calls show any sign of being under voluntary control, as Sutton and his colleagues demonstrated with some rhesus macaque (*Macaca mulatta*) calls (Sutton, Larson, Taylor, & Lindeman, 1973). Here we approach for the first time the issue of behavioral context. Are the alarm calls involuntarily and inextricably bound together with emotional behaviors concerned with fearfulness and escape, or can the vervets voluntarily call or remain silent, depending on the circumstances? Several lines of evidence converge to suggest that production of alarm calls by vervets is, in fact, flexibly dependent on social context and that alarm calling can be decoupled from the other responses evoked by a predator.

First, vervets producing alarm calls do not invariably also engage in other types of antipredator behavior, such as fleeing to cover. For example, a monkey that spots a distant eagle may call and then simply resume feeding (Cheney & Seyfarth, 1990). This result could be explained by an emotion-based model that simply incorporated different thresholds for the various components of response to a predator, so that calling could be more readily elicited than fleeing. Such a model clearly predicts that vervets should not be able to express the nonvocal responses to a predator without call production.

It is therefore striking that isolated vervets are capable of inhibiting production of alarm calls, even when being chased by a leopard (Cheney & Seyfarth, 1990), although, because vervets are highly social, such observations under field conditions are inevitably rare. However, subsequent experiments with a captive vervet colony have produced comparable results, confirming that both male and female adults are able to modulate alarm call production depending on the nature of their "audience." Females called at higher rates in the presence of their offspring than when only unrelated juveniles were adjacent. Similarly, subordinate adult males called more when their audience was a female than when it was the dominant male (Cheney & Seyfarth, 1985).

Finally, although field playbacks of alarm calls were highly effective, and consistently elicited appropriate escape responses, the vervets being tested very rarely produced alarm calls themselves (Seyfarth, Cheney, & Marler, 1980a).

Thus, alarm calling does not seem to be an obligatory component in a cluster of emotionally based escape behaviors. Rather, the calls seem to be under voluntary control. Perhaps they do indeed reflect a cognitive appraisal of the nature of different causes of danger, implying an assessment of the most appropriate responses in the circumstances.

If this is a correct interpretation, it helps us to understand the otherwise astonishing behavior of captive chimpanzees (*Pan troglodytes*) trained with languagelike systems of signaling and thus susceptible to interrogation by the experimenter (R. A. Gardner & B. T. Gardner, 1969; D. Premack, 1976; Rumbaugh, 1977). These animals clearly exhibit a capacity for voluntary symbolic signaling, and it would be remarkable if this were never manifest under natural conditions, where signaling behavior is often a matter of life or death. Descriptions of the behavior of free-ranging chimpanzees at the Gombe Stream Research Center in Tanzania suggest an example of just such flexibility. During "patrols" in the periphery of their home range, when the risk of discovery by another group, and consequently of a dangerous fight, is high, all members of the group inhibit their vocalizations, sometimes maintaining silence for periods of several hours. Adult males perform "charging" aggressive displays, omitting the "pant-hoots" that normally accompany them (Goodall, 1986).

It became clear to us that the next phase in the study of the psychological and physiological basis of communication in animals should be developmental in nature. We need to explore the ontogeny of alarm calling behavior and the possible roles of learning and of social instruction indepth. This is virtually impossible in the field, and the predator responses of monkeys have proved to be difficult to study under captive conditions. We therefore began searching for a subject that would be more amenable to laboratory investigation.

D. Input Specificity 2: Bird Calls

Birds are more suitable than monkeys for laboratory investigation of the subtleties of communication and their development, and we had indications from field studies that, like primates, they also display input specificity in both alarm calls and food calls. Galliform birds, in particular, such as pheasants, partridges and quail, tend to have unusually large vocal repertoires, perhaps in part as a correlate of their rich social life.

After considering various galliforms as possible subjects for pursuing questions of call meaning, we chose the domestic chicken. Jungle fowl, the wild ancestor of the chicken, proved to be difficult to handle experimentally, but some strains of domestic chicken such as the Golden Sebright bantam, which have been bred not for eating or egg production, but for their showy appearance, are more tame and yet still possess essentially the same vocal repertoire as their wild ancestors.

We began with studies of food calling, and the results were promising. A specific call was identified, which has a high-pitched, pulsatile structure and is used in two situations: by males courting females, and by broody hens in attracting their chicks to food. We focused on the courtship situation, exemplified in the so-called tidbitting display of cockerels. A male repeatedly seizes a food item, holds it in view of a female, food calls, and then drops the food before her, refraining from consuming it himself, however highly preferred it might be, allowing her to take it from him and eat it.

Experiments with a range of foods revealed that rates of food calling varied with the preference ranking of the food. Tests were conducted in which hens could hear a male with food but could not see the food itself. They approached more quickly and reliably when a male was calling to a preferred food than when he was given a nonfood item (Marler, Dufty, & Pickert, 1986a, 1986b). Observational studies of birds maintained in large outdoor pens provided potential cases of functional deception in the use of food calling. For example, males sometimes called while holding inedible twigs in their beaks, rather than the usual invertebrate. Such "deceptive" calling was most frequent when a male encountered a new female, and attempted to induce her to join his harem, this being a polygymous species. Intriguingly, it occurred especially when the female was at a distance and it was consequently more difficult for her to identify the proffered item (Gyger & Marler, 1988).

Pressing the issue of input specificity further, we shifted our attention to alarm calls. Like many birds, chickens have two classes of alarm calls, one for aerial predators and one for ground predators. They are acoustically distinct, and do not intergrade. We then set out to devise methods for eliciting these two call types under controlled conditions in the laboratory.

First, we borrowed an idea from the classic experiments of Lorenz, Tinbergen, and Schleidt (Schleidt, 1961) and passed a hawk silhouette overhead. As long as certain requirements of image size and angular velocity were satisfied, a cockerel reliably produced aerial alarm calls in response to this simulation of a soaring hawk. Seeking to gain more control over the visual stimuli presented, we generated graphic displays of hawk images for video presentation. By placing a large video monitor overhead so that the cockerel could look up at it, we found that computer-generated animation of a hawk moving across the screen was as effective as a model in eliciting this pattern of calling (C. S. Evans, Macedonia, & Marler, 1993; C. S. Evans & Marler, 1992). By studying the effects on alarm calling of varying image size and velocity, we have been able to specify precisely the parameters of size and movement necessary to elicit the call (C. S. Evans, Macedonia, & Marler, 1993).

In a typical test, males were initially standing in a relaxed posture. They then panicked as the hawk silhouette first appeared, called, crouched, and peered upward, adopting the characteristic cryptic posture displayed by a bird that is attempting to hide, with both the head and the tail lowered.

Devising stimuli for eliciting ground alarm calls in the laboratory proved to be more difficult. We experimented with snakes and trained dogs, but the inevitable complications from using live stimuli made it difficult to get reproducible results, so we again decided to try video images of predators. We videorecorded a raccoon in a glassfronted cage that was constructed to match the size of the video monitor, so that the image presented was life-sized. We then edited raw footage to obtain a sequence containing almost continuous movement. This proved to be a reliable stimulus for eliciting the ground alarm call (C. S. Evans, L. Evans, & Marler, 1993).

When the raccoon image appeared, the cockerels typically adopted the posture of a bird that is highly alert and aroused, with both head and tail raised. They then began to produce the ground alarm call, turned away and fled to the side of the cage furthest from the video screen, calling at a high rate. From subsequent experiments we now know that if we had provided an area of cover, there would have been movement into it with the hawk, and away from it with the raccoon.

The results from these laboratory experiments replicate those obtained earlier from observational studies of interactions between chickens maintained in large outdoor enclosures and their potential predators (Gyger, Marler, & Pickert, 1987): Only aerial alarm calls were elicited by the simulated hawk and only ground alarm calls were evoked by the videorecorded raccoon. There was also an interesting degree of within-category variation in call structure that merits further study.

The next question we addressed was that of how chickens would react if we played the alarm calls back to them with all predator stimuli absent. Could we recreate the distinctive and contrasting aspects of responsiveness to these two classes of predators solely by signal playback, as with vervet monkeys? If so, we could then begin to think of the calls as symbols, representing the different classes of predators with which they are associated.

For this purpose, we selected recordings representing the full range of within-category variation in each of the two classes of alarm call. Each of these playback exemplars was contributed by a different individual. Hens were placed in a test cage, with an area of brush in one corner to constitute cover. The responses to playback of the two call types were strikingly different. For example, the frequency with which subjects ran into the area of cover was high in response to the aerial alarm call, but low in response to the ground alarm call, which had no more effect than a control sound.

The data on gaze direction were the most striking of all. Horizontal scanning increased significantly, and to a similar degree, in response to both types of alarm call. However, looking upward, which is conspicuous in these birds because they have a limited binocular vision and use the medial fovea for inspecting objects at any distance, was elicited much more often by aerial alarm calls.

We conclude that the aerial alarm call represents danger overhead, and that this is not true of the ground alarm call, a surprising echo of the findings with the vervet monkey. Once more we have a considerable degree of input specificity, leaving us well placed to broach studies of the development of alarm calling in chickens. We intend to examine both predator recognition and call production, together with the development of responsiveness to calls. We are also preparing studies of such issues as whether or not there is a degree of plasticity in the development of call usage (see Marler & C. S. Evans, 1996). For example, we will be interested in determining whether chicks can be trained to give aerial alarm calls to a raccoon, or ground alarm calls to a hawk.

E. Behavioral Context: Are Signals and Other Responses to Referents Inextricably Linked?

We now turn to the relationship between alarm calling and its accompaniments. Can animal signals be produced independently of the other behavior with which they are associated, or are they obligatory members of a suite of emotional behaviors and physiological responses from which they cannot be separated? Our window on this problem arose from the discovery that, when we test a cockerel for food calling or alarm calling, and provide the appropriate stimuli, either food objects or predators, the rate of call production is very different when a male is alone, and when he is in the presence of another bird. We discovered this phenomenon during studies of food calling. When there is a hen nearby, males food call at a significantly higher rate than when they are alone. In contrast, the presence of other males has an inhibitory effect (Marler, Dufty, & Pickert, 1986b). This sensitivity to social context makes functional sense if food calling is part of a courtship ritual designed to elicit female approach, and consequently inappropriate in the presence of a male.

AUDIENCE EFFECTS ON ALARM CALL PRODUCTION

What are the effects of social context on alarm calls? Signaling by a solitary animal may be of some benefit to the signaler by informing the predator that it has been detected (Caro, 1986; Hasson, 1991), but putative functions of alarm calls, such as alerting kin and other companions to danger (Sherman, 1985), and diverting the attention of predators to others by causing them to panic and so reveal their presence (Charnov & Krebs, 1975), all require the presence of companions. As with food calls, we found that a companion exerts an "audience effect" on the production of alarm calls. We exposed male subjects in one cage to the hawk silhouette passing overhead. Adjacent was a second audience cage, either left empty or containing a hen. There was a significant potentiation of alarm calling in her presence, as compared with both an empty cage and a member of another species, namely a bobwhite quail, in the adjacent cage. In this case, a male companion was equally effective (Gyger, Karakashian, & Marler, 1986).

This audience effect on alarm calling is relevant to the present discussion because the effect is not general to all escape behaviors, but specific to call production. A solitary male gives full responses to the hawk overhead, crouching, sleeking his feathers, and fixating upward. However, he calls little or not at all. In the presence of a companion, other responses to the hawk are similar, but now alarm calling is specifically potentiated. This result, which we have now obtained repeatedly (C. S. Evans & Marler, 1991, 1992; Gyger et al., 1986; Karakashian, Gyger, & Marler, 1988), demonstrates that calls can indeed vary independently of the other behaviors that usually accompany them. The cockerel behaves as though he has an intent to communicate. If an appropriate audience for communication is absent, then signaling is curtailed. If it is present, calling is augmented. We now have many demonstrations of this ability to vary call production in an independent fashion, contrary to expectations from a simple "emotion-based" hypothesis.

A. What Is an Adequate Audience?

What constitutes an adequate audience? Will any animate object suffice or does it have to be a conspecific? Our data suggest that companions are classified or categorized as a potential audience for alarm calls by different criteria than in other kinds of social interactions. For example, the relative ineffectiveness of bobwhite quail as an audience for alarm calling led us to explore the role of appearance in the audience effect. We selected three same-size strains of bantam hens on the basis of their plumage characteristics. One, the Japanese Silky bantam, is very different from the Golden Sebright. Its plumage is dark gray rather than brown, its feathers have a hairlike quality, and its combs and wattles are inconspicuous. As an intermediate strain, we chose Cochin bantams, also different in color, with black plumage, but otherwise more similar to Sebrights. For the third strain we used hens of the male's own breed.

We reasoned that males might use an internalized standard based on phenotype matching for judging the adequacy of an audience bird prior to alarm calling (e.g, Holmes & Sherman, 1983; Sherman & Holmes, 1985). If this were so, then a Silky bantam hen should be the least effective, with a Cochin hen intermediate, and a Golden Sebright hen the most effective of all. We found no such effect. Hens of all three strains significantly potentiated alarm calling, relative to an empty cage, but they did not differ from one another in their audience effectiveness (C. S. Evans & Marler, 1992).

However, when we studied the courtship responses of males to these same hens, their reactions differed strikingly, and here the prediction was verified. Silky bantams were weak stimuli for courtship, Sebright hens were strong stimuli, and Cochin hens were intermediate. Moreover, males responded more vigorously in every case to hens that were strange to them than to hens that were familiar. In contrast, audience familiarity had no effect on alarm calling. Thus, in a courtship situation, males were responsive to subtle characteristics of hens that were simply overlooked when they served as audiences for alarm calling. This supports our suspicion that less specific criteria are used in judging appropriateness of companions as an audience for alarm calls than when judging them as objects for sexual interaction.

There are intriguing hints that this judgment may vary in different communicative contexts. The criteria defining an adequate audience for food calling seem quite different from those employed for alarm calling. For example, when males are presented with a food stimulus, female companions potentiate calling, whereas males inhibit it. There is no such effect of audience gender when males are responding to aerial predators. Similarly, audience familiarity, which has no effect on alarm calling, has a significant negative influence on food calling—males food call most to a strange female. The overall pattern is thus of audience characteristics being more specifically defined during food calling than during alarm calling. It may be that each communicative subsystem has its own audience "rules," varying according to the functional requirements of the situation.

In studying audience effects, perhaps the most intriguing prospect is the possibility that an animal might modulate the frequency or form of signal production according to the behavior of the audience. Does a cockerel that spots a hawk overhead curtail his alarm calling if he sees that his neighbor is already alarmed? Does he perseverate with calling if a neighbor remains relaxed and unalarmed in the face of danger? We took a preliminary look at this possibility by arranging a test situation in which one or other of the birds, subject or audience, was prevented from seeing the hawk by a screen overhead. There was a slight, but nonsignificant, tendency for a male to call more when his female audience did not see the hawk than when she did. This was, however, a difficult experiment to conduct and interpret because of the inevitable variation in the behavior of the audience hen. In the ideal experiment, one would have independent control over the behavior of the audience. To accomplish this, we set about substituting videorecorded images with sound for live audience hens.

B. Is a Video Image of an Audience Effective?

Males were presented with hawk models overhead while one of three audience types (Sebright hen, bobwhite quail, and empty cage) was present. Audiences were live birds during some test trials and videotaped images with recorded soundtracks on others. Our goal was to replicate with video stimuli the pattern of results obtained in earlier experiments (Gyger et al., 1986; Karakashian et al., 1988). We found that the video audience mimicked effects of the live audience almost perfectly (C. S. Evans & Marler, 1991). Again, a video of a chicken was more effective than a video of a bobwhite quail, and both were better than an empty cage.

We began to exploit the advantages of video stimuli by selecting clips so that the bobwhite sequences contained substantially more vocal and locomotor activity than the chicken sequences. We reasoned that if potentiation of alarm calling was dependent principally on the amount of gross visual and acoustic stimulation provided, then the videorecorded bobwhite sequences should be more effective. The fact that the conspecific video stimuli were nevertheless superior as audiences suggests that potentiation of alarm calling is mediated by species recognition, rather than simply by the level of noise and movement in the immediate environment.

Although the live and videorecorded bobwhite quail were significantly less effective than Sebright hens, they did increase alarm call production, relative to the empty cage. This result adds the further impression that relatively unspecific social stimuli may suffice for an audience effect on alarm calling.

In a subsequent experiment, we found a decrement in the audience effect when either the optical or the acoustic component was removed, although visual stimulation alone and auditory stimulation alone both exerted significant effects on the potentiation of alarm calling, in comparison with the empty cage (C. S. Evans & Marler, 1991).

Thus, chickens do indeed respond to images of other chickens seen on a video monitor. We are currently assembling a library of videotapes of chickens behaving in various ways, in preparation for tests of whether a male's signal production is influenced by moment-to-moment changes in the behavior of his audience. This approach offers new ways of addressing questions about whether animals emit signals reflexively, or whether they actually intend to communicate. Meanwhile, it is clear that animals can withhold or emit some signals independently of their other behavioral accompaniments. This finding reveals a significant deficiency of the simple emotional model.

DOES SOCIAL FACILITATION PLAY A ROLE
IN AUDIENCE EFFECTS?

There are complications in the interpretation of audience effects and of male food calling in chickens. First, how certain are we that this is a "food" call and not a "social" call? The response of a hen is to approach and share the food and the male often then courts her (Kruijt, 1964). How can we be sure that this is not actually a generalized signal inviting social interaction, rather than a signal specifically about food?

To explore this question, we sought to gain independent control of a male's access to food and his access to a female by employing operant techniques. We arranged for a light to signal when the male was able to obtain food by pecking a key. When the light was off, pecks delivered to the key had no effect and food was unavailable. We placed males in the chamber with a female in the adjacent cage and the signal light off. All of the males courted the hen with the stereotyped "waltzing" display, but they did not give food calls significantly until the signal light was illuminated. Food calling began as the males approached and pecked the key, and increased to a high rate once the food was delivered. Evidently food calling is specifically linked to food and to cues that reliably predict the presence of food, such as the signal light. Calls were not evoked by the hen, even when males were engaging in high levels of sexual display (C. S. Evans & Marler, 1994).

Further analyses of these data address the possibility that an audience influences call production by social facilitation (Zajonc, 1965); that is, by affecting the level of general arousal. Calling rates with successive food deliveries provide clear evidence of an audience effect; significantly more food calls were produced after each of six food presentations when a hen was present than when the males were alone. In contrast, the female had no effect on the rate at which males pecked the key. In other words, the audience facilitated signal production specifically, but had no effect on a concurrent instrumental response. Because enhanced performance on a well-learned task is the hallmark of social facilitation (Zajonc, 1965), this contrast suggests to us that audience effects on food calling are not attributable to changes in general arousal.

Once more, we have evidence not only of input specificity, but also of the dissociation of signal production from other associated behaviors. The call is not an integral part of the caller's general physiological state, but rather a commentary on that state that can be given or withheld according to communicative demands.

A. Emotion Is a Significant Factor in Animal Signaling

In making the case that some animal calls encode highly specific information, we do not intend to eliminate emotional content from consideration. This is clearly an important dimension of animal signals. For example, food call rate appears, in part, to reflect motivational state with regard to food, because it varies with the preference ranking of a food item and declines with habituation. Similarly, if we present a raccoon image repeatedly, the general alarm call response wanes. Calling bouts become shorter and call structure changes somewhat as well, both serving as potential sources of information about the *intensity* of the response, as opposed to the *category* of response. Although the appropriate playback experiments have yet to be done, we think it likely that such acoustic correlates of the level of the caller's response will in fact prove to influence the intensity of responses elicited in animals receiving the signals, much as we suspect proponents of the emotion-based view of animal communication had in mind.

Increasingly, we find suggestions that animal signals encode both referential information and affective information, with the balance shifting according to functional requirements (Marler, C. S. Evans, & Hauser, 1992). In much the same way, our own speech encodes not only linguistic information but also information about the speaker's mood and state of mind, as well as the speaker's intentions.

Thus the conclusion we reach is that animal signals are not necessarily emotion bound. Some signals are subject to physiological or perhaps cognitive controls that are distinct from those controlling affect. The input specificity of animal signals can be high, especially in situations that have become overwhelmingly important to them in nature, such as encounters with food and predators. Whether or not emotions are aroused, the signaler's social circumstances have a strong influence on signal production, independently of the involvement of affect. The experience of emotion may be inexorable in the appropriate circumstances, but the communication signals of animals are not necessarily emitted unless there is an appropriate receiver. In retrospect, this hardly seems surprising. What is surprising is that it has taken us so long to realize that this attribute of an efficient communication system is present in animals, not only in nonhuman primates, but even in the lowly chicken.

REFERENCES

Caro, T. M. (1986). The functions of stotting in Thompson's gazelles: Some tests of the predictions. *Animal Behaviour, 36,* 477–486.

Charnov, E. L., & Krebs, J. R. (1975). The evolution of alarm calls: Altruism or manipulation? *American Naturalist, 109,* 107–112.

Cheney, D. L., & Seyfarth, R. M. (1981). Selective forces affecting the predator alarm calls of vervet monkeys. *Behaviour, 76,* 25–61.

Cheney, D. L., & Seyfarth, R. M. (1985). Vervet monkey alarm calls: Manipulation through shared information? *Behaviour, 93,* 160–166 .

Cheney, D. L., & Seyfarth, R. M. (1990). *How monkeys see the world: Inside the mind of another species.* Chicago: Chicago University Press.

Eisenberg, J. F. (1976). Communication mechanisms and social integration in the black spider monkey *Ateles fusciceps robustus,* and related species. *Smithsonian Contributions to Zoology, 213,* 1–108.

Evans, C. S., Macedonia, J. M., & Marler, P. (1993). Effects of apparent size and speed on the response of chickens (*Gallus gallus*) to computer-generated simulations of aerial predators. *Animal Behaviour, 46,* 1–11.

Evans, C. S., & Marler, P. (1991). On the use of video images as social stimuli in birds: Audience effects on alarm calling. *Animal Behaviour, 41,* 17–26.

Evans, C. S., & Marler, P. (1992). Female appearance as a factor in the responsiveness of male chickens during anti-predator behavior and courtship. *Animal Behaviour, 43,* 137–145.

Evans, C. S., & Marler, P. (1994). Food calling and audience effects in male chickens (*Gallus gallus*): Their relationships to food availability, courtship and social facilitation. *Animal Behaviour, 47,* 1159–1170.

Evans, C. S., Evans, L., & Marler, P. (1993), On the meaning of alarm calls: Functional reference in an avian vocal system. *Animal Behaviour, 46,* 23–38.

Gardner, R. A., & Gardner, B. T. (1969). Teaching sign language to a chimpanzee. *Science, 165,* 664–672.

Goodall, J. (1986). *The chimpanzees of Gombe: Patterns of behavior.* Cambridge, MA: Harvard University Press.

Gould, J. L., & Marler, P. (1987). Learning by instinct. *Scientific American, 255,* 74–85.

Green, S. (1975). Variation of vocal pattern with social situation in the Japanese monkey (*Macaca fuscata*): A field study. In L. Rosenblum (Ed.), *Primate behavior* (Vol. 4, pp. 1–102). New York: Academic Press.

Gyger, M., Karakashian, S., & Marler, P. (1986). Avian alarm calling. Is there an audience effect? *Animal Behaviour, 34,* 1570–1572.

Gyger, M., & Marler, P. (1988). Food calling in the domestic fowl (*Gallus gallus*). The role of external referents and deception. *Animal Behaviour, 36,* 358–365.

Gyger, M., Marler, P., & Pickert, R. (1987). Semantics of an avian alarm call system: The male domestic fowl, *Gallus domesticus. Behaviour, 102,* 15–40.

Hasson, O. (1991). Pursuit-deterrent signals: Communication between prey and predator. *Trends in Ecological Evolution, 6,* 325–329.

Holmes, W. G., & Sherman, P. W. (1983). Kin recognition in animals. *American Scientist, 71,* 46–55.

Karakashian, S. J., Gyger, M., & Marler, P. (1988). Audience effects on alarm calling in chickens (*Gallus gallus*). *Journal of Comparative Psychology, 102,* 129–135.

Kruijt, J. P. (1964). Ontogeny of social behaviour in Burmese red jungle fowl (*Gallus gallus spadiceus* Bonaterre). *Behaviour Supplement, 12,* 1–201.

Marler, P. (1961). The logical analysis of animal communication. *Journal of Theoretical Biology, 1,* 295–317.

Marler, P. (1977). Primate vocalization: Affective or symbolic? In G. Bourne (Ed.), *Progress in ape research* (pp. 85–96). New York: Academic Press.

Marler, P. (1978). Affective and symbolic meaning: Some zoosemiotic speculations. In T. Sebeok (Ed.), *Sight, sound and sense* (pp. 113–123). Bloomington: Indiana University Press.

Marler, P. (1992). Functions of arousal and emotion in primate communication: A semiotic approach. In T. Nishida, W. C. McGrew, P. Marler, M. Pickford, & F. B. de Waal (Eds.), *Topics in primatology: Vol. 1. Human origins* (pp. 225–233). Tokyo: University of Tokyo Press.

Marler, P., Zoloth, S. & Dooling, R. (1980). Comparative perspectives on ethology and perceptual development. In M. Bornstein (Ed.), *The comparative method in psychology: Ethological, developmental and cross-cultural viewpoints* (pp. 189–230). Hillsdale, NJ: Lawrence Erlbaum Associates.

Marler, P., Dufty, A., & Pickert, R. (1986a). Vocal communication in the domestic chicken. I. Does a sender communicate information about the quality of a food referent to a receiver? *Animal Behaviour, 34,* 188–193.

Marler, P., Dufty, A., & Pickert, R. (1986b). Vocal communication in the domestic chicken. II. Is a sender sensitive to the presence and nature of a receiver? *Animal Behaviour, 34,* 194–198.

Marler, P., & C. S. Evans (1996). Bird calls: Just emotional displays or something more? *IBIS, 138,* 26-331.

Marler, P., Evans, C. S., & Hauser, M. D. (1992). Animal signals: Motivational, referential, or both? In H. Papoušek, U. Jürgens, & M. Papoušek (Eds.), *Nonverbal vocal communication: Comparative and developmental approaches* (pp. 66–86). Cambridge, UK: Cambridge University Press.

Marler, P., Zoloth, S., & Dooling, R. (1981). Innate programs for perceptual development: An ethological view. In G. Gollin (Ed.), *Developmental plasticity. Behavioral and biological aspects of variations in development* (pp. 135–172). New York: Academic Press.

Premack, D. (1976). *Intelligence in ape and man.* Hillsdale, NJ: Lawrence Erlbaum.

Rumbaugh, D. (Ed.). (1977). *Language learning by a chimpanzee. The Lana project.* New York: Academic Press.

Schleidt, W. M. (1961). Reaktionen von Truthühnern auf fliegende Raubvögel und Versuche zur Analyse ihrer AAM's (Reactions of turkey-hens to flying predatory birds, and experiments to analyse their AAAM). *Zeitschrift für Tierpsychologie, 18,* 534–560.

Seyfarth, R. M., & Cheney, D. L. (1980). The ontogeny of vervet monkey alarm-calling behaviour: A preliminary report. *Zeitschrift für Tierpsychologie, 54,* 37–56.

Seyfarth, R. M., & Cheney, D. L. (1986). Vocal communication and its relation to language. In B. B. Smuts, D. L. Cheney, R. M. Seyfarth, R. W. Wrangham, & T. T. Struhsaker (Eds.), *Primate societies* (pp. 440–451). Chicago: Chicago University Press.

Seyfarth, R. M., Cheney, D. L., & Marler, P. (1980a). Monkey responses to three different alarm calls: Evidence for predator classification and semantic communication. *Science, 210,* 801–803.

Seyfarth, R. M., Cheney, D. L., & Marler, P. (1980b). Vervet monkey alarm calls: Semantic communication in a free-ranging primate. *Animal Behavior, 28,* 1070–1094.

Sherman, P. W. (1985). Alarm calls of Belding's ground squirrels to aerial predators: Nepotism or self-preservation? *Behavioral Ecological Sociobiology, 17,* 313–323.

Sherman, P. W., & Holmes, W. G. (1985). Kin recognition: Issues and evidence. In
    B. Hölldobler & M. Lindauer (Eds.), *Experimental behavioral ecology and socio-
    biology* (pp. 437–460). New York: Fischer Verlag.
Struhsaker, T. T. (1967a). Auditory communication among vervet monkeys (*Ceropithecus
    aethiops*). In S. A. Altmann (Ed.), *Social communication among primates* (pp. 281–
    324). Chicago: University of Chicago Press.
Struhsaker, T. T. (1967b). Behavior of vervet monkeys (*Ceropithecus aethiops*). *University
    of California Publication in Zoology, 82,* 1–74.
Struhsaker, T. T. (1967c). Ecology of vervet monkeys (*Ceropithecus aethiops*) in the Masai-
    Amboseli Game Reserve, Kenya. *Ecology, 48,* 891–904.
Sutton, D., Larson, C., Taylor, E. M., & Lindeman, R. C. (1973). Vocalizations in rhesus
    monkeys: Conditionability. *Brain Research, 52,* 225–231.
Zajonc, R. B. (1965). Social facilitation. *Science, 149,* 269–274.

9

THE SOCIAL FUNCTION OF "SMILE" AND "LAUGHTER": VARIATIONS ACROSS PRIMATE SPECIES AND SOCIETIES[1]

Signe Preuschoft
Jan A. R. A. M. van Hooff
University of Utrecht

When communicating emotional states and social attitudes, humans rely heavily on nonverbal signals. Among these facial expressions or facial displays play an important role. Like humans also nonhuman primates use facial displays for social communication. In addition, they even share essentially similar facial expressions with us (Chevalier-Skolnikoff, 1973; Darwin, 1872; van Hooff, 1962, 1972; S. Preuschoft, 1992). Darwin (1872) supposed that these similarities were due to common descent; that is, that they were homologies. There is nevertheless appreciable variation in the facial displays across the primates, both in morphology and meaning. This variation is found especially in the bonding displays that indicate submission, affiliation, and playfulness; that is, in various types of smile and laughter. In biology, such variation can be explained in two ways: It can either result from common descent of

---

[1] This is an abridged version of a longer paper entitled *Variations in Primate Affiliative Displays: An Exercise in Behavior Phylogeny.*

present displays from the same ancestor (i.e., homology), or it can be the result of systematic adaptation where ecological and social influences have driven the evolution of the displays in a certain direction (i.e., analogy). (Note that homologous and analogous are not absolute attributes of displays, but are relational properties in a certain phylogenetic horizon.)

In this chapter, we consider variation in the contexts and social functions of bonding displays across the primates. We restrict ourselves to those taxa that have been studied more or less extensively, namely certain Old World primates, the cercopithecoids (e.g., macaques, baboons), and hominoids (great apes and humans).

We know from previous studies how ecological factors mold social organization (e.g., van Hooff & van Schaik, 1992; van Schaik & van Hooff, 1983; Wrangham, 1980). In particular, the types of competition that appear within and between groups have recently been shown to be important, ecologically determined factors in the differentiation of social systems (van Schaik & van Noordwijk, 1988), resulting, for example, in different dominance styles (van Schaik, 1989; de Waal, 1989a). Here, we examine to what extent the variations in facial displays can be attributed to varying characteristics of social organization; that is, how social ecology affects the choice of displays for particular communicatory functions.

Primates possess a number of facial expressions to communicate submission, affiliation, and playful attitude. Among the best studied facial behaviors are smiling in humans (e.g., Ekman & Keltner. chap. 2, and K. Schneider, chap. 6, both this volume), the "silent-bared-teeth" display of nonhuman primates, which is the likely homologue of our human smiling, and the "relaxed open-mouth" display of the nonhuman primates, the likely homologue of human laughter (van Hooff, 1972; S. Preuschoft, 1992). In addition, there are a few displays that have received less attention. One is the "pout face," used primarily by infants as a signal expressing the need for care and contact with the mother. The "lip smacking" display is used in a broad range of affiliative contexts by a large number of primate species. It is thought to be a ritualized intention movement of the functional lip smacking employed during grooming (van Hooff, 1962), or, perhaps, of the sucking of the mother's nipple by an infant (Redican, 1975). Its reference to a desire for intimate contact made this behavioral element a very suitable candidate to express bonding motivation. In a number of species the "teeth chattering" display has evolved. Teeth chattering can be understood as an intermediate between lip smacking and silent bared-teeth display, both morphologically and contextually.

DESCRIPTION OF PRIMATE "SMILE" AND "LAUGHTER"

Silent bared-teeth display (also *grin, grimace* or *smile*) is a soundless and extreme baring of the teeth and is associated with inhibited loco-motion, with evasive and protective body movements and postures, with smooth body dynamics (e.g., Fig. 9.1), and with body contact (e.g., grooming, embraces, see Fig. 9.2). Relaxed open-mouth display (also "play face") is characterized by a widely opened mouth, without pro-nounced baring of the teeth (e.g., Fig. 9.3). A remarkable variant in some species is the open-mouth bared-teeth display (also "laughter-face"). With its often extreme baring of the teeth combined with an opened mouth it represents an intermediate between the silent bared-teeth and the relaxed open-mouth display (e.g., Fig. 9.4 and 9.5). It thus bears a striking resemblance in form with our human laughter. Both the relaxed open-mouth and the open-mouth bared-teeth display may be ac-companied by staccato breathing that in some spe-cies develops into bursts of vocalizations. Associated body postures and move-ments are never tense but may be boisterous, espe-cially during gnaw wres-tling and playful chasing. Brusque, explosive body movements or biting may

Fig. 9.1.   A female Barbary macaque performs a submissive silent bared-teeth display.

Fig. 9.2.   During a polyadic affiliative interaction among Tonkean macaques the silent bared-teeth display of one female (right) is answered with lip smacking by another (left).

Fig. 9.3. During social play in immature Barbary macaques relaxed open-mouth display (rom) is reciprocal. The juvenile to the right performs a low-intensity rom.

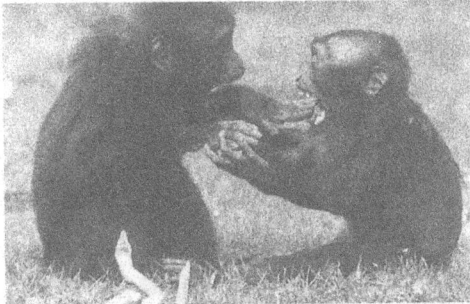

Fig. 9.4. A relaxed open-mouth display is reciprocated by an open-mouth bared-teeth display in playing juvenile Tonkean macaques.

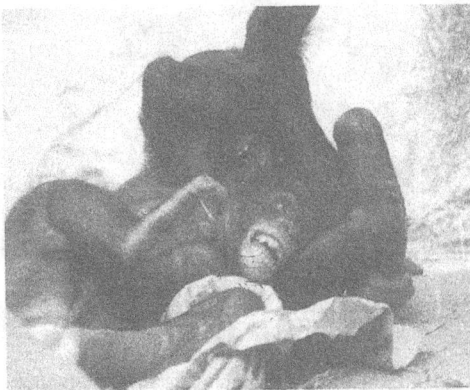

Fig. 9.5. Reciprocal open-mouth bared-teeth displays in two wrestling bonobos (courtesy T. Dielentheis).

also be observed but usually seem controll ed or inhibited. Each of these displays are accompanied by particular gaze patterns. These range from evasive glancing through rapid and repetitive peering from an oblique angle to direct and open looking at the partner's face or body. Staring with a tense gaze is never observed.

Relaxed open-mouth (play face) and silent bared-teeth (grin, grimace, smile) displays seem to be universal to all macaque and baboon species (S. Preuschoft & van Hooff, 1995). Relaxed open-mouth is also found in each of the great apes and humans (common chimpanzee, *Pan troglodytes*: van Hooff, 962, 1972; bonobo, *P. paniscus*: de Waal, 1988; orangutan, *Pongo pygmaeus* and gorilla, *Gorilla g. gorilla*: Chevalier-Skolnikoff, 1982; van Hooff, 1967; *G. g. beringei:* Schaller, 1963; humans, *Homo sapiens*: Blurton Jones, 1972; Lockard, Fahrenbruch, Smith, & Morgan, 1977). Moreover, it is found in species more distantly related to humans such as vervets (*Cercopithecus aethiops*), guerezzas (*Colobus guerezza*), and squirrel monkeys (*Saimiri sciureus*; Marriott & Salzen, 1978). In turn, silent bared-teeth display is reported to occur in the two chimpanzee species (van Hooff, 1962, 1972; de Waal, 1988), and in orangutans (Chevalier-Skolnikoff, 1982). It is, of course, well known for our own species (e.g., Ekman & Keltner, chap. 2, this volume).

It is thus possible to trace a smile and a play face in various species of Old World monkeys and apes. To a biologist, this regular occurrence of silent bared-teeth and relaxed open-mouth displays in various, sometimes remotely related species suggests that these two displays are ancestral characters and can be regarded as homologous in all the species (S. Preuschoft & van Hooff, 1995). Open-mouth bared-teeth display (laughter face), on the other hand, is found only in some species, where it seems to complement or to replace relaxed open-mouth, while taking over the characteristic staccato breathing vocalization.

SITUATIONAL CONTEXTS OF SMILE AND LAUGHTER

The term *facial expression* implies that an individual expresses an internal state, an emotion; or a motivation, in overt behavior. As a consequence, many investigations on facial displays have focused on the message of a display as expressed by the sender (for animals see Caryl, 1982; for humans, see Ekman & Keltner, chap. 2, and K. Schneider, chap. 6, both this volume). In order to detect that message, the antecedents of the display and the sender's subsequent tendencies to act are explored. To a biologist, however, the reason an individual should announce emotion to conspecifics is not at all evident. Dawkins and Krebs (1978) emphasized that a display should better be viewed as a cheap device to manipulate receivers. This proposition shifts the focus of research from the underlying motivation of the sender to the meaning the display has to the receiver, as it is evident from the receiver's reaction to the display. Hinde (1981, 1985a, 1985b) argued that a display expresses a sender's *conditional* tendency to act. The condition the future behavior depends on is simply the reaction of the receiver to the display in the sense of "If you don't attack me, I may groom you." Thus, although a facial display may express an emotion, it may also be a signal in a process of negotiation between two individuals.

A. Motivational Background and Social Function of Silent Bared-Teeth Display (Smile)

The silent bared-teeth display has often been called the "fear grin" or "fear grimace," because in many monkeys (but also sometimes in humans: Goldenthal, Johnston, & Kraut, 1981; Kraut & Johnston, 1980) it is clearly associated with tense social situations and because its sender is usually the inferior partner. There are, however, remarkable species differences with respect to the exact social function of silent bared-teeth display:

In some species it is almost exclusively confined to a fearful situation of *submission,* where the sender demonstrates the inhibition of his aggressive tendencies. This may have an *appeasing* function, such that the display may lead to an inhibition of aggression in the receiver. In this function, silent bared-teeth display has been observed in pigtail, longtailed, rhesus, Japanese, toque, bonnet, Barbary (Fig. 9.1), and stumptail macaques (*Macaca: nemestrina, fascicularis, mulatta, fuscata, sinica, radiata, sylvanus, arctoides*; Angst, 1974; Chevalier-Skolnikoff, 1973; Hinde & Rowell, 1962; van Hooff, 1962, 1967; Kaufman & Rosenblum, 1966; Masataka & Fujii, 1980; S. Preuschoft, 1992; de Waal & Luttrell, 1985) and in chacma and hamadryas baboons (*Papio c.ursinus:* Hall & deVore, 1965; *P. hamadryas:* Kummer, 1957). In these species it is usually the lower ranking interaction partner who performs this signal. In some species, at least in longtailed (Angst, 1975; de Waal, 1977; S. Preuschoft, Gevers, & van Hooff, 1995) and rhesus macaques (de Waal & Luttrell, 1985), silent bared-teeth display is uttered as a signal of formal subordination, thus indicating the sender's evaluation of a long-term relationship, rather than expressing an acute emotional state of fear.

In cases where silent bared-teeth display is employed as an appeasement signal it may eventually lead to *reconciliation* of the interactants, that is, affiliative replaces conflict behavior (Barbary macaques: S. Preuschoft, 1992; common chimpanzees: de Waal & van Roosmalen, 1979). The silent bared-teeth display can also acquire a *reassuring function* (Tonkean macaques: Thierry, Demaria, S. Preuschoft, & Desportes, 1989; chimpanzees: van Hooff, 1972). In these cases, it is performed by a higher ranking individual to mollify a lower ranking interaction partner.

Silent bared-teeth display may also be performed in the context of sexual or caregiving behaviors, which can be considered the germ cells of social affiliation. In other species, silent bared-teeth display extends into clearly *affiliative contexts*, such as greeting, grooming, embracing, or huddling with the receiver (Fig. 9.2). In these contexts, silent bared-teeth display may be observed in Sulawesi macaques (*M. nigra, M. maura, M. tonkeana:* Dixson, 1977; van Hooff, 1967; Petit & Thierry, 1992; Thierry et al., 1989), Barbary (S. Preuschoft, personal observations) and stumptail macaques (Blurton Jones & Trollope, 1968), mandrill, drill, geladas (Dücker, 1996; van Hooff, 1967), and both chimpanzee species (van Hooff, 1972; de Waal, 1988).

In Tonkean macaques, silent bared-teeth display is a primarily affiliative display that fails to correlate with measures of dominance and subordination (Desportes, Demaria, & Thierry, 1990; S. Preuschoft, 1995; Thierry et al., 1994). This species also performs an open-mouth bared-teeth display that shows considerable overlap with silent bared-teeth display, both morphologically (by varying degrees of mouth aperture) and contextually. After a conflict, either of two former opponents may embrace the other wearing silent bared-teeth display and may continue the interaction with playfull gnaw wrestling (Thierry et al., 1989). This strongly resembles the manner in which humans may use a joke in order to relieve a tense situation. An extension of silent bared-teeth display into the play context has also been observed for Sulawesi macaques (Dixson, 1977; Petit & Thierry, 1992; Thierry et al., 1989), mandrills and gelada baboons (Dücker, 1996; van Hooff, 1967), and, possibly also in orangutans (Chevalier-Skolnikoff, 1982; Rijksen, 1978).

B. Motivational Background and Social Function of Relaxed Open-Mouth and Open-Mouth Bared-Teeth Display (Laughter)

Irrespective of the species concerned, relaxed open-mouth display seems to be rather strictly confined to the context of *social play* (e.g., Fig. 9.3). Performance of a ritualized open-mouth display in which the teeth are bared in the context of play has been documented for Sulawesi macaques, mandrills (Fig. 9.4), geladas (Dixson, 1977; van Hooff, 1967; Petit & Thierry, 1992; S. Preuschoft, 1995; Thierry et al., 1989), and two apes: the orangutan (Chevalier-Skolnikoff, 1982) and the bonobo (de Waal, 1988; Fig. 9.5). In social play relaxed open-mouth or open-mouth bared-teeth display typically accompanies play fighting, gnaw wrestling, catch hands, and play chasing. In some species, relaxed open-mouth has been observed to accompany solitary play (acrobatics and object play; e.g., Haanstra, Adang, & van Hooff, 1984), suggesting that relaxed open-mouth may be a spontaneous expression of joy and amusement. However, because in every case conspecifics were close by, it is likely that the presence of an audience is a necessary or at least a facilitating factor for releasing the display.

To summarize, an ethological approach comparing different species of primates shows that homologous displays can occur in *different situational contexts*, which points to a wide range of motivational backgrounds and social functions. Fig. 9.6 illustrates differences between the species and the distribution of silent bared-teeth display and relaxed open-mouth display in various contexts. It suggests that there is a convergence of the displays in several species. This convergence concerns the functions of displays, and it is also expressed morphologically in the open-mouth bared-teeth display. Such a convergence of smile and play face is found in some macaques, some baboons, and some apes. This finding raises the question: How did the homologous silent bared-teeth and relaxed open-mouth displays come to be associated with these vary-

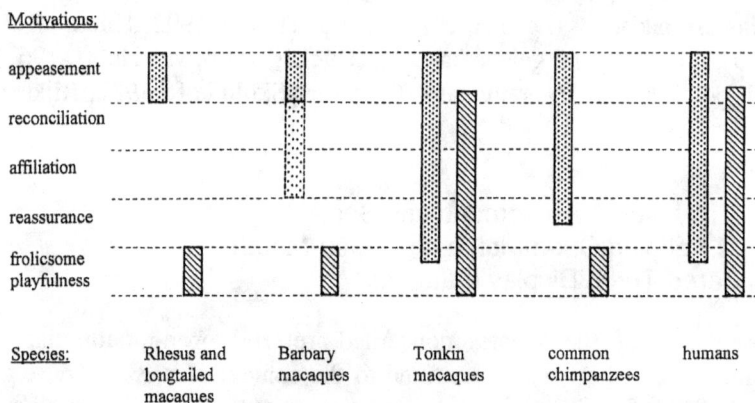

Fig. 9.6:   Graphic representation of the full range of social contexts in which silent bared-teeth display (dotted) and relaxed open-mouth display (hatched) have been observed in a variety of primate species. The classifications are based on quantitative data (*Macaca fascicularis:* Angst, 1975; S. Preuschoft, Gevers, & van Hooff, 1995; M. mulatta: de Waal & Luttrell, 1985; Symons, 1978; *M. sylvanus:* S. Preuschoft, 1992; *M. tonkeana:* S. Preuschoft, 1995; Thierry et al., 1989; *Pan troglodytes:* van Hooff, 1972; *Homo sapiens,* silent bared-teeth display: Kraut & Johnston, 1980; Goldenthal et al., 1981; Fridlund, 1991; relaxed open-mouth in the context of play: Blurton Jones, 1972; Lockard et al., 1977). For definitions of motivations, see the text.

ing social functions? Why is it that this occurred in some species, but not in others? In other words: Are there certain socioecological conditions that have favored this development?

Van Hooff (1967, 1972) suggested that the original motive for grins and smiles may have been fearful appeasement. He interpreted the usage of silent bared-teeth display in the context of affiliation and reassurance as *emancipation* from its original context of social conflict. On the other hand, as we have seen, the contextual variation does not follow taxonomic boundaries. This suggests that the observed motivational similarities are due to analogous developments; that is, at different points during evolution, the same motivational emancipation occurred independently in different species. This invites us to look for a common environmental condition that gave rise to these convergences. It was primarily the presence of conspecifics (i.e., the social environment) that provided the selective pressure for the evolution of communication.

Recent progress in social ecology provides more and more insight into the factors governing group life in animals. In the following section, we show how the variation in the social function of smile and laughter is related to variation in the social relationships among primates.

THE POWER ASYMMETRY HYPOTHESIS
OF MOTIVATIONAL EMANCIPATION

A. Ecological Determinants of Social Aggregations and the Degree of Power Asymmetry Among Interactants

There is convincing evidence that animals live in groups rather than alone when ecological conditions force them to do so (e.g., Alexander, Hoogland, Howard, Noonan, & Sherman, 1979; Wrangham, 1980). The distribution of vital resources (safety from predators, food, mates, etc.) plays a key role in shaping the pattern of animal dispersal and cohesion through the appearance of particular types of competition. Competition is an inevitable by-product of social aggregations and may take two forms, contest and scramble (disorderly struggle) (Nicholson, 1954). In short, concentrated resources are monopolizable and can be contested. The winner of the contest can exclude the loser from the resource. Contest competition can occur among members of a social group (within-

group contest) or among social groups (between-group contest), depending on the size of a monopolizable resource. If resources occur in
scattered, small patches, competition by effective exclusion is replaced
by basically hazardous consumption, or scramble.

The degree of contest competition in a society strongly influences
the degree of social stratification. On the one hand, there are highly
stratified or despotic societies, characterized by strong power asymmetries among individuals. This is evident from the unequal distribution of
profits in competition and results in strict and formalized dominance hierarchies. In egalitarian societies, on the other hand, individual power
asymmetries are less pronounced and the status hierarchy is shallow and
not necessarily linear. The associated differences in dominance styles
(de Waal, 1989a) are clearly rooted in ecological conditions (e.g., van
Schaik, 1989; Vehrenkamp, 1983; Wrangham, 1980).

However, whenever there is contest over larger resource patches,
there is the potential for animals to engage in cooperative resource defense (between-group contest). In cases where obtaining a resource depends on cooperation, an animal's fighting power is no longer the only
crucial capacity. Instead, the vital capability becomes the ability of an
animal to keep its group members motivated to continue contributing to
the common goal of cooperative resource defense. This can only be
achieved if dominants allow their allies to have a fair share. In other
words, it forces them to exercise restraint in intragroup competition,
thus ensuring that subordinates can also profit from their membership
in the group (Hand, 1986; Vehrenkamp, 1983).

B. Degree of Power Asymmetry Among Interactants
Determines the Social Function of Homologous Displays

It is our contention that it is in egalitarian societies (see previous discussion) that the same expressions can be used in submission as well as
in affiliation or even play. We think that the relationship of submission,
appeasement, affiliation, and play to different aspects of social bonding
constitutes the theoretical basis for the explanation of the motivational
shifts in the performance of displays. In social evolution there may have
been an emphasis on either making concessions in competition or exert-
ing full exploitative coercion. Primates can choose between submission
and conflict. Concessions allow the inferior a peaceful, although subordinate, social integration, where the fright resulting from relentless
power exertion would have caused him simply to run away and avoid

future encounters (Schenkel, 1967). This also means that submission should be viewed as one of the bonding mechanisms (see de Waal, 1986).

In the typical bonding behaviors involving care, sex, and affiliation, the success of the interaction depends crucially on the capacity to emphasize shared interests and to de-emphasize competition. This is also characteristic for reconciliation and play. In play, each participant can reach a satisfactory outcome only if it can maintain the subtle balance of stimulation that motivates the partner to remain engaged in the interaction (Bischof, 1985). This stimulation is provided by the the partner's unexpected performance of an expected behavioral act (van Hooff, 1976). The essence of play seems to be to actively bring about incongruous and unexpected behaviors and to interpret them as nonthreatening. In this way, the incongruencies are affectively and cognitively mastered and appreciated as nonthreatening and nonserious (van Hooff, 1989). On the other hand, the use of the play face in contexts of social tension should be possible only under the condition of strong bonding and mutual trust. In this way, an individual may express that it appreciates the relentless assertion of its partner as incongrous but not overly threatening.

Play interactions are typically symmetrical. This symmetry results either from instant reciprocation of behavioral acts (S. Preuschoft, 1992) or from subsequent role changes (Fagen, 1981); that is, from a bidirectionality of actions. In contrast, agonistic interactions are clearly one-sided and may in despotic relationships remain unidirectional across various contexts. In egalitarian relationships, however, the roles may be reversed in that the superior interactant may show the "appeasement" signal—this is what we call reassurance. Thus in relaxed relationships, the same signals may be used up and down the hierarchy, or bidirectionally.

EMPIRICAL EVIDENCE FOR THE POWER ASYMMETRY HYPOTHESIS OF MOTIVATIONAL EMANCIPATION

The existence of dominance—subordination hierarchies has been documented for most macaque and baboon species (e.g., Chapais, 1992) and for chimpanzees (Noë, de Waal, & van Hooff, 1980). However, we also find considerable differences in the extent to which this

Fig. 9.7   Social tolerance and marked relaxation of dominance characterize the social behavior in Tonkean macaques: Group members crowd to share a clump of fruit and vegetables (Experiments by B. Thierry).

dominance is exerted (e.g., Aureli, 1992; Thierry, 1985, 1990; de Waal, 1982, 1989a, 1989b). The proposed model seems to fit the data on the four species of macaques well, where silent bared-teeth display and relaxed open-mouth display have been studied in some depth: Extension of silent bared-teeth display from a submissive fear grin into a reassuring and even friendly expression is associated with a more egalitarian organization of relationships, as is the case in Tonkean macaques (Desportes et al., 1990; Petit & Thierry, 1994; Thierry, 1985; see Fig. 9.7) and, to a lesser degree, in Barbary macaques (Küster & Paul, 1992; S. Preuschoft, Paul, & Küster, 1993). It is also associated with the occurrence of communal group defense and the formation of male coalitions, for example, in the common chimpanzee (Goodall, 1986; Nishida & Hiraiwa-Hasegawa, 1987; Noë et al., 1980; de Waal, 1982). The limited evidence available also suggests that this relaxation of dominance facilitates the inclusion of the element of teeth-baring in the advertisment of playfulness, and the use of play signals as nonhostile and affiliative displays in the establishment and maintenance of cooperative relations, as is the case in humans and Tonkean macaques. On the other hand, when strict dominance relations prevail (e.g., Fig. 9.8), silent baring of the teeth remains restricted to appeasement and the communication of subordination, and shows no overlap with relaxed open-mouth display, which remains restricted to the context of social play. This is the situation we find in rhesus and longtailed macaques (Angst, 1975; de Waal, 1977, 1989b; de Waal & Luttrell, 1985).

Fig. 9.8:   Rhesus monkeys' interaction are shaped by strict dominance exertion: A small part of the group feeds on a clump of food, as monkeys not tolerated at the feeding site form a waiting queue (background) (Experiments by B. Thierry).

DISCUSSION

The overview presented here lends further support to van Hooff's (1972, 1976) conclusion that from a phylogenetic point of view, the human smile cannot be regarded as a diminutive of laughter. Instead, human smile and laughter should be viewed as two converging displays, which are rooted in two distinct ancestral facial displays, the silent bared-teeth display and the relaxed open-mouth display, respectively. Both displays are found in most Old World primates, where they have also undergone changes—as is evident from evolved modifications, for example, of the silent bared-teeth display in drill, mandrill, and geladas, or by the open-mouth bared-teeth display of Sulawesi macaques, bonobos, or orangutans. The fact that a morphological as well as a functional convergence of silent bared-teeth and relaxed open-mouth display can be observed in different phyletic groups shows that also in this respect humans are not at all unique.

In this chapter, we have hypothesized that the evolutionary emancipation of silent bared-teeth display from its originally fearful motivation, and the extension of the relaxed open-mouth display from its original motivation of frolicsome playfulness toward affiliative and even polite smoothing of social tension, may have occurred by virtue of a reduction of power asymmetry and an increased overlap of interests among interactants. The hypothesis presented here may also explain other parallel developments in the evolution of the social function of displays, for instance the use of "coo" contact calls in different species of macaques.

An unresolved problem concerns the fixation of a display's function in the repertoire of a species. As Wickler (1976) showed, the criteria by which homology is established do not differentiate between common ancestry due to social tradition and that due to genetic descent. Whereas their production seems to be fairly robust against different conditions of upbringing (Miller, Caul, & Mirsky, 1967), correct understanding of species-specific facial expressions is not innate in primates. It is at present unclear whether there are primates that are able to voluntarily control their visual signaling (but see Tanner & Byrne, 1993). It should be stressed here that systematic investigation of the information content of visual displays lags far behind research carried out on vocalizations (Marler & Evans, chap. 8, this volume). It is extremely tedious to design experiments for visual displays that parallel playback experiments in that a signal is decoupled from its situational context, or from its sender, while at the same time maintaining a reasonable degree of ecological validity. The active participation and seemingly passionate involvement of monkeys in social events obscures the distinction between the external social context of a display and the emotional attitude this context elicits in the sender (see S. Preuschoft & H. Preuschoft, 1994). The experiments by Miller and colleagues (Miller et al., 1967) show that there may be some degrees of freedom. This view is supported by the observation that *cercopithecines* (macaques and baboons) kept in a mixed taxa group were able to adapt to interspecies differences in communication (Bernstein & Gordon, 1980). De Waal and Johanowicz (1992) showed that juvenile rhesus macaques housed with slightly older, dominating stumptails adjusted their social manners to those of stumptails and exhibited raised levels of reconciliation. In sum, there seems to be some flexibility with respect to both primate dominance style and the social function a facial display can adopt. However, this flexibility does not affect the relationship between power asymmetry and the meaning of displays as hypothesized earlier, quite the contrary.

CONCLUSIONS

1. Similarities and pattern of distribution in the usage of facial displays for bonding across taxa of Old World primates cannot be explained exhaustively by phylogenetic inertia, and hence homologies. Consequently, an explanantion in terms of analogous developments is called for.

2. Earlier studies have shown that dominance style results from the type of competition induced by the pattern of dispersion of vital resources. The degree of social stratification, or type of dominance style, seems to be a promising factor for explaining the analogous developments in the usage of facial displays.

3. The following hypothesis is deduced: Under the condition of hierarchical and strongly asymmetrical social relationships and a formalized dominance style, distinct displays of submission and appeasement, of affiliation, and of playfulness will be present. In case of symmetrical, egalitarian relations, the displays of submission and affiliation and those of appeasement and friendly inclination will converge and will be used more symmetrically as well. Eventually, the distinctiveness of play from other sociopositive contexts will be blurred.

4. The number of species for which the quantitative evidence to test this hypothesis is available is still limited. The information that is available is in agreement with the hypothesis. Clearly, more data are needed before our results can be more firmly supported.

ACKNOWLEDGMENTS

Dr. N. Herrenschmidt and O. Petit have, by their friendly cooperation and hospitality, enabled the first author to study the Tonkean macaques at the Centre de Primatologie, Strasbourg. Special thanks are due to Dr. B. Thierry for generously sharing his knowledge of the Tonkean macaques. The first author has profited from discussions with Drs. F. Aureli, I. Bernstein, L. Jäncke, A. Paul, B. Thierry, and C. P. van Schaik. We would also like to express our thanks to Helga Schulze for drawing the figures, to Professor Peter Weingart, Sabine Maasen, and the staff of the Center for Interdisciplinary Research for their friendly and cooperative attitude.

REFERENCES

Alexander, R. D., Hoogland, J. L., Howard, R. D., Noonan, K. M., & Sherman, P. W. (1979). Sexual dimorphism and breeding systems in pinipeds, ungulates, primates and humans. In N. A. Chagnon & W. A. Irons (Eds.), *Evolutionary biology and human social behavior: An anthropological perspective* (pp. 402–603). Belmont, CA: Wadsworth.

Angst, W. (1974). Das Ausdrucksverhalten der Javeneraffen *Macaca fascicularis Raffles* (The expressive behavior of the longtailed macaques *Macaca fascicularis Raffles*). *Fortschritte der Verhaltensforschung, Heft 15*. Berlin: P. Parey.

Angst, W. (1975). Basic data and concepts on the social organization of *Macaca fascicularis*. In L. A. Rosenblum (Ed.), *Primate behavior* (pp. 325-388). New York: Academic Press.

Aureli, F. (1992). *Reconciliation, redirection and the regulation of social tension in macaques*. Unpublished doctoral dissertation, University of Utrecht, Netherlands.

Bernstein, I. S., & Gordon, T. P. (1980). Mixed taxa introductions, hybrids and macaque systematics. In D. G. Lindburg (Ed.), *The macaques: Studies in ecology, behavior and evolution* (pp. 125-148). New York: van Nostrand Reinhold.

Bischof, N. (1985). *Das Rätsel Ödipus (The puzzle of Oedipus)*. Munich: Piper.

Blurton Jones, N. G. (1972). Non-verbal communication in children. In R. A. Hinde (Ed.), *Nonverbal communication* (pp. 271–296). Cambridge, UK: Cambridge University Press.

Blurton Jones, N. G., & Trollope, J. (1968). The behavior of stump-tailed macaques in captivity. *Primates, 9*, 365–394.

Caryl, P. G. (1982). Animal signals: A reply to Hinde. *Animal Behaviour, 30*, 240–244.

Chapais, B. (1992). Role of alliances in the social inheritance of rank among female primates. In A. Harcourt & F. B. M. de Waal (Eds.), *Cooperation in contests in animals and humans* (pp. 29–59). Oxford, UK: Oxford University Press.

Chevalier-Skolnikoff, S. (1973). Facial expressions of emotion in nonhuman primates. In P. Ekman (Ed.), *Darwin and facial expression* (pp. 11–89). New York: Academic Press.

Chevalier-Skolnikoff, S. (1982). A cognitive analysis of facial behavior in Old World monkeys, apes, and human beings. In C. T. Snowdon, H. Brown, & M. R. Peterson (Eds.), *Primate communication* (pp. 303–368). Cambridge, UK: Cambridge University Press.

Darwin, C. (1872). *The expression of the emotions in man and animals*. London: Murray.

Dawkins, R., & Krebs, J. R. (1978). Animal signals: Information or manipulation? In R. Krebs & N. B. Davies (Eds.), *Behavioral ecology: An evolutionary approach* (pp. 282–309). Oxford, UK: Blackwell.

Desportes, C., Demaria, C., & Thierry, B. (1990). *Measures of dominance in a semi-free group of Tonkean macaques*. Unpublished report, University of Strasbourg, France.

Dixson, A. F. (1977). Observation on the displays, menstrual cycles and sexual behaviour of the "Black ape" of Celebes (*Macaca nigra*). *Journal of Zoology London, 182*, 63–84.

Dücker, S. (1996). *Soziale Funktion der affiliativen Gesichtsausdrücke bei* Theropithecus gelada *(Social function of the affiliative facial expressions of* Theropithecus gelada*)*. Unpublished thesis, University of Bochum, Germany.

Fagen, R. (1981). *Animal play behavior*. New York: Oxford University Press.

Fridlund, A. J. (1991). Sociality of solitary smiling: Potentiation by an implicit audience. *Journal of Personality and Social Psychology, 60*, 229–240.

Goldenthal, P., Johnston, R. E., & Kraut, R. E. (1981). Smiling appeasement, and the silent bared-teeth display. *Ethology and Sociobiology, 2*, 127–133.

Goodall, J. (1986). *The chimpanzees of Gombe: Patterns of behavior*. Cambridge, MA: Harvard University Press.

Haanstra, B., Adang, O., & van Hoof, J. A. R. A. M. (1984). *The family of chimps.* Laren, The Netherlands: Haanstra Films.

Hall, K. R. L., & deVore, I. (1965). Baboon social behavior. In I. deVore (Ed.), *Primate behavior* (pp. 53–110). New York: Holt, Reinhart & Winston.

Hand, J. L. (1986). Resolution of social conflicts: Dominance, egalitarianism, spheres of dominance, and game theory. *Quarterly Review of Biology, 61,* 201–220.

Hinde, R. A. (1981). Animal signals: Ethological and games theory approaches are not incompatible. *Animal Behaviour, 29,* 535–542.

Hinde, R. A. (1985a). Expression and negotiation. In G. Zivin (Ed.), *The development of expressive behavior* (pp. 103–116). Orlando, FL: Academic Press.

Hinde, R. A. (1985b). Was "The Expression of the Emotions" a misleading phrase? *Animal Behaviour, 33,* 985–992.

Hinde R. A., & Rowell, T. E. (1962). Communication by postures and facial expressions in the rhesus monkey (*Macaca mulatta*). *Proceedings of the Zoological Society London, 138,* 1–21.

Hooff van, J. A. R. A. M. (1962). Facial expressions in higher primates. *Symposia of the Zoological Society London, 8,* 67–125.

Hooff van, J. A. R. A. M. (1967). The facial displays of Catarrhine monkeys and apes. In D. Morris (Ed.), *Primate ethology* (pp. 7–68). Chicago: Aldine de Gruyter.

Hooff van, J. A. R. A. M. (1972). A comparative approach to the phylogeny of laughter and smile. In R. A. Hinde (Ed.), *Nonverbal communication* (pp. 209–241). Cambridge, UK: Cambridge University Press.

Hooff van, J. A. R. A. M. (1976). The comparison of facial expressions in man and higher primates. In M. von Cranach (Ed.), *Methods of inference from animal to human behavior* (pp. 165–196). Chicago: Aldine de Gruyter.

Hooff van, J. A. R. A. M. (1989). *Laughter and humor, and the "due-in-uno" of nature and culture* (pp. 120–149). Bochum, Germany: Brockmeyer.

Hooff van, J. A. R. A. M. & van Schaik, C. P. (1992). Cooperation in competition: The ecology of primate bonds. In A. H. Harcourt & F. B. M. de Waal (Eds.), *Coalitions and alliances in humans and other animals* (pp. 357–389). Oxford, UK: Oxford University Press.

Kaufman, C., & Rosenblum, L. A. (1966). A behavioral taxonomy for *Macaca nemestrina* and *Macaca radiata*: Based on longitudinal observation of family groups in the laboratory. *Primates, 7,* 205–258.

Kraut, R. E., & Johnston, R. E. (1980). Social and emotional messages of smiling. An ethological approach. *Journal of Personal and Social Psychology, 57,* 431–475.

Kummer, H. (1957). *Soziales Verhalten einer Mantelpavian-Gruppe (Social behavior of a group of hamadryas baboons).* Bern: Huber.

Küster, J., & Paul, A. (1992). Influence of male competition and female mate choice on male mating success in Barbary macaques (*Macaca sylvanus*). *Behaviour, 120,* 192–217.

Lockard, J. .S., Fahrenbruch, C. E., Smith, J. L., & Morgan, C. J. (1977). Smiling and laughter: Different phyletic origins? *Bulletin of the Psychonomic Society, 10,* 183–186.

Marriott, B. M., & Salzen, E. A. (1978). Facial expressions in captive squirrel monkeys (*Saimiri sciureus*). *Folia Primatologica, 29,* 1–18.

Masataka, N., & Fujii, H. (1980). An experimental study on facial expression and interindividual distance in Japanese macaques. *Primates, 21,* 340–349.

Miller, R. E., Caul, W. F., & Mirsky, J. A. (1967). Communication of affect between feral and socially isolated monkeys. *Journal of Personality and Social Psychology, 7,* 231–239.

Nicholson, A. J. (1954). An outline of the dynamics of animal populations. *Australian Journal of Zoology, 2,* 9–65.

Nishida, T., & Hiraiwa-Hasegawa, M. (1987). Chimpanzees and bonobos: cooperative relationships among males. In B. Smuts, D. L. Cheney, R. Seyfarth, R. W. Wrangham, & T. Strushaker (Eds.), *Primate societies* (pp. 165–177). Chicago: University of Chicago Press.

Noë, R., de Waal, F. B. M., & van Hooff, J. A. R. A. M. (1980). Types of dominance in a chimpanzee colony. *Folia Primatologica, 34*, 90–110.

Petit, O., & Thierry, B. (1992). Affiliative function of the silent-bared teeth display in moor macaques *(Macaca maurus)*: Further evidence for the particular status of sulawesi macaques. *International Journal of Primatology, 13*, 97–105.

Petit, O., & Thierry, B. (1994). Aggressive and peaceful interventions in conflicts in Tonkean macaques. *Animal Behaviour, 48*, 1427–1436.

Preuschoft, S. (1992). "Laughter" and "smile" in Barbary macaques *(Macaca sylvanus)*. *Ethology, 91*, 200–236.

Preuschoft, S. (1995). *"Laughter" and "smiling" in macaques.* Doctoral dissertation, University of Utrecht, The Netherlands.

Preuschoft, S., & van Hooff, J. A. R. A. M. (1995). Homologizing primate facial displays: A critical review of methods. *Folia Primatologica, 65*, 121-137.

Preuschoft, S., Gevers, E., van Hooff, J. A. R. A. M. (1995). Functional differentiation in the affiliative facial displays of longtailed macaques *(Macaca fascicularis)*.

Preuschoft, S., Paul, K., & Küster, J. (1993) *Dominance styles of female and male Barbary macaques (Macaca sylvanus)* (submitted).

Preuschoft, S., & Preuschoft, H. (1994). Primate nonverbal communication: Our communicatory heritage. In W. Nöth (Ed.), *Origins of semiosis* (pp. 66–100). Berlin: Mouton de Gruyter.

Redican, W. K. (1975). Facial expressions in non-human primates. In L. A. Rosenblum (Ed.), *Primate behavior, developments in field and laboratory research, IV* (pp. 103–194). New York: Academic Press.

Rijksen, H. D. (1978). A field study on Sumatran orangutans *(Pongo pygmaeus abelii* LESSON 1972): Ecology, behaviour and conservation. Doctoral dissertation, Agricultural University, Wageningen, The Netherlands.

Schaik van, C. P. (1989). The ecology of social relationships amongst female primates. In V. Standon & R. A. Foley (Eds.), *Comparative socioecology* (pp. 195–218). Oxford, UK: Blackwell.

Schaik van, C. P., & van Hooff, J. A. R. A. M. (1983). On the ultimate causes of primate social systems. *Behaviour, 85*, 91–117.

Schaik van, C. .P., & van Noordwijk, M. A. (1988). Scramble and contest among female longtailed macaques in a Sumatran rain forest. *Behaviour, 105*, 77–89.

Schaller, G. (1963). *The mountain gorilla: Ecology and behavior.* Chicago: University of Chicago Press.

Schenkel, R. (1967). Submission: Its features and function in the wolf and dog. *American Zoologist, 7*, 319–323.

Symons, D. (1978). Play and aggression. A study of rhesus monkeys. New York: Columbia University Press.

Tanner, J. E., & Byrne, R. W. (1993). Concealing facial evidence of mood: Perspective taking in a captive gorilla? *Primates, 34*, 451–457.

Thierry, B. (1985). Patterns of agonistic interactions in three species of macaque *(Macaca mulatta, M. fascicularis, M. tonkeana)*. *Aggressive Behavior, 11*, 223–233.

Thierry, B. (1990). Feedback loop between kinship and dominance: The macaque model. *Journal of Theoretical Biology, 145*, 511–521.

Thierry, B., Demaria, C., Preuschoft, S., & Desportes, C. (1989). Structural convergence between silent bared-teeth display and relaxed open-mouth display in the Tonkean macaque *(Macaca tonkeana)*. *Folia Primatologica, 52*, 178–184.

Thierry, B., Anderson, J. R., Demaria, C., Desportes, C., & Petit, O. (1994). Tonkean macaque behavior from the perspective of the evolution of Sulawesi macaques. In J. J. Roeder, B. Thierry, J. R. Anderson, & N. Herrenschmidt (Eds.), *Current primatology: Vol. II. Social development, learning and behaviour* (pp. 103–117). Strasbourg, France: Université Louis Pasteur .

Vehrenkamp, S. (1983). A model for the evolution of despotic versus egalitarian societies. *Animal Behaviour, 31,* 667–682.

Waal de, F. B. M. (1977). The organization of agonistic relations within two captive groups of Java-monkeys *(Macaca fascicularis). Zeitschrift für Tierpsychologie, 44,* 225–282.

Waal de, F. B. M. (1982). *Chimpanzee politics.* New York: Harper & Row.

Waal de, F. B. M. (1986). The integration of dominance and social bonding in primates. *Quarterly Review of Biology, 61,* 459–479.

Waal de, F. B. M. (1988). The communicative repertoire of captive Bonobos *(Pan paniscus)* compared to that of chimpanzees. *Behaviour, 105,* 183–251.

Waal de, F. B. M. (1989a). Dominance "style" and primate social organization. In V. Standon & R. A. Foley (Eds.), *Comparative socioecology* (pp. 243–264). Oxford, UK: Blackwell.

Waal de, F. B. M. (1989b). *Peacemaking among primates.* Cambridge, MA: Harvard University Press.

Waal de, F. B. M., & Johanowicz, D. L. (1993). Modification of reconciliation behavior through social experience. *Child Development, 64,* 897–908.

Waal de, F. B. M., & Luttrell, L. (1985). The formal hierarchy of rhesus monkeys: An investigation of the bared-teeth display. *American Journal of Primatology, 9,* 73–85.

Waal de, F. B. M., & van Roosmalen, A. (1979). Reconciliation and consolation among chimpanzees. *Behavioral Ecology and Sociobiology, 5,* 55–66.

Wickler, W. (1976). The application of homology—reasoning to behaviour. In M. von Cranach (Ed.), *Methods of inference from animal to human behaviour* (pp. 62–72). Paris: Mouton.

Wrangham, R. W. (1980). An ecological model of female-bonded primate groups. *Behaviour, 75,* 262–300.

10

PRIMATE COMMUNICATION AND THE ECOLOGY OF A LANGUAGE NICHE

Alexandra Maryanski

University of California, Riverside

In 1871, the linguist Max Muller wrote: "the one great barrier between the brute and man is *language*. Language is our Rubicon, and no brute will dare to cross it" (p. 403). Today, many students of language still echo Muller's time-honored belief, although in these post-Darwinian times it might be more appropriate to view language as a product of selection with antecedents in other modes of primate communication. Unfortunately, primate communication—that is, the exchange of information among conspecifics—is normally viewed as irrelevant for understanding speech sounds, in part because of an "oral bias" that focuses only on the acoustic forms of primate communication but, in large part, because of a "technical bias" that regards language mostly as a formal set of operations for learning grammatical rules rather than a social skill for effective discourse between conspecifics (Chomsky, 1986; Fodor, Bever, & Garrett, 1974). Even the reality that laboratory chimpanzees *(Pan)* and gorillas *(Gorilla)* have learned to use complex arbitrary visual symbols for communication, while employing the grammatical rules for perceiving speech sounds (in the case of bonobos), has not shaken the conviction that language is a special creation that is unique to humans (see Gardner, Gardner, & Cantfort, 1989; Matsuzawa, 1991; Savage-Rumbaugh et al., 1993).

To rekindle interest in the social dimensions of language, this chapter begins with a summary of primate communication channels by drawing, in part, from the research of S. Preuschoft and H. Preuschoft (1994), and then exploring: (a) the design features that distinguish each mode of nonverbal communication, (b) the criteria for each channel to transmit a successful message, (c) the type of information best suited for each mode of communication, and (d) the components comprising each modality code. In particular, I attempt to show that primates choose their mode of communication in accordance with the sophistication of their major sensory organs—that is, the olfactory, tactile, visual, and auditory—and the demands of the environment. Then, the thesis to be developed argues that the pressures of forest zones long ago equipped higher primates with a distinctive communication system that allows for the dual transmission of emotional states and cognitive states when channeled through the visual and haptic sensory systems. Only later, under the selection pressures of an opencountry adaptive zone was the system upgraded for the articulation of voluntary sounds, which eventually evolved into the distinctly human side of speech.

PRIMATE CHANNELS OF NONVERBAL COMMUNICATION

A. Classification and Distribution of Primates

The primate order is composed of nearly 190 species. The *Prosimii* or lower primates evolved first and today constitute about 25% of all primate species, most of whom are grouped into Lorisiformes or lorises and Lemuriformes or lemurs. As a suborder, the prosimians are rather primitive-looking primates with their wide staring eyes, placid facial expressions, moist doglike nasal patch, and their locomotion pattern of vertical clinging, leaping, or hopping. The suborder Anthropoidea or higher primates are monkeys, apes, and humans. New and Old World monkeys make up about 70% of all primate species, and despite differences between New and Old World forms, both share the same skeletal anatomy with immobile shoulder joints, a narrow rib cage, a short collarbone, and front and rear limbs of near equal length, which permits all monkeys quadrupedal movement along the tops of tree branches, or when on the ground, locomotion with palms and soles flat on the surface (for general references, see Fleagle, 1988; J. R. Napier & P. H. Napier, 1985; Tattersall, Delson, & van Couvering, 1988).

Apes and humans make up Hominoidea, a superfamily composed of gibbons, *(Hylobatidae)*, orangutans *(Pongo)*, gorillas *(Gorilla)*, chimpanzees *(Pan)*, and humans *(Homo)*. Whereas living hominoid species constitute only 5% of all primate species, they are set apart from other primates by their much larger size (with the exception of the gibbon), their bigger brains, their much greater capacity to learn complex tasks, and their more flexible communication patterns. Further, all hominoids are morphologically similar, with an enlarged and more developed collarbone, shorter spine, unequal limbs (in apes front limbs are longer than rear limbs, and in humans the reverse), lack of tail, short and wide trunk, along with specialized shoulders, wrists, and hands for greater flexibility and mobility. With these morphological traits, all hominoids share the capacity to use their forelimbs alone for locomotion, and unlike monkey anatomy which reflects selection for an "above branch" locomotor pattern, hominoid anatomy reflects selection for a "below branch" locomotor pattern (Conroy, 1990; K. Hunt, 1991; J. R. Napier & P. H. Napier, 1985). These distinctions between monkeys and hominoids will take on significance later when we turn to the hominid adaptive niche, nonverbal communication, and the selection pressures for hominid linguistic vocalizations.

B. Primate Modes of Nonverbal Communication

Primates convey information to conspecifics utilizing four basic modes that correspond to the major mammalian sensory modalities: the olfactory, visual, auditory, and general somatic (especially, haptic or active touch discrimination). In mammals, the olfactory bulbs are part of the limbic system, a collection of heterogeneous subcortical structures that are specialized for visceral functions and for maintenance of the organism, with mostly emotionally based responses to environmental stimuli (Horel, 1988; Isaacson, 1982; MacLean, 1990). In contrast, the visual, auditory, and haptic modalities are part of the cerebral cortex, a cortex that connects with limbic zones but is specialized for problem solving, learning, and rational intentional behaviors to cope more efficiently with the external world (Gilinsky, 1984; MacLean, 1990). Each modality is specialized to detect and respond to crucial aspects of an animal's environment (e.g., finding food, mates, avoiding predators, etc.), and each one is sensitive only to particular stimuli, in order for an organism to perceive the different qualities of objects. Moreover, because of the diversity in ecological zones, the type of sensory equipment will vary dramatically among taxa (see Stephan, Baron, & Frahm, 1988). That is, from a selectionist perspective, the kind and quality of an animal's sensory organs is a function of environmental demands. As an order of mammals, primates reflect the pressures of an arboreal zone. The evolution of primate sense modalities cannot be reviewed here (but see Maryanski & J. H. Turner, 1992). However, by making use of some of Hockett's (1960) and S. Preuschoft and H. Preuschoft's (1994) *design features*, the sensory architecture and communication channels of present-day primates are summarized, highlighting the following features within a comparative framework:

1. *Broadcast transmission:* Is the communication channel used for long distance, short distance, or is it primarily a physical contact transmitter?

2. *Rapid fading or lingering:* Is the communication channel able to bridge temporal gaps or is it restricted to rapid decay?

3. *Accessibility:* Is the communication channel highly sensitive to external influences (light, darkness, noise, wind, water)?

4. *Functionality:* Is the channel of communication of primary or secondary importance over other modes? How is it best utilized?

5. *Directionality:* Is the communication broad and sweeping (e.g., open to every possibly receiver) or selective (directed toward specific individuals)?

6. *Voluntary:* Is the communication channel under cortical control?. That is, are responses voluntary (e.g., purposeful, rational, and intentional), or are they largely emotionally based responses (e.g., a fight or flight reaction, sexual response, or aggression)?

Let me begin this review with the olfactory organ, a subcortical structure, and then turn, respectively, to the tactile, auditory, and visual communicative modes in the cerebral cortex.

Olfactory Communication.   The olfactory organ is well developed in terrestrial mammals, but among primates, only prosimians come equipped with a moist, glandular area on their snout for olfactory functions. Prosimians rely heavily on olfactory communication, transmitting and receiving olfactory cues for information about age, sex, reproductive states, and other information, especially through "scent signals" or direct depositing of odors within their habitat (J. R. Napier & P. H. Napier, 1985).

In higher primate evolution, the olfactory bulb underwent selection for a substantial reduction (Beard, Krishtalka, & Stucky, 1991; Jerison, 1990; Radinsky, 1970). As a result, monkeys, apes and humans do not scent mark or otherwise make extensive use of the olfactory sense for communication, although smell still plays an important role in food analysis, and some aspects of reproduction such as in sending scent signals regarding female hormonal states (Fleagle, 1988).

In design features, olfactory information from lingering scent marks is open to anyone with an operative smell receiver. Further, the olfactory modality is an excellent long distance communicator that can transmit information either actively or passively. Although odorous solutions can be altered by such external factors as heavy rain or evaporation by strong winds, this communication mode is rather resistant to environmental impediments (see S. Preuschoft & H. Preuschoft, 1994). Thus, although smell sensations project directly to limbic zones (rather than neocortical zones) for predominately emotionally based responses, most mammals make extensive use of the olfactory modality for communication (Fleagle, 1988). The relative silencing of this powerful communication system in higher primates is one clue to the evolution of speech when early proto-hominids left a forest zone for a terrestrial zone.

Tactile Communication.   Touch is only one of the general somatic senses located in the primate neocortex. The receptors for tactile communication can be grouped into (a) information available through general body contact and transmitted through the skin, tendons, muscles, joints, and so on, which also provides fine sensorimotor coordination; (b) communication through the hands, especially the prehensile hands of monkeys, apes, and humans. Sensations transmitted through touching and other body contact readily disclose the internal state of an interactional partner; that is, whether a conspecific is calm, animated, friendly, or hostile.

In addition to information obtained through body contact, monkeys, apes, and humans have highly sophisticated prehensile hands for active or haptic touch—that is, the reaching out and touching of a stationary object. Haptic touch also refers to the exploratory nature of the prehensile hand and the use of the sensitive fingertips for tactile impressions about the properties of the outside world. For example, in hominoids (i.e., apes and humans), haptic touch has an inherent and pronounced adeptness to locate and recognize objects in space by stringing together a succession of independent chunks of information, and hence recognizing the relationship of individual parts to each other in time rather than space. The haptic sense is also an excellent resonator for the detection of vibrations, along with superior tactile perception for determining what lies under the surface of objects. Higher primates also extensively use their prehensile hands for social communication, especially for establishing and maintaining social relationships. For example, mothers groom offspring extensively to seemingly establish a social bond, whereas adult grooming communicates to both groomer and groomee, as well as to observers, whether a social relationship is sexual, kinship-based, friendship-based or a dominant–subordinate relationship (for discussions see Goosen, 1980; Kaas & Pons, 1988; Maryanski & J. H. Turner, 1992; S. Preuschoft & H. Preuschoft, 1994).

In design features, tactile interactions are usually contingent on direct contact between sender and receiver. Touch also decays rapidly, which makes it largely impractical for bridging temporal or spacial gaps. However, tactile communications are expedient for conveying information both privately and indiscriminately, and knowledge transmitted through touch is not environmentally sensitive, except under low temperature conditions, which impedes perception (see S. Preuschoft & H. Preuschoft, 1994). The use of the haptic organ for detecting vibrations also provides useful information. In primates, tactile perception is under cortical control for learned, purposeful, and voluntary responses to environmental stimuli.

Visual Communication.   In higher primates, vision is the dominant sense, having displaced the olfactory organ, which underwent a substantial reduction in primate evolution (Conroy, 1990; Martin, 1990; Radinsky, 1974). As a product of this dominance shift, monkeys, apes, and humans are equipped with binocular, stereoscopic perception for depth function and such retina specializations as color vision and the ability to perceive the intricate details of objects and scenes (J. R. Napier & P. H. Napier, 1985; Rodieck, 1988; Wolin & Massopust, 1970).

Not surprisingly, with such visual sophistication, this modality is also the principal communicator in higher primates (J. R. Napier & P. H. Napier, 1985; Simonds, 1974). For in anthropoids, most social interactions are interfaced with body language, especially posturing, which involves the use of the limbs, tail, head, chest, hips, and so on, for communication. For example, signals that communicate fear, low status, and anxiety include the crouch posture (i.e., a stance that enwraps body parts, signifying that the sender is a victim in an extreme agonistic situation); the raised tail (i.e., a signal that indicates apprehensiveness in a social interaction), and the present (i.e., a pose which involves the ano-genital regions, signaling an inferior status in a dominant–subordinate interaction); S. Preuschoft & H. Preuschoft, 1994). In addition to visual posturing, both Old World monkeys and apes manifest a large repertoire of facial displays that include the lips, jaws, cheeks, and ears. For example, lip smacking (i.e., where the mouth is opened and closed rapidly) is often a prerequisite to sexual relations (J. R. Napier & P. H. Napier, 1985), whereas the play face (where the mouth is open wide with only the lower teeth exposed) is an affable, placating expression, and is the likely precursor of human laughter (van Hooff, 1972; S. Preuschoft, 1992).

In addition to broadcasting information about the internal state of a sender, vision is also extensively used to communicate pragmatic information about the external world. For example, experiments indicate that visual cues are used by chimpanzees for intended messages about the environment, for as Menzel (Menzel, 1971) noted: "One chimpanzee can convey to others, who have no other source of information, the presence, direction, quality, and relative quantity or preference value of distant hidden objects that he himself has not seen for several minutes" (p. 220).

In design features, vision is a splendid long-distance transmitter, although unlike tactile perception, which is automatically activated by touch or auditory perception, which is automatically activated by sound, the visual modality requires the active attention of both sender and receiver. The visual mode is also highly sensitive to environmental influences, decays rapidly, and lacks temporal stability. However, it is well suited for fine-tuned negotiations among conspecifics, and within groups it is flexible both in its ability to be directed toward specific individuals or accessible to every likely receiver. Moreover, when using this highly sophisticated cortical sense, information from visual receptors is projected directly to the neocortex, a structure primarily geared toward the understanding of a variable and changing external environment. Thus, a dominant visual modality for general information processing and for communication would tend to suppress species-specific behavior and promote voluntary and purposeful patterns of response (see Maryanski & J. H. Turner, 1992).

Vocal Communication.   The primate auditory modality is sensitive to low-frequency sound waves, which travel further than high frequencies, facilitating the use of the primate ear as a wide-ranging, early warning detection system to localize a sound, and, in turn, to alert the primate visual system to attend to the object in space (Masterton, 1992). In primate evolution, the auditory system has been a conservative organ, and according to Stebbins (1965), with regard to the hearing potential of all higher primates, the "final stages of human hearing have taken place in the primates, and thus, it is not surprising that the differences in auditory sensitivity between man and non-human primates is small" (pp. 186f.; see also Newman, 1988).

Primates evidence a large range of diverse vocalizations that vary with respect to their acoustic properties and contents. Contact calls are useful within groups, whereas spacing calls are useful for localizing neighboring groups (J. R. Napier & P. H. Napier, 1985). Within groups, primates often engage in loud screams, which immediately attract the support or intervention of group members. In particular, immature monkeys will often vary their vocalizations depending on whether their adversary is a blood relative or an individual of a higher or lower status. Individual vocalizations can also also distinguish group members, such that in some monkey species, infant and juvenile voices are immediately recognized not just by their own mothers but by all group members (S. Preuschoft & H. Preuschoft, in press).

Primate alarm calls are used for both close and long-distance communication with some intriguing findings. One studied Old World monkey species, the vervets *(Cercopithecus aethiops),* are able to vocally distinguish between predators and nonpredators. Further, they are able to warn conspecifics about menacing predators using vocalizations with encoded semantic qualities. For example, there is seemingly a leopard alarm call to inform conspecifics to flee to the top of the canopy; a bird of prey call to inform conspecifics to take cover out of the canopy, and a snake alarm call to warn conspecifics to stay out of thickets (see Cheney, 1984; Marler & Evans, chap. 8, this volume; S. Preuschoft & H. Preuschoft, 1994; Cheney & Seyfarth, 1980). This signaling behavior must be learned (Cheney & Seyfarth, 1980).

In design features, acoustic information fades quickly, along with sensitivity to environmental influences such as air currents, and background noise. However, primate auditory signals provide a flexible and speedy means to communicate at close range or over long distances, especially when visibility is low. Moreover, the primate ear is especially

tuned for localizing a sound and the auditory system overall is specialized to respond to brief, abrupt, or arrhythmic sounds that potentially
signal the presence of an animate object (Masterton, 1992). It would
appear that the self-alerting capacity of the auditory system is so crucial
for higher primates that, according to Masterton and Diamond (1973),
"it is virtually impossible to truncate the central auditory system in such
a way as to make an animal completely incapable of responding to a
brief sound" (p. 431). Finally, in common with the visual and haptic
systems, the auditory system for sound perception is under neocortical
control. However, primate acoustic responses—that is communication
through the vocal-auditory channel–is largely under limbic control.
And, although recent experiments have shown that higher primates
have some faculty for voluntary and semantic vocalizations, most calls
are largely limbic controlled vocalizations (Cheney & Seyfarth, 1990;
Steklis, 1985; Sutton & Jurgens, 1988).

In summary, the primates evidence sophisticated sensory modes
that are also utilized to fulfill specific communicative tasks. Among
primates, only prosimians rely extensively on olfactory communication
that is automatically activated, can bridge temporal gaps, and is also a
long-distance receptor. As a noncortical sense, however, it is housed in
phylogenetically older cortex that is primarily involved with monitoring
the environment with regard to protection and preservation purposes
(MacLean, 1990). In contrast, touch and visual communication are under cortical control, although tactile perception usually involves face-
to-face interactions and cannot bridge time gaps. For monkeys and
apes, vision is the primary cortical sense both for object recognition and
communication. As a communication channel it works best at moderate
distances, cannot bridge time gaps, and requires active attention to
transmit or receive information. The auditory modality, although a cortical sense for acoustic input, is still mostly under limbic control for vocal responses (Snowdon, 1990). It is a splendid long-distance receiver,
but information decays rapidly. Although each modality is a distinct
system in own right, primates often utilize more than one modality simultaneously, increasing the likelihood that a message will be properly
received.

Multichannel communication also characterizes human primates.
For example, emotionally laden sentiments are often best received
when transmitted through touch and vision. Moreover, when verbal
messages are ambiguous or when contradictory messages are received
simultaneously from verbal and nonverbal communication, all humans

rely heavily on a nonverbal code, especially their visual sense in the form of intimate eye contact and facial expressions (see Freides, 1974, for a discussion). Although the dominance of the visual system in anthropoids is seemingly an adaptation to an arboreal habitat, the later movement of proto-hominids to an open-country habitat can provide important insights into the emergence of propositional speech.

THE HOMINID ECOLOGICAL ZONE

When a lineage of proto-hominids left the forests for the African savanna, the process of hominidization was initiated. In reconstructing hominid evolution, African apes provide an important source of indirect data. For in recent years, such "human" behavioral traits as tool making and use, meat eating, hunting behavior, warfare (defined as systematic conflict between groups), and linguistic-based communication have all been reported for chimpanzees (see Goodall, 1986; Savage-Rumbaugh et al., 1993; Tuttle, 1986). It is important to emphasize that although both Pan and Gorilla are the evolutionary end points of their own equally long lineages, as the forest belt has remained relatively stable since before the Miocene, niche theory would predict relative morphological and neurological stasis, especially for primary forest chimpanzees (for a discussion of niche theory see Vandermeer, 1972). Moreover, at the molecular level, recent work on chromosomes, serum proteins and hemoglobin, and calibration of immunological distance all report that humans, gorillas, and chimpanzees share a close genetic affinity, which at the genic level meets the established criterion for a sibling species (Goodman et al., 1990; King & A. Wilson, 1975; Sibley, Comstock, & Ahlquist, 1990).

A. The Vocal Tract Anatomy of Chimpanzees,
Gorillas and Humans

The vocal tracts of higher primates—that is, the stretch between the vocal cords and lips—show a common morphology and work in the same manner (Bastian, 1965; Negus, 1949). Primates vocalize by the manipulation of air, lip movements, and vibrations in their vocal cords. Thus the hoots of chimpanzees are, at a gross functional level, produced in the same manner as speech sounds in humans, and in fact, chimpanzees can make the rudiments of vowels and consonants (Andrew, 1973,

1976). Yet, chimpanzees and gorillas cannot produce the wide variety of sounds, nor generate them as rapidly, as can humans (J. Hamilton, 1974). Thus, vocal tract elaborations involving the larynx, pharynx, and other related structures have given humans the facility for rapid production and easy sequencing of phonemes. What are these alterations? Anatomically, the larynx (which houses the "voice box" or vocal cords) is positioned in the lower neck area in humans, whereas it is high up in the neck in other primates. This descent of the larynx in humans (which only occurs after infanthood) greatly augments the space between the larynx and *velum* (i.e., expanding the pharynx), resulting in the much greater capacity of humans to make and modify sounds than is the case with other primates (Bone, 1977; DuBrul, 1976; Laitman, 1983).

These alterations of the human vocal apparatus are correlated with the evolution of hominid bipedalism (see Hill, 1972; Negus, 1949). Upright posture created a curvature of the vocal tract, which, in turn, seemingly forced the descent of the larynx. Only later when selection pressures for linguistically mediated organization increased did other changes in the vocal tract probably occur. These selection pressures must have been intense, because aside from its phoneme-producing qualities, human vocal tract anatomy is considerably less efficient than that in other primates. For example, comparative studies clearly indicate that the alterations in the human vocal tract have increased the susceptibility of the respiratory system to blockage when swallowing and, hence, to choking (J. Hamilton, 1974; Lieberman & Crelin, 1971). Apparently, selection for speech in human ancestors had greater adaptive value than an efficient respiratory system.

B. The Hominoid Brain

Alterations in basic hominoid vocal anatomy were essential for an assortment of acoustic sounds, but alterations to the hominoid brain were also crucial. The discovery that chimpanzees and gorillas have the complex neurological apparatus to use symbols referentially for objects not present underscores the evolutionary continuity of higher order cognitive functions in the hominoid lineage. And, the remarkable discovery that when repeatedly exposed to verbal stimuli, young bonobo chimpanzees *(Pan panicus)* can spontaneously learn to comprehend speech sounds at the level of a 2½- to 3-year-old human child points to the role of the social environment in passively assimilating a linguistic code to both chimpanzees and humans (see Gardner et al., 1989; Savage-Rumbaugh et al., 1993).

But, we might ask: Why is this so? Why should apes possess a neurological capacity for symbolic representation through their visual-tactile modalities, whereas bonobo chimpanzees possess a full-blown capacity to link a phonological code with sounds and images? Could it be that our cognitive boundaries of what is considered "language" from "nonlanguage" need to be redrawn? Indeed, the *hominoid line* seems to share a number of homologous cognitive structures that, with the right selection pressures, can seemingly utilize any cortical modality as a vehicle for symbolic representation. For on the one hand, it is now difficult to deny that chimpanzees and gorillas reveal complex linguistic skills when they are channeled through the visual modality. On the other hand, ape vocalizations are never mistaken for speech signals because they lack a phonemic system.

C. Selection Pressures for Human Speech

This overview of the primate sensory organs and modes of communication can now provide a framework for informed speculation on the origins of verbal communication. As emphasized, the primate order originally evolved in a forest zone. The movement of proto-hominids to an open-country zone thus opened the door for evolutionary opportunism. However, those early proto-hominids that left the African forest for the open terrain were already enormously complex primates, being the product of 50 million years of primate evolution. This heritage was to place enormous constraints on any evolutionary changes (see Maryanski, 1992, 1993). Of equal significance is the general nature of evolution itself, which is conservative, working on already existing characters for adaptation in a particular habitat. In other words, there is a "conservation of organization" such that "once a particular level of organizational complexity has been achieved, mutations that elaborate upon this complexity have a much greater chance of success than do mutations tending to destroy it, simplify it, or start a trend toward lower levels of complexity" (Stebbins, 1965, p. 124). For example, human locomotion clearly evolved through Darwinian descent with modification by undergoing alterations from the occasional pongid "bent-knee posture" (i.e., an upright stance where the knees are slightly bent), to the hominid "straight leg" striding gait by triggering modifications of the hominoid postcranial skeleton in the vertebral column, pelvis, lower limbs, and feet (and this would be matched by changes in the adjacent muscles like the lower back; for a detailed discussion see Lewin, 1993). Equally important, a hominoid with hindlimb dominant locomotion would then have the forelimbs freed for other activities, such as tool making and use.

In tandem with bipedalism, when proto-hominids confronted the challenges of an open terrain, they not only transported the basic hominoid skeletal anatomy but the basic hominoid *neuroanatomy* that had also facilitated their adaptation in a forest zone (Maryanski & J. H. Turner, 1992). Thus early proto-hominids came to the savanna with a greatly reduced olfactory organ that had inconsequential utility for olfactory communication. However, they did come equipped with: (a) a voluntary (cortical) system of control over their visual and haptic modalities for communicating rational and intended responses, (b) a dominant visual organ both for object recognition and for communication, and (c) an auditory faculty with cortically based sound perception but with oral responses largely under limbic control.

We can now address the intriguing question: How and why did the auditory modality become linked to the process of symbolization? In considering this issue, we should first focus our attention on the information-processing qualities of higher mammals in general by considering the following: Which modality is best suited for a savanna adaptive zone? In a mammalian head count, the overwhelming favorite is the olfactory organ (see Fleagle, 1988), probably because of its keen long-distance receptors, its automatic alerting properties, and its lingering chemical cues that allow for the detection of predators and prey. Although the primate optical system is also excellent for long-distance perception, it requires active attention. In addition, where visibility is low or absent such as at night, the visual organ is completely deficient as a sensory organ. The primate haptic organ is also a long-distance receiver for vibrations, but once bipedalism became a way of life, the utility of the haptic organ for detecting predators through ground vibrations would be greatly diminished, because a bipedal creature moves along on the basis of visual cues alone. Thus, early hominids in their transition from the forest to the savanna were initially biologically ill-equipped for an open-country lifestyle with a lack of built-in defense weapons, a low-alerting visual sense, a less effective tactile sense (at least for processing environmental information) and a greatly reduced olfactory organ. However, because the auditory modality had originally evolved as an early warning detection system, it had the capacity for long-distance reception with fine low-frequency discrimination. Thus, it is not unreasonable to envision a heightened auditory system to enhance perception, especially where the dominant visual system was sensory deficient (see Jerison, 1973). And, the easiest evolutionary pathway for functionally enhancing the auditory sense was to place the vocal-auditory channel directly under cortical control. Thus, the initial step toward linguistic-based sounds probably involved only a quantitative alteration in the primate acoustic system, because the auditory system was already housed in the neocortex with sound perception already under cortical control (see Newman, 1988). Once vocal responses were under cortical control, voluntary sounds became possible, especially in light of the fact that bipedalism had already opened up the vocal tract. But selection for intended sound (or intended silence, which is an equally valuable attribute) probably evolved over time as the entire vocal apparatus had to become modified.

But why would selection favor in hominids an oral language for communication? After all, vision is the primary sense for primates, and the chimpanzee and gorilla are good examples of how easily proto-hominids could have handled a visual and gestural language. It is possible that a visual and gestural language was initially used to communicate (see Hewes, 1973; Poizner, Bellugi, & Klima, 1990). However, the peculiar changes in the hominid vocal tract signal that, at some point in time, heavy selection pressures were operating for more complex vocalization. Thus, it would be useful here to highlight two key modifications to the vocal-auditory channel and to what surely approximated a basic hominoid call system, but, which over time, evolved into a highly specialized auditory-based linguistic system that is unique to humans.

1. *Volitional control of response.* Speech is normally under voluntary control. Sounds are selected and this selection of sounds in response to an environmental stimulus is learned.
2. *Non-emotional response.* Language is rationally—and logically—based; and like the primate tactile and visual organs, it is a system primarily geared toward obtaining environmental information to generate ideas about the physical world.

Thus, human vocalizations are mostly under cortical-auditory control and nonemotionally based, unless the sensations received become overly stimulating. However, even emotionally arousing sensations do not necessarily put the vocal system under limbic control, for the neocortex seemingly has the ability to regulate, constrain, and even suppress certain sensations. On the other hand, intense sensations override a cortical vocal response and directly engage the limbic system for an instinctive vocal response, such as screaming in the face of grave danger.

Of equal importance, however, is to once again return to an appreciation of language as a social skill for human primates to communicate (rather than just a technical skill for syntactic capability). As such, like all true communication, language rests on social *consensus*—that is, a common definition of the situation. In humans, symbols and their meanings are built up over time and stabilized though social interactions that following George Herbert Mead (1934), necessitate the following behavioral capacities:

1. The ability to represent objects in the environment symbolically.
2. The ability to learn precisely which symbols are appropriate in a particular social environment.
3. The ability to use these acquired symbols to signal individual acts and dispositions to act in certain ways.
4. the ability to read symbols emitted by other individuals that signal their individual acts, and dispositions to act in certain ways.
5. The ability to use and read symbols in ways that allow for mutual adjustment and cooperation among symbol-using individuals that unites individuals and allows for social interaction and social solidarity to occur.

In many ways the language studies of apes have demonstrated how chimpanzees (and to a lesser degree gorillas) already possess these five linguistically based social capacities when channeled through the visual-haptic modalities—albeit in much more modified form. Thus, the first stage of spoken language did not involve a radical spontaneous mutation in hominids; instead, it represented an extension of cognitive abilities already present in the hominoid visual-haptic system (see Burling, 1993, for an alternative tack on this issue, but one that also supports the relationship between primate cognitive abilities and language origins). However, what began as a quantitative modification–that is, the shifting of the auditory-vocal channel to a cortical zone—ushered in a qualitative change over the communication systems of nonhuman primates. For vocal sounds under volitional control allowed for the accumulation of a storehouse of vocally based information that could be shared by members of a linguistic community. And, although speaking itself is an individual act, it relies on a cultural tradition for consensus on the meanings of symbols and for intergenerational transmission.

Thus, spoken language is not a mysterious property of humans, but the result of a series of changes to primate sensory modalities that evolved first in an arboreal zone and were later selectively modified and expanded on with the adaptation of hominids to a terrestrial zone. Thus, in trying to understand the properties of verbal communication, more emphasis should be directed to the ecology of nonhuman primates and to primate nonverbal communication within a broad evolutionary framework.

ACKNOWLEDGMENT

A thank you to Signe Preuschoft for her comments and for granting me permission to summarize primate communication data from her forthcoming publication "Primate Nonverbal Communication: Our Communicatory Heritage" (S. Preuschoft & H. Preuschoft, 1994).

REFERENCES

Andrew, R. J. (1973). Comment on primates communication and the gestural origin of language. *Current Anthropology, 14,* 12.

Andrew, R. J. (1976). Use of formants in the grunts of baboons and other non-human primates. *Annals of the New York Academy of Sciences, 280,* 673–693.

Bastian, J. (1965). Primate signaling systems and human languages. In I. Devore (Ed.), *Primate behavior* (pp. 585–606). New York: Holt, Rinehart & Winston.

Beard, C., Krishtalka, L., & Stucky, R. (1991). First skulls of the early eocene primate shoshonius cooperi and the anthropoid-tarsier dichotomy. *Nature, 349,* 64–67.

Bone, E. (1977). Palaeontological indications of the appearance of speech. *Journal of Human Evolution, 6,* 279–291.

Burling, R. (1993). Primate calls, human language, and nonverbal communication. *Current Anthropology, 34,* 25–53.

Cheney, D. L. (1984). Category formation in vervet monkeys. In R. Harre & V. Reynolds (Eds.), *The meaning of primate signals* (pp. 58–74). Cambridge, UK: Cambridge University Press.

Cheney, D. L., & Seyfarth, R. M. (1980). Vocal recognition in free-ranging vervet monkeys. *Animal Behavior, 28,* 739–751.

Chomsky, N. (1986). *Knowledge of language: Its nature, origin and use.* New York: Praeger.

Conroy, G. (1990). *Primate evolution.* New York: Norton.

DuBrul, E. (1976). Biomechanics of speech sounds. *Annals of the New York Academy of Sciences, 280,* 631–642.

Fleagle, J. (1988). *Primate adaptation and evolution.* New York: Academic Press.

Fodor, J. A., Bever, T. G., & Garrett, M. F. (1974). *The psychology of language: An introduction to psycholinguistics and generative grammar.* New York: McGraw-Hill.

Freides, D. (1974). Human information processing and sense modality: Cross-modal functions, information complexity, memory, and deficit. *Psychological Bulletin, 81(5),* 284–310.

Gardner, R., Gardner, B., & Cantfort, T. (1989). *Teaching language to chimpanzees.* Albany: State University of New York Press.

Gilinsky, A. (1984). *Mind and brain: Principles of neuropsychology.* New York: Praeger.

Goodall, J. (1986). *The chimpanzees of Gombe: Patterns of behavior.* Cambridge, MA: Harvard University Press.

Goodman, M. D. A., Tagle, D. H., Fitch, A., Bailey, W., Czelusnak, J., Koop, B. F., Benson, P., & Slightom, J. L. (1990). Primate evolution at the DNA level and a classification of hominids. *Journal of Molecular Evolution, 30,* 260–266.

Goosen, C. (1980). *On grooming in Old World monkeys.* Delft, The Netherlands: W. D. Meinema 2.

Hamilton, J. (1974). Hominid divergence and speech evolution. *Journal of Human Evolution, 3,* 417–424.

Hewes, G. (1973). Primate communication and the gestural origin of language. *Current Anthropology, 14,* 5–11.

Hill, J. (1972). On the evolutionary foundations of language. *American Anthropologist, 74,* 308–315.

Hockett, C. (1960). *The origins of speech* (pp. 1–10). New York: Freeman.

Hooff van, J. A. R. A. M. (1972). A comparative approach to the phylogeny of laughter and smile. In R. A. Hinde (Ed.), *Nonverbal communication* (pp. 209–241). Cambridge, UK: University Press.

Horel, J. (1988). Limbic neocortical interrelations. In H. Steklis & J. Erwin (Eds.), *Neurosciences 4* (pp. 81–97). New York: Liss.

Hunt, K. (1991). Positional behavior in the hominoidea. *International Journal of Primatology, 12,* 95–118.

Isaacson, R. (1982). *The limbic system.* New York: Plenum.

Jerison, H. (1973). *Evolution of the brain and intelligence.* New York: Academic Press.

Jerison, H. (1990). Fossil evidence on the evolution of the neocortex. In E. Jones & A. Peters (Eds.), *Cerebral cortex* (pp. 311–362). New York: Plenum Press.

Kaas, J., & Pons, T. P. (1988). The somatosensory system of primates. In H. Steklis & J. Erwin (Eds.), *Neurosciences* (pp. 426–468). New York: Liss.

King, M., & Wilson, A. (1975). Evolution at two levels in humans and chimpanzees. *Science, 188,* 107–116.

Laitman, J. T. (1983, August). The anatomy of human speech. *Natural History,* pp. 20–27.

Lewin, R. (1993). *Human evolution.* Boston: Blackwell.

Lieberman, P., & Crelin, E. (1971). On the speech of Neanderthal man. *Linguistic Inquiry, 2,* 203–222.

MacLean, P. (1990). *The triune brain in evolution.* New York: Plenum.

Martin, R. D. (1990). *Primate origins and evolution: A phylogenetic reconstruction.* London: Chapman & Hall.

Maryanski, A. (1992). The last ancestor: An ecological network model on the origins of human sociality. *Advances in Human Ecology, 1,* 1–32.

Maryanski, A. (1993). The elementary forms of the first protohuman society: An ecological/social approach. *Advances in Human Ecology, 2,* 215–241.

Maryanski, A., & Turner, J. H. (1992). *The social cage: Human nature and the evolution of society.* Stanford, CA: Stanford University Press.

Masterton, B. (1992). Role of the central auditory system in hearing: The new direction. *Trends in Neurosciences, 15,* 280–285.

Masterton, B., & Diamond, I. (1973). Hearing: Central neural mechanisms. In E. Carterette & M. Friedman (Eds.), *Handbook of perception* (Vol. 3, pp. 408–448) New York: Academic Press.

Matsuzawa, T. (1991). The duality of language-like skill in a chimpanzee. In A. Ehara, T. Kimura, O. Takenara, & M. Iwamoto (Eds.), *Primatology today* (pp. 703–704). Amsterdam: Elsevier.

Mead, G. H. (1934). *Mind, self and society.* Chicago: University of Chicago Press.

Menzel, E. W. (1971). Communication about the environment in a group of young chimpanzees. *Folia Primatologica, 15,* 220–232.

Muller, F. M. (1871). *Lectures on the science of language* (Vol. 1). London: Longmans, Green.

Napier, J. R., & Napier, P. H. (1985). *The natural history of the primates.* Cambridge, MA: MIT Press.

Negus, V. E. (1949). *The comparative anatomy and physiology of the larynx.* New York: Grune & Stratton.

Newman, J. (1988). Primate hearing mechanisms. In H. Steklis & J. Erwin (Eds.), *Neurosciences* (Vol. 4, pp. 469–499). New York: Liss.

Poizner, H., Bellugi, U., & Klima, E. (1990). Biological foundations of language. *Annual Review of Neuroscience, 13,* 283–307.

Preuschoft, S. (1992). "Laughter" and "smile" in Barbary macaques, *Macaca Sylvanus. Ethology, 91,* 220–236.

Preuschoft, S., & Preuschoft, H. (1994). Primate nonverbal communication: Our communication heritage. In W. Nöth (Ed.), *Origins of semiosis* (pp. 66–100). Berlin: Mouton de Gruyter.

Radinsky, L. B. (1970). The fossil evidence of prosimian brain evolution. In C. R. Noback & W. Montagna (Eds.), *The primate brain* (pp. 209–224). New York: Appleton Century Croft.

Radinsky, L. B. (1974). The fossil evidence of anthropoid brain evolution. *American Journal of Physical Anthropology, 41,* 15–28.

Rodieck, R. W. (1988). The primate retina. In H. Steklis & J. Erwin (Eds.), *Neurosciences.* New York: Alan Liss, 203–278.

Savage-Rumbaugh, S., Murphy, J., Seveik, R., Brakke, D., Williams, S., & Rumbaugh, D. (1993). *Language comprehension in the ape and child,* volume 58 (Monographs of the Society for Research in Child Development). Chicago: University of Chicago Press.

Sibley, C., Comstock, J., & Ahlquist, J. (1990). DNA hybridization evidence of hominoid phylogeny: A reanalysis of the data. *Journal of Molecular Evolution, 30,* 202–236.

Simonds, P. (1974). *The social primates.* New York: Harper and Row.

Snowdon, C. (1990). Language capacities of non-human animals. *Yearbook of Physical Anthropology, 33,* 215–243.

Stebbins, L. (1965). *The basis of progressive evolution.* Chapel Hill: The University of North Carolina Press.

Steklis, H. (1985). Primate communication, comparative neurology, and the origin of language re-examined. *Journal of Human Evolution, 14,* 157–173.

Stephan, H., Baron, G., & Frahm, H. (1988). Comparative size of brains and brain components. In H. Steklis & J. Erwin (Eds.), *Neurosciences* (Vol. 4, pp. 1–38). New York: Liss.

Sutton, D., & Jurgens, U. (1988). Neural control of vocalization. In H. Steklis & J. Erwin (Eds.), *Neurosciences* (Vol. 4, pp. 625–647). New York: Liss.

Tattersall, I., Delson, E., & van Couvering, J. (1988). *Encyclopedia of human evolution and prehistory*. New York: Garland.

Tuttle, R. (1986). *Apes of the world*. Park Ridge, NJ: Noyes.

Vandermeer, J. (1972). Niche theory. In R. Johnston, P. Frank, & C. Michener (Eds.), *Annual Review of Ecology and Systematics* (pp. 107–132).

Wolin, L., & Massopust, L., Jr. (1970). Morphology of the primate retina. In C. R. Noback & W. Montagna (Eds.), *The primate brain* (pp. 209–224). New York: Appleton Century Croft.

11

THE EVOLUTION OF EMOTIONS: THE NONVERBAL BASIS OF HUMAN SOCIAL ORGANIZATION

Jonathan H. Turner
University of California, Riverside

From a sociological perspective, human social organization is created and sustained by the capacity for symbolically mediated interaction among individuals. Such interaction is, ultimately, a "conversation of gestures" in which the emission of both verbal and nonverbal signs by one individual is seen, interpreted, and used as a basis for the emission of gestures by another individual (G. H. Mead, 1934). Such conversations of gestures enable individuals to align their behaviors and to sanction each other in ways that facilitate cooperation or, if desired, to initiate more antagonistic relations. Many studies of interaction document that nonverbal gestures—body positioning, body countenance, facial expressions, hand movements, and the like—are as important to effective cooperation as spoken words, indicating that interaction is a highly complex and subtle *set* of processes (J. H. Turner, 1988). As Darwin (1872/1934) recognized long ago, much of what is signaled via these nonverbal channels is emotional, involving those affective states that mobilize individuals to act in particular ways and with varying degrees of intensity and feeling. Thus, accompanying verbal utterances are nonverbal conversations of gestures that not only communicate but also arouse emotions. Emotions are, therefore, fundamental to human interaction and social organization, a conclusion that eventually compels sociologists to examine the evolution of emotions in the biology of humans in the course of mammalian and primate history.

Evolutionary psychology (e.g., Daly, M. Wilson, & Weghorst, 1982; R. Thornhill & N. W. Thornhill, 1989; Tooby & Cosmides, 1989) offers one avenue of investigation: Emotions exist because they maximize reproductive fitness of individuals. For sociologists, such explanations seem incomplete because the effects of group structures on selection processes are underemphasized. For sociologists, then, an alternative avenue of investigation is to shift attention toward group selection dynamics: That is, those hominid ancestors of humans that could develop more adaptive patterns of group organization were more likely to survive, with the existence of such groups and competition among groups circumscribing the processes of selection on individuals. As I argue, the control and elaboration of emotional responses greatly facilitated the development of flexible and adaptive group structures, and conversely, the existence of group structures circumscribed the forces of selection as these worked on individual phenotypes. This line of argument need not contradict sociobiological positions, but it nonetheless forces the recognition that selection often works at the group level for humans.

WHY ARE HUMANS SO EMOTIONAL?

Lower mammals appear to display just a few emotional states, whereas humans reveal many such states. What accounts for the differences? There are several possible answers.

One is that the complex array of emotions in humans is an artifact of selection processes among humans' hominid ancestors on the African savanna that operated to create cortical control over undisciplined emotional displays, because a loud and emotional primate in the predator-ridden savanna was soon a dead primate. Thus, there was a fundamental "rewiring" of the brain so that limbic system processes (MacLean 1990) came under cortical, or conscious, control (Maryanski & J. H. Turner, 1992). However, control of emotion is very different than diversity of emotions and although it is likely that the larger neuronet represented by the neocortex sitting on top of the older limbic system could allow such diversity to be a possibility, there must have been additional selection pressures to translate this possibility into an evolutionary reality.

Another answer to the question of why humans reveal so many emotions is that they are the key mechanism that enabled humans' hominid ancestors to overcome a basic feature of all apes: genetic propensities for low sociality and high individual autonomy (Maryanski, 1992; Maryanski & J. H. Turner, 1992). That is, in contrast to monkeys who reveal biological propensities for comparatively rigid group organization, apes are less group-oriented, are not particularly social, and are highly individualistic. Therefore, as intense selection for group organization sought to overcome phylogenetic inertia, emotions evolved to "connect" and "bind" individualistic hominids to each other and to those group structures necessary for their survival. Selection clearly worked to enable hominids to gain cortical control over limbic outbursts of emotion, as noted earlier. As an artifact of this selection process, or more likely, as a converging selection process of its own, the development and control of complex arrays of emotional responses facilitated the attachments of otherwise individualistic hominids to each other and group structures. In fact, there must have been intense selection pressure for mechanisms that could create structure among rather loosely organized hominids. For without a well-organized structure, survival would be problematic in open-country savanna. Selection for an increased array of emotions was, no doubt, one crucial force foraging increased attachments among individuals.

A third answer to the question of why humans have so many emotions is that emotions greatly facilitate the process of interaction, and hence, group organization. Emotions denote and demark propensities to act in certain ways; and if emotions can be differentiated and fine-tuned, subtle behavioral dispositions can be communicated and used to construct fluid and flexible patterns of interaction and organization—a capacity that not only facilitated adaptation to the dangers of the African savanna but also accommodated to genetic tendencies toward loose and fluid social relations (Maryanski, 1992). Indeed, unlike monkeys, such as the baboon, who used their tendencies for male hierarchy and female matrilines to create a rigid, militarylike pattern of social organization for survival on the savanna, apes would have to build structure on the tendency to form weak and fluid ties. Hominid structures would have to be loose and flexible, because 30 million years of phylogenetic inertia for apes could not be undone; and the best way to create coherence rather than chaos is to give animals the emotional capacity for diversity, nuance, and subtlety in their emotional responses. This greater array of emotionally-laden responses could create strong ties needed for survival and, yet at the same time, accommodate the phylogenetic tendency among apes for individualism, looseness, and weak tie formation.

All of these answers are highly compatible. The expanding neocortex was probably the result of selection for language among *Homo habilis* (where the first big jump in brain size on the human line occurs) and this increase in the size of the neocortex would allow for the elaboration of many differentiated emotions. Yet, part of this increase in the neocortex would have to be the result of intense selection favoring the development and display of more robust configurations of emotions that could complement those selection processes for language (and later speech) and, thereby, greatly increase the subtlety, fluidity, and effectiveness of gestural interaction, overcoming genetic propensities for low sociality and for loose social relations.

SELECTION, GROUP FITNESS, AND EMOTIONS

The end result of these simultaneous selection pressures was to produce capacities for nonverbal communication of a wide array of emotions facilitating group organization and group fitness for hominid gatherers-hunters in the Pleistocene. In what way, then, did the elaboration of nonverbal, emotional behavioral responses increase group fitness?

One major consequence for group fitness of the capacity for nonverbal, emotionally-laden responses is the dramatic increase in *attunement* of individuals to each other. Emotions offer signs of behavioral readiness, significance, texture, and nuance, and they do so rapidly, as studies show that the pickup of emotional signals is very rapid on nonverbal channels. Moreover, as still other studies document, much emotion is unconsciously emitted and received, thereby increasing the speed and range of emotions that are nonverbally communicated. In fact, the more information about states of affect and readiness to respond can be communicated without recourse to either conscious deliberation or language, the more communication can avoid the log jam or, in Luhmann's (1982) terms, the "bottleneck" of sequentially uttered speech or conscious thought. As a consequence, communication can revolve around complex, robust, and subtle alignments of behaviors, at the same time freeing cognition and speech for expressly instrumental activity. The end result is that individuals can interact and coordinate activities in ways that facilitate flexible and adaptive patterns of group organization and, hence, group fitness in competition with other group-organizing and, hence, group fitness in competition with other group-organizing species. This was especially important for early hominid survival in predator-ridden environments where competition with other primates for resources was at times intense.

Another aspect of attunement in hominid evolution became particularly important as the neocortex expanded. Increasingly, infants would have to be born neurologically immature (in order for the head of a large-brained organism to pass through the female's cervix), with little early ability to use verbal gestures. As numerous studies demonstrate, adult-infant emotional attunement is almost instantaneous, and as a consequence, biologically immature infants have access to nonlinguistic channels for early learning. Such capacities of infants and adults for early emotional attunement obviously promoted fitness for both the individual and the groups on which they depended for survival.

A second major consequence of nonverbal, emotional responses for group fitness is the capacity for *sanctioning*. Both positive and negative sanctions are essential to viable group structures; for without sanctions, conformity and cooperation are not possible among symbol-using organisms. Such capacities for sanctioning would have been critical for humans' hominid ancestors who innately displayed comparatively low sociality and high individualism; for without mutual sanctioning, cohesive patterns of social organization necessary for survival could not be sustained. Emotions are the stuff of effective sanctions, both to the sanctioning and sanctioned individual; and so, without feeling and affect, positive or negative sanctions could not be effectively used to organize behavioral responses, especially for somewhat individualistic hominids who might simply have walked away from the group rather than conform.

A third major consequence of emotion for group fitness, especially among a symbol-using primate, is in the development and use of *moral codes*. Without cultural, as opposed to genetic codes, hominid groupings would not have been fit, for there would have been insufficient information guiding and coordinating the activity of individualistic primates. Emotions are the psychological force behind such moral codes, for their power to regulate conduct and organizational patterns resides in the affect-driven desire to conform to the instructions in shared symbol systems.

In sum, then, hominid evolution on the line to humans involved selection for a group-organizing primate who could overcome the individualism, low sociality, and preference for loose structures of the ancestor common to present-day apes and humans (Maryanski, 1992; Maryanski & J. H. Turner, 1992). This selection favored hominids who could control limbic outbursts and yet reveal a complex array of emotions that facilitated interindividual attunement, positive and negative sanctioning, and conformity to moral codes. Hence, contemporary analyses in the sociology of emotion and nonverbal communication must keep these long-range evolutionary considerations in mind.

THE EVOLUTION OF THE EMOTIONS AND NONVERBAL COMMUNICATION

The complex array of emotions that humans exhibit and use in both verbal and nonverbal attunement, sanctioning, and conformity to moral codes is built on a small number of primary emotions that, in turn, represent evolutionary elaborations of more basic aversive, aggressive, and passive dispositions of lower mammals. Yet, there is far from complete consensus over which emotions are primary, although all researchers would agree that fear, anger, and happiness are universal to humans. Depending on the research tradition, additional primary emotions are added, including sadness, depression, surprise, disgust, and anticipation (e.g., Ekman, 1982; Franks & Gecas, 1992; Franks & McCarthy, 1989; Kemper, 1978, 1981, 1987, 1991; Plutchik, 1962; Plutchik & Kellerman, 1980; Scherer & Ekman, 1984). I could construct an ad hoc scenario for the selection pressures behind each of these emotions—for example, fear to mobilize in the face of danger, aggression to cope with threat, satisfaction to rest and recuperate, sadness to withdraw and avoid, surprise to deal with the unexpected, disgust to respond to the unpleasant or dangerous, anticipation to be ready, and so on. Such scenarios would, no doubt, exhibit considerable plausibility, although once we started adding elaborations of primary emotions to our list—jealousy, pride, shame, joy, envy, wonder, awe, hope, shyness, contempt, nostalgia, grief, love, gratitude, yearning, hate, vengeance, and the like—the number of scenarios would become long. I propose to analyze, instead, emotions with respect to their consequences for the three group-organizing processes that guided selection during the course of human evolution: attunement, sanctioning, and moral coding. For me, selection worked to elaborate a basic set of mammalian and primate emotions—at a minimum, happiness, fear, anger, sadness, and surprise—to increase capacities for attunement, sanctioning, and moral coding.

A. Selection and Emotional Attunement

As a general hypothesis, selection would favor high degrees of emotional differentiation among organisms with a large neocortex and with little genetic propensity for close social relations or rigid social structures—as was the case with those hominoids who were on the present-day human line. In the absence of genetic programming for high sociality and structure, a robust configuration of emotions would facilitate flexible attunements of relatively individualistic apelike hominids into adaptive group structures. There would be limits to how much differentiation of emotions could occur, however, because too many emotional states could overload cognitive processes and get in the way of effective sanctioning and moral coding. It is not surprising, therefore, that most investigators isolate a few primary emotions that are then differentiated and elaborated into just a few dozen additional emotions (usually somewhere between 35 and 50).

Pursuing a strategy outlined by Kemper (1987), Table 11.1 presents a perspective on the differentiation of human emotions. Column 1 lists five primary emotions, although others might be added. Column 2 offers a sense for the range of variation in these primary emotions. Column 3 presents prominent examples of what can be termed first-order combinations of emotions where one primary emotion is combined with another primary emotion (indicated in the parentheses of Column 3) to form a more complex emotion. Other first-order combinations could be hypothesized, and perhaps even second-order ones as well (i.e., combinations among first-order combinations). Selection operated, it is argued here, to differentiate primary emotions, then variations on these, and finally combinations of these primary emotions and their variations. Expansion of the hominid neocortex from Australopithecus through *Homo habilis* to *Homo sapiens sapiens* was not just the result of selection for more cognitive capacity to symbolize and use language. Also involved was selection for an expanded emotional repertoire so that much signaling and communication could be nonverbal, robust, and partially subconscious, thereby enabling interpersonal attunement that would not overload conscious verbal communication (which, by its sequential nature, is rife with potential log jams and bottlenecks that can get in the way of effective interaction).

TABLE 11.1

Selection for Interpersonal Attunement and the
Differentiation of Emotions

Primary Emotions	Range of Emotions	First-Order Combinations
Happiness	Satisfaction Pride Love	Gratitude, hope, wonder (fear) Vengeance (anger) Nostalgia (sadness) Joy (surprise)
Fear	Anxiety Apprehensiveness Aversiveness	Awe (happiness) Guilt, envy (anger) Worry (sadness) Panic (surprise)
Anger	Contempt Distaste Aggressiveness	Snobbing (happiness) Shame, hate, jealousy (fear) Depression (sadness) Rage (surprise)
Sadness	Resignation Ennui Sorrow	Yearning (happiness) Hopefulness (fear) Grief, boredom (anger) Crestfallen (surprise)
Surprise	Startlement Amazement Astonishment	Delight (happiness) Shock (fear) Disgust (anger) Disappointment (sadness)

In fact, the capacity to read instantaneously and simultaneously a robust array of emotions—both outside the verbal track as well as inside it via voice inflections—is an enormous evolutionary achievement. Talk and discourse are slow, sequential, and inefficient as mechanisms for attuning and aligning individuals (this becomes particularly evident when emotional "body language" cannot be observed, as in a "conference call" over the phone lines where attunement is always awkward);

and if there was a need for rapid mobilization of responses and flexible alignment and attunement of responses to external threats on the African savanna, the elaboration of emotions would be the easiest evolutionary path. Such elaboration would have to build on existing primary emotions in higher mammals, and it would need to be channeled to accommodate other aspects of group structure—sanctioning and moral coding.

B. Selection and Interpersonal Sanctioning

Group structures cannot remain viable without sanctions that reward conformity and punish nonconformity to expectations. Emotions are central to this process because they provide the psychological force that drives both the bestowal of sanctions and the responses of those who are sanctioned. Thus, the evolution of emotions among hominids on the line to humans was intimately connected to the sanctioning processes as these promoted group fitness.

Not all emotions are, however, equally relevant to sanctioning processes. The emission of negative sanctions is built on the primary emotion of anger, whereas the emission of positive sanctions is ultimately tied to happiness; conformity to sanctions is fueled by fear of the consequences of nonconformity, especially to negative sanctions but to positive ones as well. Because negative sanctioning is connected to anger and fear, it is less effective in the long run than positive sanctioning in generating continued conformity, unless these combine to produce shame and guilt, which are somewhat different mixtures of fear about the negative consequences of one's behavior, and anger toward oneself (or others) for failing to conform. If negative sanctioning generates suppressed anger on the part of those receiving the sanctions, then sadness and sluggish conformity ensue, often punctuated by outbursts of anger or fear, and then shame or guilt. However, the critical point is that negative sanctioning arouses complex sequences of disruptive emotions based on anger and fear, or ultimately flight and aggressiveness; and as such, these emotional dispositions are potentially disruptive to ongoing, coordinated interpersonal activity and hence group fitness.

In contrast, positive sanctioning is tied to emotions springing from happiness on the part of those sending and receiving the sanction. They generate pride on the part of those receiving the sanctions, and even if there was some fear of nonconformity, the act of conformity in response to positive sanctions produces in others such positive emotions as gratitude or even delight that represent, themselves, positive sanctions. Thus, it should not be surprising that groups with high solidarity have much higher ratios of positive to negative sanctioning. We can conclude, therefore, that emotions such as pride, shame, guilt, delight, and gratitude are salient to humans today because of intense selection in the distant past for emotions that would make sanctioning an effective tool for group organization and fitness among somewhat individualistic hominids.

If we imagine a phylogenetic tendency for autonomy among hominids, coupled with basic emotions for fear and flight, anger and aggression, and satisfaction and contentment, how is it possible to use this emotional base to give sanctioning flexibility and power? The evolutionary answer was to elaborate new variations of these emotions and then to combine them in various combinations (as is illustrated in Columns 2 and 3 for Table 11.1).

Happiness would be crucial because of its connection to positive sanctions, and so in the evolutionary history of hominids, it would first be elaborated into new variants like "pride" and "love," which would add extra emotional power to positive sanctions. Then, it would be combined with fear and anger to produce other emotions, such as gratitude, hope, wonder, and fear of vengeance, that give positive sanctions an additional force. Fear would first be elaborated into variants like generalized anxiety and apprehensiveness that give negative sanctions an extra edge; and in turn, such first-order combinations of emotions as guilt, worry, and awe would provide even more force behind negative sanctions. Anger is a complex emotion because it is what underlies the giving of negative sanctions, but it is also an emotion that is evoked when people are made to experience fear or when expected happiness is denied. However, despite this complexity, its evolution would involve initial elaboration into such variants as contempt and distaste that give negative sanctions both increased diversity and extra thrust, and then, it would be combined with fear to produce "shame," which is perhaps the key emotion behind effective negative sanctioning.

C. Selection and Moral Coding

Viable human groupings must create value premises and normative codes as functional equivalents of genetic codes. Such codes are more than cognitive exercises, however. Those codes critical for maintenance of the group and, hence, group fitness, are always moral and laden with emotion. To violate moral codes generates both anger and fear, and all the potential variations and combinations of these, whereas conformity brings happiness, satisfaction, and all the many variants of these more positive emotions. As with sanctions, positive or prescriptive moral codes about what should and can be done are more effective than pro-scriptive ones for organizing groups, especially when sanctioning is also positive. Proscriptive codes always hold the specter of negative sanctions, and as such they invite complicated emotional cycles revol-ving around fear, anger, guilt, and shame. These emotions can seeming-ly make moral codes more powerful, and yet, because they are built on rudimentary mammalian propensities for aversiveness and aggressive-ness, they always contain the seeds of emotional arousal that reduce the morality of cultural codes and invite disruptive group conflict. In the face of this prospect, particular emotions—happiness, satisfaction, and pride, on the more positive side, or fear, anger, shame, and guilt, on the negative side—evolved as a way to put "teeth" into codes necessary for group organization and fitness. Other emotions—awe, vengeance, and wonder, for instance—may also have evolved to make moral codes highly salient, but the point is clear: Selection favored those hominids who organized in terms of moral codes that effectively organized rather individualistic primates into flexible but well-regulated groups that could outcompete less fit groups.

Without emotions, moral codes have no real power to cause con-formity, so to the extent that these kinds of codes were to become the organizing force of hominids, there would be intense selection for those emotions that would give power to constructed cultural codes. More-over, as Durkheim (1912) first recognized and later Goffman (1967) fully understood, moral codes are reinforced by rituals, both larger cere-monial and smaller interpersonal, and such rituals activate the relevant and appropriate emotions, as Collins (1986, 1988) sought to demon-strate. Thus, emotions are more than the force behind sanctions as these are applied to moral codes, they are the force of moral codes, and they are the force behind the constant displays of rituals that worship and re-inforce moral codes.

Why would humans need to reinforce moral codes with sanctions and rituals? The answer lies in our evolutionary history as somewhat autonomous primates who have no biologically based propensity to bond or conform. However, if moral codes are to force bonds and con-formity, they must be given emotional content. Yet, an organism cannot be emotionally mobilized all of the time, because this produces severe pathologies (especially in a large-brained organism like a higher mammal). Therefore, there must be mechanisms to activate the relevant emotions when needed to give moral codes their special force. Interpersonal sanctions and rituals represent the two mechanisms by which this activation occurs, and given their importance in maintaining the moral order, it should not be surprising that they are a part of every interaction among humans. For without them, emotions cannot be attached to cultural codes, and without this attachment, these codes lose their moral force.

CONCLUSION

The complex arrays of emotions evident among humans exist because they had selective advantages in the past among those individualistic and loosely structured hominids who were the ancestors of humans. Considerations of group fitness are essential to understanding why emotions evolved in humans; for without the capacity to control emotions and to emit them both consciously and unconsciously on nonverbal communication channels, humans' hominid ancestors could not have survived. Thus, the necessity for attunement among low sociality primates, for effective sanctioning, and for codes with a moral impact generated selection pressures for the differentiation and elaboration of complex arrays of emotions. The high salience in human affairs of particular emotional dynamics revolving around happiness, pride, shame, guilt, anger, and fear is the result of selection for emotions that could facilitate attunement, give sanctions power, and make moral codes meaningful. My argument does not contradict more extreme arguments in sociobiology, but it does shift attention to imperatives for group organization as these created selection pressures for attunement, sanctioning, and moral coding. Such considerations must be part of any Darwinian explanation for the evolution of the emotions, as these are used in nonverbal communication among human beings.

REFERENCES

Collins, R. (1986). Interaction ritual chains, power and property. In J. Alexander, B. Giesen, R. Münch, & N. Smelser (Eds.), *The micro-macro link* (pp. 177–192). Berkeley: University of California Press.

Collins, R. (1988). *Theoretical sociology.* San Diego, CA: Harcourt Brace Jovanovich.

Daly, M., Wilson, M., & Weghorst, S. J. (1982). Male sexual jealousy. *Ethology and Sociobiology, 3,* 11–27.

Darwin, C. (1934). *The expression of the emotions in man and animals.* London: Watts & Co. (Original work published 1872).

Durkheim, E. (1912). *The elementary forms of religious life.* New York: The Free Press.

Ekman, P. (1982). *Emotions in the human face.* Cambridge, UK: Cambridge University Press.

Franks, D. D., & Gecas, V. (Eds.) (1992). *Social perspectives on emotion* (Vol. 1). Greenwich, CT: JAI.

Franks, D. D., & McCarthy, E. D. (Eds.) (1989). *Emotions: Original essays and research papers.* Greenwich, CT: JAI.

Goffman, E. (1967). *Interaction ritual: Essays on face-to-face behavior.* Garden City, NY: Anchor.

Kemper, T. D. (1978). *A social interaction theory of emotions.* New York: Wiley.

Kemper, T. D. (1981). Social constructionist and positivistic approaches to the sociology of emotions. *American Journal of Sociology, 87,* 336–362.

Kemper, T. D. (1987). How many emotions are there? Wedding the social and the autonomic components. *American Journal of Sociology, 93,* 263–289.

Kemper, T. D. (1991). *An introduction to the sociology of emotions: International review of studies on emotion.* London: Wiley.

Luhmann, N. (1982). *The differentiation of society.* New York: Columbia University Press.

MacLean, P. (1990). *The triune brain in evolution.* New York: Plenum.

Maryanski, A. R. (1992). The last ancestor: An ecological-network model on the origins of human sociality. *Advances in Human Ecology, 2,* 1–32.

Maryanski, A. R., & Turner, J. H. (1992). *The social cage: Human nature and the evolution of society.* Stanford, CA: Stanford University Press.

Mead, G. H. (1934). *Mind, self, and society.* Chicago: University of Chicago Press.

Plutchik, R. (1962). *The emotions: Facts, theories and a new model.* New York: Random House.

Plutchik, R., & Kellerman, H. (Eds.) (1980). *Emotion: Theory, research, and experience.* New York: Academic Press.

Scherer, K. R., & Ekman, P. (Eds.) (1984). *Approaches to emotion.* Hillsdale, NJ: Lawrence Erlbaum Associates.

Thornhill, R., & Thornhill, N. W. (1989). The evolution of psychological pain. In R. Bell (Ed.), *Sociobiology and the social sciences* (pp. 73–103). Lubbock: Texas Tech University Press.

Tooby, J., & Cosmides, L. (1989). Evolutionary psychology and the generation of culture: Part I. Theoretical considerations. *Ethology and Sociobiology, 10,* 29–49.

Turner, J. H. (1988). *A theory of social interaction.* Stanford, CA: Stanford University Press.

PART IV

Nonverbal Communication as a Mediator Between Nature and Culture

In the final part, we once again bring up the central question of this book: How can nonverbal communication act as a mediator between nature and culture? The earlier parts of this volume already addressed this question in different ways. In Part I, we discussed how humans seem to be preprogrammed for emotional, nonverbal social interaction and also how already existing biologically grounded mechanisms may be turned into cultural signals (e.g., the nose wrinkle) or form a basis for social bonding (e.g., grooming). Part II gave various examples of how an appropriate social context turns the initially 'biological' infant into a competent, communicative social being. Part III looked at the nature–culture continuum from two directions: On the one hand, it identified voluntary and symbolic communication in animals; on the other, it discussed emotions, nonverbal communication, and spoken language as evolutionary advantages for humans. The final part of this volume approaches the question of nature and culture from yet another angle. Here we are interested in the direct role of nonverbal communication as a mediator or interface between human cultural practices and various biological givens.

The anthropologist Walter Goldschmidt discusses the importance of childrearing practices for nonverbal transmission of culture-specific emotional attitudes. Reinterpreting material from his own firsthand observations among the Sebei in Uganda in the 1950s in the light of recent theory on the role of mother–infant interaction for child development, he shows how the mothers' "idle hands and absent eyes" may produce the typical lack of affective ties and commitments in Sebei culture. He also reinterprets earlier studies, such as Bateson and Mead's (1942) famous book on Balinese character.

Heller's chapter looks at concrete ways in which cultural and social aspects of human behavior interact with anatomical and biological constraints. His theoretical framework is partly that of Leroi-Gourhan (1964, 1965), partly the "structural" approach in nonverbal communication (see chap. 1, this volume). Heller notes that culture may directly affect biology in the sense that posture (and backache) is a product of interaction between anatomy and work requirements. Using a detailed method of observation (Siegfried Frey's Bernese System for Movement Notation, which he helped develop), Heller's own studies show how in nonverbal interaction, body movement and posture are simultaneously influenced by type of profession, status, role, and individual style.

The historian August Nitschke introduces us to an intricate world of medieval signs and gestures, particularly in monasteries and courts of justice. A special case is the code of silence. The allowable gestures are well described—enticing the reader to try them out on the spot. More provocatively, Nitschke suggests that the social order and organization typical for an epoch is reflected in body movements, as seen in illustrations from the time. Thus, with Nitschke we re-enter the discussion of human universals across cultures and epochs. However, to the extent universals are seen as human predispositions or capabilities, historical observations of changing behaviors can also be accommodated.

Finally, Robert Frank, an economist, suggests an answer to the question how, from an evolutionary point of view, cooperative behavior could

227

have possibly won out over selfish behavior, and thus evolved. Frank here points to the importance of nonverbal communication for the evolution of moral sentiments and trust. In his scenario, it is genuine emotions rather than the deceptive strategies typically championed by sociobiologists (e.g., Krebs & Dawkins, 1978) that are important. Our ability to detect nonverbal signs of lying and embarrassment (cf. also Ekman & Keltner, chap. 2, this volume) helps us select those individuals whom we can trust and involve in long-term cooperative relationships.

REFERENCES

Bateson, G., & Mead, M. (1942). *Balinese character: A photographic analysis.* New York: New York Academy of Sciences.

Krebs, J. R., & Dawkins, R. (1978). Animal signals: Information or manipulation? In: R. Krebs & N. B. Davies (Eds.), *Behavioral ecology: An evolutionary approach* (pp. 282-309). Oxford: Blackwell.

Leroi-Gourhan, A. (1964). *Le geste et la parole: Technique et language (Gesture and word: Technique and language).* Paris: Sciences d'Aujourd'hui, Albin Michel.

Leroi-Gourhan, A. (1965). *Le geste et la parole: La mémoire et les rythmes (Gesture and word: Memory and rhytms).* Paris: Sciences d'Aujourd'hui, Albin Michel.

12

NONVERBAL COMMUNICATION AND CULTURE

Walter Goldschmidt
University of California, Los Angeles

Communication through gesture, facial expression, and physical contact is as ontogenetically prior to verbal communication as it is phylogenetically. Elsewhere in this volume the patterns of nonverbal communication among primates has been discussed. Here I examine the patterns of such communication between mothers and infants to show that they draw the child into the sphere of social interaction and that the subtle differences in the handling of infants sets that emotional character and tone in the infant that is suited to the expectations of its own culture.

THE ETHOLOGY OF HUMAN INFANCY

We must first review the biologically based characteristics of the infant that make the transferral of cultural attitudes possible and, indeed, inevitable. I briefly review the literature on this subject that indicates what these human qualities are. We may take as text for this discussion the statement by Trevarthen (1979) who said that "human infants are *intentional, conscious* and *personal;* that above all they have a faculty of *intersubjectivity* which is in embryonic condition in the neonate and which soon becomes the central motivator and regulator for human mental growth" (p. 530).

Meltzoff (1985) summarizing a decade of work on neonate behavior, said: "It appears that even the youngest infant is not an asocial creature in a state anything akin to the normal autism or radical egocentrism that has been described. On the contrary, young infants, even newborns, can recognize certain human acts as like their own, and have a rich set of tools for building further bridges between themselves and others" (p. 27). He is here arguing against the *tabula rasa* infancy of Skinner and Piaget. More importantly, he is laying the groundwork for understanding what biological features the human infant brings with it that lead it into participation in social life long before it is capable of speech, from the first days and even minutes of postpartum existence. We might call these the *sociophilic* biological features of infancy. The relevant matters that have been researched include the physiological need for grooming, the centrality of the face, the ability to imitate facial expressions, the unconscious "dialogue" between mother and infant, the phenomenon of attachment, and the early ability to express affective states, including the early ability to evoke positive response by smiling. We must remember that although this research focuses on the needs and capacities of the infants, it also involves the appropriate responses of the adult caretakers.

The work of Spitz (1965) on human infants and the famous studies of Harlow (1959) on rhesus monkeys had long ago established that the human infant has a built-in affective need that I call *affect hunger*. Both Spitz, for humans, and Harlow, for rhesus monkeys, showed that infants deprived of normal quanta of affective response from their caretakers simply did not grow into normal adults—that they were not only psychologically retarded, but physically impaired. Nothing is as convincing of the vital importance of the physiological need for parental physical contact (licking, grooming, caressing) as the fact that infants deprived of tactile stimulation have less fully developed dendrites and fewer synapses per nerve cell; that is, that the behavior of the mother not only affects the behavior of the offspring but also its psychophysical development. This strongly implies that the grooming patterns (which are universal between mother and infant among nonhuman primates) are the evolutionary precursors to the socialization needs of human infants, with deep roots in the mammalian line; for grooming by licking is widespread if not universal among mammals. Being caressed as a physiological need and its counterpart, the adult propensity to do so, must be seen as the first of these sociophilic attributes.

The human face plays a most significant role in human sociality. There is an area of the brain specifically devoted to facial recognition (Geschwind, 1979). Spitz simply asserted that the human infant will track on a face—any face—but not on any other object. This has subsequently been subjected to intense and careful research and the present state of inquiry is that "the newborn brain is predisposed to track patterns that have certain face-like properties" (Johnson, Dziurawiec, Ellis, & Morton, 1991, p. 11) but that this biological propensity is extinguished or reduced by the time the infant is a month old, only to reappear later in infancy. It is not necessary to go into the history of the research on this subject here, but we may note that carefully controlled experiments on tracking propensities of infants as young as 45 minutes old show that they will track on a facelike representation but not on a similarly shaped object with the features of the face scrambled or absent. That this highly artificial situation provokes statistically significant responses suggests how very robust the underlying propensity must be. Spitz was right in asserting that the face has great importance to human sociality; the infantile proclivity to be stimulated by the face from the moment of birth is an innate sociophilic characteristic.

Meltzoff and Moore (1977) first demonstrated that infants of 2 to 3 weeks of age were capable of imitating the facial expressions of adults; more particularly that they would, with statistically reliable results, imitate lip protrusion, mouth opening, and tongue protrusion. This early research was subjected to severe criticism (Anisfeld, Masters, Jacobson, & Kagan, 1979), with the result that increasingly carefully controlled studies have been made on increasingly younger infants. The issue is particularly important to the perception of infantile neural behavior, because it involves the use of more than one sensory modality, namely sight and proprioception. A study conducted in 1983 demonstrated that babies under 72 hours old imitated the facial expression of tongue protrusion, mouth opening, and lip protrusion (Meltzoff, 1985). Field and associates (Field, Woodson, Greenberg, & D. Cohen, 1982) showed that infants with an average age of 36 hours imitated the expression of adult models. This research not only reinforces the importance of the face in human social interaction, but adds three elements: (a) innate imitativeness, (b) early affective discrimination, and (c) coordination of two informational modalities.

The first of these needs no elaboration. With respect to affective discrimination, Ekman, Levenson, and Friesen (1983) showed the physiological ties between the formation of facial expressions and the differential physiological response appropriate to the emotion. They had subjects artificially form diverse facial expressions and found that their physiological responses were appropriate to the expressions they had thus produced. Molnár (1990), however, measured the heart rate during neonates' mimicking responses and found that the patterns they displayed indicate that this mimicking does not involve some kind of conscious activity, but is merely a directly triggered response and hence that this early imitation does not have affective involvement. Yet even the capacity to differentiate expressions is itself an indication of a biological preparedness for that emotional discrimination that is so essential to the acquisition of culture.

The third implication of these studies is that the infant's neurological development includes the capacity to bring together information from two separate sensory modalities in what is known as the Molyneux Problem (Meltzoff, 1985); in this case specifically the visual and the proprioceptive. (Molyneux wrote to John Locke asking whether a person blind from birth who had only recognized shapes by feel would be able to identify them should he suddenly become endowed with sight. Locke thought not; the matter has long been debated.) This was demonstrated by experiments that showed the infant would turn its head in imitation of the experimenter. Evidence also came as an incidental outcome of an experimental protocol investigating the infant's auditory perception. In this experiment (DeCasper & Fifer, 1980) the subjects (all younger than 72 hours) were to respond to voices by sucking on differently shaped teething rings. That they were able to respond to the auditory and tactile stimulations in association provides such evidence. The results of the experiment are themselves relevant. The infants could discriminate voices and showed preference for recordings of their own mother's voice over that of another mother in the experimental group. Whether this is prenatal habituation or some imprinting mechanism is not known, but in either case it is a further example of sociophilic capabilities.

The phenomenon of *attachment* was first set forth by Bowlby (1971). The infant, by the 12th week, focuses its attention on specific familiar individuals (normally the mother), so that it responds differentially to her and to other persons in its social arena. This attachment is not a matter of dependency; it is not a response to nurturance, but a social response. The nature of the attachment varies from child to child, in response to the quality of the mother's treatment. Bowlby's ideas inspired Ainsworth (1967) to investigate attachment among the Baganda of Uganda. She found that infants varied in their patterns of attachment to their mothers in response to parental treatment and her method of investigation inspired a series of clinics dealing with children who fail to make satisfactory attachments. The research on attachment demonstrates or gives evidence for (a) the importance of the mother–infant dialogue, (b) maternal variance in the treatment of their children, (c) the infant's emotional response in relation to maternal treatment, (d) the continuity of patterns of behavior over time, and (e) cultural variation in such treatment.

The mother–infant interaction may appropriately be called a dialogue, for it has the qualities of two persons engaged in speech, except that language is absent or irrelevant. That is, it involves turn taking, response, and other manifestations of interaction outside the awareness of the mother (and, we may certainly presume, the child). The research of H. Papoušek and M. Papoušek (1979), using frame-by-frame analysis of these interactions, showed unexpected behavioral changes in the mother that were responsive to the needs of the infant—changes so subtle and transitory that the mother was herself unaware of them. They found that the child at 1 week is capable of learning (although not as fast as later) and that this learning has an emotional component, because the neonate's signs of displeasure and pleasure were situationally appropriate.

We conclude this review of infantile capabilities with a brief mention of the most obvious of all: the neonate's capacity to express displeasure by crying and the baby's early capacity to express pleasure by smiling. Because everybody in the world knows about this, it would not be worth mentioning except for the fact that its full implications have not been appreciated. These are (a) that the infant is capable of feeling the emotions of pleasure and displeasure, (b) that it associates these early on not only with physical comfort and discomfort but with social gratification and dissatisfaction, (c) that it is motivated to express itself about these matters, and, (d) that adults are programmed to be responsive to these infantile communications. A baby's smile universally evokes pleasure in the adult.

This large body of research, which I have only sampled, shows that the human infant is endowed with a number of capabilities and predispositions that make it responsive to its social environment and together constitute a preadaptation for becoming a culture-bearing person. Most crucial in all these sociophilic behavioral characteristics are those that make the infant sensitive to the social response of the mother and others in the social surroundings, and that early on it engages in preverbal dialogues in which a kind of affective learning takes place.

In recounting the evidence for sociophilic traits, I have laid the groundwork for two related matters: (a) the process of transformation of the infant from a purely biological being into a culture-bearing one, and (b) the transmission of unconscious cultural attitudes and values from parent to offspring. Both are ongoing processes that continue and intensify through childhood. I have formulated the first of these carefully; being culture-bearing does not absolve the person from biological restraints and demands; it supplements them. The second of these mimics the transmission of genetic information in two ways. First, it normally goes from parent to offspring (although the mother is most important, the father and others contribute). Second, the process does not stamp out identical replicas any more than genetic transmission does. Situational factors are relevant to what takes place (e.g., presence or absence of siblings); adults bring idiosyncratic elements to the situation, as does the infant. Finally, it must be emphasized that this is a highly emotional process (can any parent doubt it?); the transition into culture may be seen as being potentially as traumatic in its way as the trip through the birth canal. What is transmitted in these early stages must be seen as entirely affective; whatever may be stored in the infant's memory must remain in the realm of the unconscious.

All of these infantile attributes involve communication. They employ vocalization, facial expressions, and gestures as modalities for interaction between the child and its caretaker. They constitute a pattern of preverbal communication that expresses good and bad, proper and improper, and reward and punishment, thus guiding the baby toward socially appropriate behavior.

THE COMMUNICATION OF CULTURAL SENTIMENTS

The communication between mother and child involves affect far more than cognition, feeling more than understanding. It transmits that part of culture that underlies the overt, pragmatic, and instrumental aspects of human learned behavior. I have elsewhere (Goldschmidt, 1990, 1993) examined the broader social implications of this transmission process.

We must stop to consider this deeper aspect of culture. As we travel from country to country in Europe, we sense the difference in the overt behavior; here they cue up at the tram station, elsewhere they push ahead; in one place one often hears shouting and angry confrontations in the street, there such public displays are rarely seen. We are dealing here with cultures that have shared histories and technology, have exchanged masses of population in the recent past, and have fought and intermarried with one another and yet these differences persist. Although we used to see them as biological (e.g., in such presumably explanatory phrases as "The Latin race is more highly emotional"), they are not. Yet the differences are real, not merely empty stereotypes. When one goes beyond these closely related societies to examine exotic cultures, even wider diversity can be observed: Here people are suspicious and witchcraft ridden, there they are aggressive and hostile and elsewhere open and friendly. The settlers in colonial Kenya would tell you that the Kitui Kamba make the best askaris and the Kikuyu make the best household servants; a pragmatic expression of the awareness of cultural differences. It is not self-evident how these social characteristics are transmitted; they are certainly not taught in the ordinary sense of that word, nor are they merely imitated behavior. There is no problem in understanding how children acquire technological competence and social rules by imitation, precept, and training but it is not easy to see how the deeper aspects of culture, their *Weltanschauung,* is transmitted.

That is the issue that a number of anthropologists addressed in the 1930s and 1940s. A not very clearly articulated or sharply focused series of studies to examine the problem was initiated. Influenced by the psychology of Freud, especially his erotic stages in infantile development, they examined childrearing practices with emphasis on toilet training and weaning, on the assumption that the emotional tonus was a product of trauma resulting from traditional practices in these matters. They found no demonstrable relationship between toilet training or weaning and adult personality characteristics, and soon this area of research was abandoned. They were good observers, however, and developed excellent data on child training in several tribal cultures. It is to this empirical material that I turn to see how nonverbal communications sets the background attitudes in different cultures. Replacing Freudian notions with an understanding of the ethology of infancy, we can seek clues to the formation of those subtle cultural differentia that are at once so self-evident and so elusive.

We enter the examination with a revised paradigm that reads as follows. The infant is programmed to be receptive to stimuli from its social surroundings and to the responses provoked by its own actions; these stimuli and responses are affect laden so that the character of the interaction influences the baby's feelings about others and most likely also about itself. The quality of the mother's performance therefore has a profound influence on the infant's outlook. The mothers from a particular culture will bring to this interaction (in addition to idiosyncratic qualities) common cultural patterns of behavior and sentiment acquired through their own enculturation so that there will be culturespecific patterns of child raising that transmit the established cultural *Weltanschauung.*

Bateson and M. Mead (1942) investigated the childrearing practices in Bali, supporting their observations with the then-new 35mm camera able to take rapid sequential pictures. They found, for instance, that Balinese women, even child caretakers, had a regular pattern of stimulating the babies and then withdrawing their attention when the baby responded, thus frustrating its desire for affective gratification. They wrote that "the mother continually stimulates the child to show emotion—love or desire, jealousy or anger—only to turn away, to break the thread, as the child, in rising passion, makes a demand for some emotional response on her part" (p. 32). They claimed this leads the infant to a sense of distrust of others and to a Balinese personality characterized by flat affect. The Balinese ability to withdraw from contact from others is demonstrated for both adults and children in their published pictures (Plate 7). They convincingly argued that this repetitive daily drama is the central element in the popular theatrical drama, *Tjalonarang*, where the mother is depicted as a fearsome witch and the father (men never treat the children thus) as the puppyish dragon. M. Mead also found that Balinese mothers frequently teased their own babies by giving primary attention to another child, thus exacerbating peer group rivalry (M. Mead & Cooke Macgregor, 1951). One manner of such teasing was to raise another child above her own child's head, expressing the Balinese obsessive concern with the status implications of relative height and inducting the child into it.

Their study inspired me to review all the photographs of the Sebei of Uganda in my files to discover whether my impressions of the distanciated Sebei mothers could be documented (Goldschmidt, 1974, 1976). A photograph I had taken had haunted me; a young mother was walking along a path, a baby suckling at her breast, her hands neither directly on the child nor otherwise engaged and her eyes off in the middle distance (see Fig. 12.1). Sebei women (even child caretakers) hold the child by encircling it with their arms, the left hand grasping the right wrist so that neither hand is in direct contact with the baby. My files yielded 28 photographs taken under a variety of circumstances and without this purpose in mind that depicted mothers holding infants either on their laps or their hips. In only one instance was the mother making eye contact with her child and in none was the hand in direct contact with the child (except one where she was cupping it under the chin and filling it with gruel in what seemed a harsh way to feed a baby). No photos, other than posed

Fig. 12.1. Sebei woman holding her child in typical depersonalized manner.

ones, showed a father holding a baby, and I have no recollection of ever seeing it. This does not mean that mothers never look at or fathers never hold their children, but it suggests an endemic sense of detachment, of emotional disengagement. This reflects an aspect of Sebei cultural demeanor: the lack of affective ties. Sebei social relations are instrumental rather than sentimental. This lack of ties, of commitment, is reflected in Sebei institutions; their rituals lack any expression of glorification of either Sebei-dom or of the clan or any other social entity within it. The wedding ritual seems calculated to intensify hostile relations between the bride and groom as well as between their respective families (Goldschmidt, 1976).

The only carefully formulated study of cultural variation in child care was conducted by Caudill on Japanese and U.S. middle-class mothers with their first child at the age of about 10 weeks (Caudill & Weinstein, 1969). The study involved a sample from each, matched as carefully as possible; observations were made of the interaction between mother and infant at strictly controlled time intervals that yielded a body of statistically analyzable data. He found that the Japanese babies whimpered more and cried less than the U.S. ones and explained this by aspects of the housing situation and customary use of space—the Japanese infant almost always being in the same room with the mother, the U.S. child most often upstairs in its own room. He also found that U.S. mothers talk to their infants more and stimulate them more with toys and the like and, reflexively, that the U.S. infants were themselves more given to babbling and were more manipulative than their Japanese counterparts. Caudill found cultural reasons for the differential behaviors of the mothers; specifically that U.S. mothers were compensating for the fact that they were frequently away from their children because they were part-time mothers, whereas Japanese mothers gave their total attention to the family and therefore did not feel the need to make such a special effort. (We must remember that these observations were made some 30 years ago and need not apply to today's customary behavior.) Caudill appears to have been more interested in the cultural determinants of maternal behavior than in the cultural outcome of their interaction with their children. He did not suggest what consequences these infantile experiences might have had for the formulation of the respective cultural outlook of the two peoples. All we can say is that the style of child care in the two cultures is different and the infants' comportment reflects these differences.

Kilbride and Kilbride (1974; also J. E. Kilbride, Robbins, & P. L. Kilbride, 1970) investigated aspects of infant care among the Baganda. They focused on smiling and sitting because earlier studies had found Baganda children to be more precocious with respect to these two attributes than U.S. children. They reported that the Baganda mothers consciously sought to develop these two traits in their children by forcing them to sit up and by actively inducing smiling responses. The former of these was important to them because at the age of 3 months, the infant undergoes a ritual in which he or she must be able to sit up in order to establish legitimacy and clan affiliation. These attributes are directly relevant to traditional Baganda cultural values, which place great emphasis on ingratiating behavior and bodily self-control. These qualities were essential to gaining preference at the Kabaka's court and set the tone for the whole culture; they are still manifested among the Baganda today. Indeed, they are equally valuable in the domestic menage, for Baganda household heads create a miniature replica of the Kabaka's court and mothers in these traditionally polygynous households want their children to have favor in the eyes of these domestic autocrats (Richards, 1964).

A study of attachment in two German cities (Grossman, Fremmer-Bombik, & Rudolph, 1988) illustrates cultural differentials and local continuity with respect to this aspect of childrearing. The authors show that women who have little or negative sense of attachment to their parents tend to have children who make unsatisfactory attachments to them. They said: "The findings reported here show strong relations between the mother's attachment representations [of her relationship with her parents] and her behaviour toward her infant as well as her infant's pattern of attachment to her" (p. 254). They presented the differential responses in the two cities, one in northern and the other in southern Germany, but did not remark on them despite the fact that they are quite at variance, for in the northern city only 25% of the mothers were on the positive side in their attitudes toward their parents, compared to 55% in the southern city. Again, only 30% of the children showed secure attachment in the north compared to 58% in the south. These differences are in accord with the stricter control of behavior in northern Germany as compared with southern Germany and reflect the public recognition of the difference in cultural tonus between these two regions. A finding that also shows the unconscious transmission of social sentiment was made in a review of the longitudinal data from the Berkeley Guidance Study (Caspi & Elder, 1988), where the researchers found a significant continuity between personal instability, marital conflict, and nonoptimal parenting and back to personal instability extending over a period of four generations. These are, of course, individual differences within a common culture.

The quality of attachment that a child receives is found to be related to its level of competence, and one study (Bretherton, Bates, Beningni, Camioni, & Volterra, 1979) has shown that the area of competence varies with the pattern of maternal stimulation. Thus those mothers that emphasize verbal behavior have children who are more verbal; those that emphasize object manipulation have children who are more dexterous. This reinforces the findings of Caudill discussed earlier.

My final example is drawn from the work of the lay analyst, Erikson (1943), among the Yurok Indians of northwestern California. The Yurok share with a few of their neighbors a remarkable culture, unique among preneolithic peoples, so far as I know. They place great emphasis on individual achievement; status and power are acquired by means of the accumulation of wealth, which ideally is obtained through personal effort (although as elsewhere in the world, a good inheritance is helpful). The wealth items are for the most part religious objects, paraphernalia for various sacred rituals, but are also used in such secular transfers as brideprice and compensation as a result of litigation. Legal conflict is a very important aspect of Yurok culture and a man is expected to take legal action and demand compensation for any delict, even if it is no more than a verbal insult. Yurok individualism is expressed not only in this endemic litigiousness, but also conversely in the absence of fixed social groups (such as clans) or of inherited social roles (even religious leadership is dependent on accumulated wealth). Social ties beyond the level of household can best be thought of as institutionalized personal networks that are always subject to renegotiation.

Under these circumstances there is, as one might expect, a strong demand for selfcontrol with respect to sex, food, and most particularly work habits. In all this they mimic, so to say, the characteristics of both the Protestant ethic and the spirit of capitalism as set forth by Weber (Goldschmidt, 1951; Weber, 1958). Yurok uptight industriousness, avarice, competitiveness, and the like, form a classic syndrome of what in Freudian theory is called the anal-compulsive personality. This was thought to be the result of traumatic toilet training, especially with respect to the bowels. In view of his Freudian training (and the spirit of the time), Erikson was seeking evidence in Yurok toilet training for the etiology of these Yurok characterological traits, but he found no tensions surrounding infantile elimination. Instead, there was a compulsive concern with eating, industriousness, and self-control that began while the mother was still carrying the infant. Not only is she subjected to food taboos, but she is supposed to be very energetic and avoid any posture that would let the infant "rest against her spine" (Erikson, 1943, p. 289). When the child is born, it is not breast-fed for ten days and is weaned much earlier than is the Native American norm. The infant is rubbed and exercised so it will become an active child. Like the Baganda, the Yurok are purposeful in their efforts to transform their infants into the kind of people that meet the Yurok ideal. In this they have apparently been quite successful, for the Yurok still demonstrate their traditional traits of character today; for instance, other California Indians find it useful to have Indian interests represented at the state capitol by Yurok, who still display their ancient manipulative skills.

Although we may fault these ethnographic studies just reviewed for their theoretical presuppositions, methodological naiveté, and lack of focus, they nevertheless give support to a number of generalizations of great significance to the transition of human beings from their biological beginnings to their adult cultural performance. First, the style of child care varies from one culture to another. Sometimes the elements of this style are consciously promulgated behavior (e.g., Baganda, Yurok); at other times they appear to be entirely outside of consciousness (e.g., Sebei), or they may be secondary consequences of other cultural elements (e.g., Japanese–American contrast). Undoubtedly in each case there is actually a mixture of all three. Second, the style of child care involves affective relations that transmit to the infant feelings about others in its social surrounding and probably also affect how it feels about its own performance and thus about itself. Third, whether consciously promulgated or not, these elements of style can be seen to be products of the cultural qualities of the community; the mother is consciously or unconsciously behaving in accordance with local norms and cultural expectations. Finally, the style sets the moral or social tone of the future adult, thus forming that feedback loop that makes for the cultural continuity that mimics genetic transfer.

CONCLUDING OBSERVATIONS

Because these studies were made with a different paradigm in mind and by scholars who, except for Caudill, did not use an experimental approach, the results can give us only limited insight into the role of nonverbal communication between parents and children in the transmission of culture. Nevertheless, they clearly tell us that such communication varies from one culture to another and that these have an effect on the outlook and emotional tonus of the child. We see in this the transmission of cultural traits carried across generations and hence the continuity of the characteristic emotional life of peoples. Like all matters cultural, they are amenable to change, although it is probably the case that, because they are so much out of awareness, they are more resistant to alteration than other aspects of culture. The studies can only be suggestive as to just what kinds of parental communication bring on what kinds of sentiments in the child. For the answer to this question it will be necessary to initiate detailed crosscultural examination of this aspect of behavior, one built on a more modern psychological paradigm.

ACKNOWLEDGMENT

I am indebted to Peter Molnár and R. A. Hinde for their helpful comments on an earlier draft of this chapter.

REFERENCES

Ainsworth, M. D. (1967). *Infancy in Uganda: Infant care and the growth of love.* Baltimore: Johns Hopkins University Press.

Anisfeld, M., Masters, J. C., Jacobson, S., & Kagan, J. (1979). Interpreting "imitative" responses in early infancy. *Science, 205,* 214–219.

Bateson, G., & Mead, M. (1942). *Balinese character: A photographic analysis.* New York: New York Academy of Sciences.

Bowlby, J. (1971). *Attachment.* London: Penguin.

Bretherton, I., Bates, E., Beningni, L., Camioni, L., & Volterra, V. (1979). Relationships between cognitions. Communication and quality of attachment. In E. Bates (Ed.), *The emergence of symbols: Cognition and communication in infancy* (pp. 223–270). New York: Academic Press.

Caspi, A., & Elder, G. H. (1988). Emergent family patterns: The intergenerational construction of problem behaviour and relationship. In R. A. Hinde & J. Stevenson-Hinde (Eds.), *Relations within families: Mutual influences* (pp. 218–240). Oxford, UK: Oxford University Press.

Caudill, W., & Weinstein, H. (1969). Maternal care and infant behavior in Japan and America. *Psychiatry, 32,* 12–42.

DeCasper, A. J., & Fifer, W. P. (1980). Of human bonding: Newborns prefer their mothers' voices. *Science, 208,* 1174–1176 .

Ekman, P., Levenson, R. W., & Friesen, W. V. (1983). Autonomic nervous system activity distinguishes among emotions. *Science, 221,* 1208–1210.

Erikson, E. H. (1943). Observations on the Yurok: Childhood and world image. *University of California Publications in American Archaeology and Ethnology, 35,* 257–302.

Field, T. M., Woodson, R., Greenberg, R., & Cohen, D. (1982). Discrimination and imitation of facial expressions by neonates. *Science, 218,* 179–181,.

Geschwind, N. (1979). Specialization in the human brain. *Scientific American, 241,* 180–201.

Goldschmidt, W. (1951). Ethics and the structure of society. *American Anthropologist, 53,* 506–524.

Goldschmidt, W. (1974). Absent eyes and idle hands. *Ethos, 3,* 157–163.

Goldschmidt, W. (1976). *The culture and behavior of the Sebei.* Berkeley: University of California Press.

Goldschmidt, W. (1990). *The human career: The self in the symbolic world.* Cambridge, MA: Basil Blackwell.

Goldschmidt, W. (1993). On the relatonship between biology and anthropology. *Man (N.S.), 28,* 341–359.

Grossman, K., Fremmer-Bombik, E., & Rudolph, J. (1988). Maternal attachment representations as related to patterns of infant–mother attachment and maternal care during the first year. In R. A. Hinde & J. Stevenson-Hinde (Eds.), *Relationships within families* (pp. 241–262). Oxford, UK: Oxford University Press.

Harlow, H. (1959). Love in infant monkeys. *Scientific American, 20,* 2–8.

Johnson, M. H., Dziurawiec, S., Ellis, H., & Morton, J. (1991). Newborns' preferential tracking of face-like stimuli and its subsequent decline. *Cognition, 40,* 1–19.

Kilbride, J. E., Robbins, M. C., & Kilbride, P. L. (1970). The comparative motor development of Baganda, American white and American black infants. *American Anthropologist, 72,* 1422–1428.

Kilbride, P. L., & Kilbride, J. E. (1974). Sociocultural factors and the early manifestation of sociability behavior among Baganda infants, *Ethos, 2,* 296–314.

Mead, M., & Cooke Macgregor, F. C. (1951). *Growth and culture: A photographic essay of Balinese childhood.* New York: P.G. Putnam's Sons.

Meltzoff, A. N. (1985). The roots of social and cognitive development: Models of man's original nature. In T. M. Field & N. Fox (Eds.), *Social perception in infants* (pp. 1–30). Norwood, NJ: Ablex.

Meltzoff, A. N., & Moore, M. K. (1977). Imitation of facial and manual gestures in human neonates. *Science, 198,* 75–78.

Molnár, P. (1990). A kapaszkodasi reflex humanetologiai megkozelitese (A human ethology explanation of clinging reflex). *Pszichologia, 3,* 441–446.

Papoušek, H., & Papoušek, M. (1979). Early ontogeny of human social interaction: Its biological roots and social dimensions. In M. von Cranach, K. Foppa, W. Lepenies, & D. Ploog (Eds.), *Human ethology: Claims and limits of a new discipline* (pp. 456–478). Cambridge, UK: Cambridge University Press.

Richards, A. I. (1964). Authority patterns in traditional Baganda. In L. A. Fallers (Ed.), *The king's men: Leadership and status on the eve of independence* (pp. 256–293). Oxford, UK: Oxford University Press.

Spitz, R. (1965). *The first year of life: A study of normal and deviant development of object relations.* New York: International Universities Press.

Trevarthen, C. (1979). Instincts for understanding and for cultural cooperation: Their development in infancy. In M. von Cranach, K. Foppa, W. Lepenies, & D. Ploog (Eds.), *Human ethology: Claims and limits of a new discipline* (pp.). Cambridge, UK: Cambridge University Press.

Weber, M. (1958). *The protestant ethic and the spirit of capitalism.* New York: Scribner's.

13

POSTURE AS AN INTERFACE BETWEEN BIOLOGY AND CULTURE

Michel Heller
University of Geneva

Classical notions of the balance between natural and cultural causes of behavior have generated two extreme formulations about body movement. On the one hand, there are the practitioners of medicine, from yoga to contemporary physiotherapy, who approach body movement as a holistic biomechanical entity regulating the body's structure and dynamics in relation to gravity: "All movement, whatever its purpose may be, like closing the eyes when remembering or thinking, is, in the last analysis, an antigravity action" involving the whole body (Feldenkreis, 1981, p. 95). Whereas any chronic deformation (lordosis, chronically shortened muscles, fat) of physioanatomy reduces the possible behavioral repertoire of an individual, the field has also accumulated an impressive list of chronic "deformations" induced by social rituals: The current "sit straight!" of European etiquette is known to have induced many crooked spines. Thus, the conclusion is that society perverts our "natural" gifts. In fact, many practitioners ask "society" to adapt its demands on behavior so that only those congruent with physical, and eventually psychological, health requirements would be supported. However, the fact is that our world does not really care for our body structure and continuously makes simultaneous contradictory demands on our organisms.

On the other hand, we have the social sciences, which have mostly analyzed the communicative functions of body parts individually, or in various configurations, without taking into account the global body configuration. This approach has been sensitive to facts showing how the body movements of a person may have strong impact on the psychophysiology of others. For instance, asking another person to modify his or her "shocking" behavior is based on such assumptions. However, we should remember that behavior is also related to our inner being. Without this, individual communicative behavior becomes meaningless. Elias (1991), for example, analysed the function of table manners in the history of European culture, but did not ask the question of what the behavior he described does to an individual.

One can think of an organism as functioning simultaneously like a robot and a puppet: moved by inner cogwheels (biomechanics) and outer strings (social interaction), the strings being made of nerves or invisible social rules. Body configurations only become meaningful in relation to issues that are being dealt with during a communicative interaction. This point was recently discussed in some detail by Lazarus (1991) in his discussion of emotional behavior. For Lazarus:

> emotions are like no other psychophysiological construct in that they express the intimate personal meaning of what is happening in our social lives and combine motivational, cognitive, adaptational, and physiological processes into a single complex state that involves several levels of analysis. The emotional reaction itself reflects and includes the perception of a changed person-environment relationship, and serves as a compelling signal that something of significance is occurring. (pp. 6ff)

POSTURE

The study of posture is a classical example of behavioral research at the interface between physiology and culture. In studies on nonverbal communication, posture is first of all related to various global configurations of the body, such as standing, sitting, squatting, and lying down. Such factors as legs crossed or not crossed, or forward or backward lean, are used to distinguish between various kinds of postures such as different ways of sitting (E. T. Hall, 1963; Mehrabian, 1969). Argyle and Kendon (1967) subdivided body communication in three hierarchically related levels:

1. "We distinguish at the *level of general orientation* how individuals may adopt a distinctive pattern of activities appropriate for, say, an interview, a cocktail party or a stroll on the beach with a friend" (p. 59). This level includes standing features defined through such variables as interpersonal distance, posture, orientation. It forms the "the backdrop for a particular flow of events, just as sitting in a particular posture at the typewriter may be said to form a backdrop to the action of typing" (p. 67).

2. "At the *level of general methods or subplans* we note, for instance, an interview may have several phases: an opening greeting phase; a phase in which rapport is established; one in which the main business of the interview may be accomplished; and a terminating phase" (p. 59). This level includes behaviors that do not require modifications at the previous level.

3. "At the *level of knacks and dexterities*, we deal with such things as sequencing of acts of communication. Below this level, we must analyse the actual muscular movements" (p. 59). These levels are taken to be *dynamic features* that are analyzed through those variables that are "framed" by standing features: specific actions involved in typing, for example (eye, hand, and finger movements).

For some psychologists who take biomechanics into account, posture is the medium through which most aspects of behavior are coordinated (see, e.g., Bullinger, 1980). It is also possible to do a biomechanical analysis of body behavior at three levels similar to those identified by Argyle and Kendon, which I describe using Rodin's "thinker" as an example:

A. Base Level

Mechanical activity is dependent on the stability of its base: how our body is supported and how it relates to this support. This aspect of behavior belongs to what Birdwhistell (1970) called "base-body phenomena" (p. 203), defined as those aspects of body movement that are "sustained throughout any interactional sequence". The main functions of this base level seem to be the organization of a situation. Musicians, for example, pay much attention to how they organize their base so that their hands can be freed as much as possible from gravity constraints. In choosing a comfortable position, they also create a certain relation with the (social) space that surrounds them. The base can be defined as including all parts of the body touching the support surfaces. In Rodin's thinker, the base is formed by feet, legs, and bottom, which distribute the body's weight on the supporting surface (ground and stool).

B. Intermediary Level

Often, although not always, parts of the body are heaped on top of the base. The weight of the thinker's head rests on the right hand; this weight is then transferred to the base via the right elbow and the right knee. The arm here forms a sort of beam connecting head and base. This intermediary *level* can be defined as including all parts of the body in autocontact, and its main function seems to be autoregulation (of breathing, blood circulation, etc.).

C. Surface Level

The base and intermediary levels are structured so as to allow certain specific actions. Given the introspective activity of the thinker, no parts of the body remain free for specific actions: All the parts of the body that could be used at this surface level are here in autoregulation. For a pianist, base and intermediary levels clearly support the freedom of head, arm, and hand movements. The surface level of posture is composed of all the parts of the body not used for the base: They are focused on objects requiring the attention of the more refined mechanisms of our motor functions (those dealing with objects, hand gestures, facial expressions, etc.).

At every moment, our actions are guided by the laws of postural dynamics: freeing some parts of the body for specific actions by using other parts to create a mechanical base.

SKELETONS

Leroi-Gourhan (1964, 1965) studied how body structure, body motion, and culture developed in constant interaction from fish to men, and from prehistoric times to today. Leroi-Gourhan (1964) distinguished the following skeletal types:

1. Horizontal *skeletons* (fish, snakes). Such skeletons have jaws that must capture, kill, cut, and swallow their prey. The rest of the body

is used for locomotion. Such a strategy requires very large jaws which weigh about as much as what a horizontal spine can carry.

2. *Horizontal skeletons with legs* (cats and dogs). The spine is higher than the ground, so that the head can drop without discomfort; it must not be attached as tightly to the spine. Limbs are used for displacement, and to capture kill and cut prey. Thus the jaws can be of a lighter structure. This mechanical organization leaves room (in terms of weight) for other functions of the head (expressiveness, more brain) than in snakes.

3. *Skeletons allowing erectness.* These skeletons are characterised by a clear differentiation between feet and hands: Feet are designed for locomotion, while hands are designed for fine manipulation of objects. The muscles attached to the spine are still required for the bearing of the head, but the head may also rest on the spine, as on a column. Hands helped by tools not only kill prey, but also cut it in small manageable pieces. When fire is discovered, food is softened, so that even lighter jaws are sufficient. Nature has now the possibility to develop even more expressive faces and a heavier brain. Erect posture, social organization more complex than that of monkeys, tools and probably language appeared simultaneously in our species at a time when our brains were smaller than those of today's chimpanzees. *Global posture* phenomena include all the levels of behaviour just described.

Leroi-Gourhan (1964) then described how the coevolution of our body design and cooperative and tool-making abilities promoted the further development of our brain. As our species developed, our stance became more erect, our societies more complex, our hands more skillful, our jaws lighter, our brains more efficient, and our faces more expressive. There is here a historical positive feedback, where the development of culture transformed our bodies as the development of our bodies transformed culture. Thus, the interaction between culture and body structure can be seen as a motor for the development of our behavioral potential.

One aspect of this history is a progressive freeing of certain parts of the body from having to deal with gravity, so that they may be more exclusively used for social activities. Culture accelerated this development by producing tools that could improve various functions of our bodies, thus freeing them even more drastically from physioanatomical constraints. Some of our actions on objects were enhanced by hammers, screwdrivers, and so on. Our mobility was increased by mastering horses, inventing steam engines, boats and planes; some of the most redundant activities related to our capacity to compute and memorize were aided by books, and today through computers. Statues, pictures, and later, film, have completely transformed how the body of a person may contact others. These examples illustrate the idea that even if some of our behaviors may have a physioanatomical similarity to other species, their functions may have been drastically modified.

CHAIRS

One of the basic questions of the conference on which this volume is based concerns the relationship between several levels of organization. I maintain that different levels may be in direct contact with each other, bypassing intermediary levels.

Let us take the example of the increasing time we spend sitting on chairs. There is an area of paramedical studies (as in Gangloff, Chan Tak Nam, & Lepoutre, 1984) centered on the design of chairs for specific professional activities. These studies show that too much sitting is bad for blood circulation, the shape of spines, lead to buildup of fat, and may cause psychological discomfort. Oversitting also seems to restrict our innate postural repertoire: Members of cultures who use "North American toilets," on which one sits, do not need to use squatting postures to survive. Indeed, many of us have become incapable of squatting or sitting in the lotus posture comfortably.

Before World War II, the Japanese had a highly varied postural repertoire for sitting, and few varicose veins. In contrast, varicose veins are already frequently observed in our societies, mostly in professions were one tends to use a single type of posture (always sitting, always standing, etc.). After World War II, as the Japanese began to use social behaviors similar to those in the United States and Europe, varicose veins increased steadily. Bourdieu (1984) described numerous examples of such mechanisms to point out how different lifestyles model our beings at the level of our physiological dynamics. He then showed how these bodily distinctions reinforce the differentiations between social groups.

Thus social trends directly influence our postural repertoire, and through this our psychophysiology and the ease with which we move. To approach such a problem, one has to start simultaneously at a physiological level and at the level of social fashions, bypassing a whole series of intermediary levels. For example, interpersonal dynamics is deeply influenced by the direct relationship between social structures and behavior: On the one hand, there are customs regulating when and how we should sit, on the other hand, a large number of people have developed an organic difficulty standing for a long time, or sitting following Japanese or Hindu customs. We have here an interaction between sociocultural customs, bodily mechanics, and physiology that seems to bypass psychological factors.

Every movement has a physiological price and every movement has a social price. The physiological price of a job is never included in the computation of a salary, but this price is then paid through medical institutions. Meanwhile, medical institutions tend to require that we only use social behaviors that follow physiological requirements. If we followed these recommendations to the letter, we might end up transforming our societies into sanatoriums. Human social behavior is in fact seldom congruent with physiological requirements as stated by such forms of knowledge as yoga or physiotherapy. There seems to be a certain independence between physiology and behavior that might be at the root of whatever freedom we have, as it allows us to explore a great variety of lifestyles, and to create social structures that have a logic of their own.

MEANING

A. Lévi-Strauss

In *Totémisme aujourd'hui*, Lévi-Strauss (1962b, see also 1962a) argued strongly against the idea that "natural" signs may have a "natural" meaning (as in totemism). One might think that a lion has the same symbolic meaning for all human beings, that a circle has the same meaning in all cultures, and so on. Indeed, as Frazer (1922) and Jung (1964) showed, one does observe a set of similar figures all around the world. Analyzing the meaning of animal symbols, Lévi-Strauss pointed out two things: (a) an animal seldom symbolizes the same thing in different cultures, and (b) it is also seldom the same aspects of an animal that are relevant. For example, in North America, certain Indians associated the sun with their good creator, whereas others compared it to a cannibal monster. Myths use already meaningful symbolic entities of a culture in a quasi-arbitrary way to form semantic dimensions. Signs then acquire their communicational meaning through the dimension they are included in, and through their capacity to distinguish and coordinate semantic dimensions.

A lion and an eagle may form a common semantic axis as kings of earthly beasts and of celestial ones, respectively. In this opposition, one concentrates on qualities such as big, powerful, beautiful, fierce, and carnivorous, to form a unit in which heaven and earth are opposed. In another culture, a lion may be opposed to a green snake to represent the difference between the dangers of the desert and the dangers of the grass. In this case, ferocity and skin color are the relevant semantic dimensions. Lévi-Strauss described a tribe in which eagles symbolize earth: They associate eagles with lightning, lightning with fire, fire with coal, coal with earth, and therefore eagles with earth.

For Lévi-Strauss, human consciousness is not capable of coordinating numerous dimensions simultaneously. Yet reality confronts us continuously with its complexity. A ritual often coordinates clan rules, marriage rules, economic considerations, regulation of food, emotional responses, phenomena related to climate and seasons, and so on. A symbolic act allows the member of a culture to adapt fairly adequately to such complexities even when he or she is not aware of all that is at stake. Available symbolic entities address our unconscious and conscious mental capacities with culturally developed know-how. The construction of these systems uses all existing devices available for symbolization, natural and social.

Against this background one interesting question is how biology may be used to communicate meaning. Research influenced by Darwin has accumulated evidence showing that human behavior uses at least two communication systems developed through phylogeny. The first system is related to *physiological mobilizations* associated with emotional displays through vegetative modifications of skin and hair, posture, and facial expressions (e.g., fear). The second system, used for *status display*, is based on set ways of regulating behavior and *gravity* (e.g., posture).

Through these systems we have automatic ways of associating psychophysiological states with various types of nonverbal communication, generated by us or by those who interact with us. Bodily configurations generated by such communication systems are often called *expressions*. This term may be misleading, because it suggests that these displays are mostly ways of providing information and an autoregulation of a person's feelings. As Siegfried Frey (1996) suggested, the major function of such communicative devices may be to regulate psychophysiologies interpersonally.

In the following, I illustrate some modalities of these systems. Imagine a person who sits straight during a meal. He or she avoids distributing weight on the table through arms and hands. The weight of the upper body (head, neck, shoulders, arms, and trunk) is transmitted directly to the base (bottom and feet) through back muscles and spine. Everybody has a personal experience of what such behavior requires, and how it "frees" a maximum of surface posture for social interaction.

Imagine now instead that you are attending a very formal scientific lecture. Suddenly the speaker produces a clear "apish expression" of disgust as described by Darwin and Ekman. Several things will occur at once:

- You will not only perceive the disgust, but also suppose that other members of the audience have perceived it.
- You will undoubtedly feel an emotional charge rise in you, and assume that others have a similar reaction.
- Although your emotional reaction may have more individual connotations, you may still have a tendency to think the other members of the audience feel the same.
- If the speaker uses such expressions often, you will probably suppose that other members of the audience also find this speaker unconventional, or even exotic.

This has been picked up by some theater schools. Some of these—like Stanislavsky's—use apish expressions often, whereas other schools such as Craig's or Bob Wilson's tend to avoid using them even when they want to create emotional sensations in their public. From the latter point of view it is the atmosphere created by a coordination of music, gesture, and use of space and light that is effective; and "expressions" are only one of the means through which a given atmosphere can be created.

Darwin (1872/1965) repeatedly wrote that as a "package" the expressions he described may not "be of the least use" (p. 28) for humans. The implication of such a statement is that an individual probably has other more resourceful means of regulating his or her emotional life than the "apish" behaviors just discussed. For example, Elias (1991) mentioned how good manners can also be used to regulate and self-regulate emotions.

The idea I am trying to convey through these examples is that these innate biological behavior modalities are in themselves culturally conditioned *repertoires*. They are ready-made sets of communicative possibilities. The fact that someone is using one of these possibilities invariably elicits two different reactions in us: On the one hand, a reaction to the very fact that such a repertoire is being used (the fact that "apish" expressions are indeed addressed by culture is clearly seen, e.g., when parents ask their children to "behave" and show less emotion, be it anger, sadness, happiness, etc.), and on the other hand, a reaction to the specific emotion exhibited.

Thus, applying Lévi-Strauss' model to behavior implies first describing the general repertoire of a species, a culture, a person, and then seeing how such biological communication packages are used to convey a particular meaning. By relating these biological repertoires to other types of repertoires, we might evaluate the importance and the functions of these communicative devices.

REPERTOIRE VERSUS SIGNALS

Most researchers interested in nonverbal behavior gather an immense amount of information on a few samples of behavior in the form of coded data. Next, they process the data with the hope of finding statistically significant distinctions, which can be related to relevant hypotheses. The end product may be a few stunning results that give no idea of the vast amount of material collected for the study. Methodology seems to require that we act as if what we present is the only data we have collected. This research strategy often turns out to be a complicated way of showing the existence of phenomena we have known about for centuries, in this case the existence of standardized behavior patterns such as body signals. That certain standardized behaviors are used in communication, and that some of these have a biological history, seems to be an empirically sound finding. However, publications seldom mention what a small part of all the coded data is covered by these findings, and therefore what a vast amount of communicative behaviors cannot be described by research on body signals, a point I illustrate empirically in the following.

The mass of data sleeping in forgotten files contain what is required to carry out the first part of Lévi-Strauss' program: a description of the immense, but not infinite, body repertoire of our species. The interest of such a huge research program, if it could be carried out, would be to gather information on those a priori structures of our communicative behavior that make communication possible. What I would now like to present is the notion that, for our species, repertoire may often be a more relevant communication unit than signals.

Repertoire is the listing of all the observed behavior configurations of a group of subjects. There is a repertoire of eye positions, of facial configurations, and so on; each part of the body can only take a restricted number of clear-cut positions; postural configurations are numerous, but again not infinite. Hewes (1955, 1957) showed that postural repertoire varies culturally. An example of this has already been discussed: In Far Eastern cultures people use various forms of squatting comfortably, whereas in European cultures these postures are today often avoided.

The notion of behavior repertoire implies that in one group subjects have access to a series of possible postures, whereas in another group they have access to another series of possible postures. The two repertoires are like two packs of cards. There may be common postures in both packs, but taken as a whole the choice of cards that the members of a group can draw is not the same. In this metaphor a sign is a card, a repertoire a pack of cards. My thesis is that communication implies first of all the choice of a game and a pack of cards; it is only then that the presentation of a card begins to convey a meaning.

Considering repertoire the basic unit for meaningful communication seems reasonable for at least two reasons. First, it is difficult to believe that the communication of any given social behavior would require only a specific expression (or a set of them). If we really functioned this way, studies on nonverbal behavior would already have yielded more spectacular results than what is now published. Communication by repertoire makes it possible to perceive the fact that something is being communicated, although the contribution of each individual sign to the overall meaning may be unclear, and the communication may be only partially reliable.

Second, access to repertoire does not mean that the behavior is fully determined. For instance, burial rituals are partially consciously structured (e.g. I am told where to stand), but nobody ever told me exactly how I should behave in such a situation. Yet, I somehow have a vague feeling of what sort of behaviors I dare display and which ones I would not even dream of using. Access to repertoire in such a standardized situation as a burial is not the same thing as knowig exactly what to do.

This capacity or competence only comes with experience. This seems to be similar to our competence for grammar. According to Chomsky (1980), we can produce an infinite number of grammatically correct new sentences, and just as easily detect "wrong" sentences. What he said about language could equally well be applied to the notion of repertoire: "We construct new sentences freely and use them on appropriate occasions, just as we comprehend new sentences that we hear in novel circumstances, generally bringing much more than our knowledge of language to the performance of these creative acts" (p. 222).

POSTURAL DYNAMICS AND SOCIAL STATUS

A. Method

I now move on to discuss status display, the second of the communicative systems mentioned earlier. To illustrate the notion of repertoire in this realm, I present some results from my research on postural dynamics and social status (Heller, 1992).

The research took place in two different institutions, at a university and a school of nursing. Here we recorded the body movements from the front and profile of participants in semistructured interviews that lasted about 7 minutes. In these interviews, an experimenter asked a subject whether she thought that there existed a relationship between social status and body behavior (all experimenters and subjects were female). Twelve such situations were filmed in a university. The experimenters were six first-year students, who each interviewed another first-year student as well as an assistant to the faculty. The order of these two interviews was randomized. Eigteen situations were filmed in the school of nursing. Here, the experimenters were nine first-year students, who each interviewed both another first-year student and a teacher from the school, again in a randomized order.

In all, we coded 60 samples and 45 participants. The code and method used to analyze posture were derived from Frey, Hirsbrunner, Florin, Daw, and Crawford's (1983) *Time Series Notation System*. In the following, I illustrate how this method was used to compute two measures: base surface repertoire and global posture.

I was advised to scan social behavior using the postural angle, with the hope that I might find "typical postures" for each status variable: difference between institutions, between higher and lower status within an institution, and between experimenter and subject. I ended up with the conclusion that there are probably no such typical postures unless they are produced consciously by an acted form of ritual, and that the notion of group repertoire might be more relevant. The data led me to the notion that in everyday situations what seems to be relevant is to associate social status with certain bodily dimensions that push possible bodily combinations in certain directions rather than others: thus producing a reduced group of possible postures that I call *group repertoire*.

Base surface is described as the list of parts of the body touching chair or floor at a given moment. Average base surface is the average number of parts of the body touching the chair or floor in a situation. This measure provides information on the stability of a posture in relation to gravity.

For base surface I coded the following 26 parts of the body: right and left hands, wrists, arms, elbows, upper arms, shoulders, upper back, lower back, flanks, bottom, upper legs, lower legs, and feet. For each part of the body I used a two dimension code: 0 (no touch), 1 (touch). The base surface configuration observed at a given moment is then described by a number such as this:

```
01001100110011001100110011
```

The two first numbers are right and left hands, and the two last numbers are right and left feet. I checked the position of every part of the body every half of a second. People do not move much in base posture, so coding was carried out in 6 months (one only notes down changes and the time at which they occur). Behavior was standard for such situations, which means probably less varied than in many others.

How many different ways of sitting were observed using such a simple code, in such a standardized setting, in the 60 samples? To answer this question, I just counted how many different configurations of 0 and 1 were coded. The answer is 104 different base posture configurations among university participants, 261 base posture configurations among school of nursing participants, and 346 in all.

To study *global posture* I focused on the school of nursing films. Coding was still kept as simple as possible. I needed to code more parts of the body for this coding (head, belly, knees, etc.), amounting to 47 items. The 36 school of nursing samples yielded 984 configurations of autocontact, and 1.501 different global postural configurations.

RESULTS

A few results will show what sort of phenomena can be considered common denominators of group repertoire. I first discuss base surface results (1–5) and thereafter autocontact results (6–10)

A. Base Surface Results

1. University and school of nursing participants had clearly different base surface behavior. Nurses had a tendency to use bigger average base surfaces than university participants.
2. Nurses had a clear tendency to touch the back of their seats with more parts of their backs than university participants.
3. Nurses often touched the side of their chairs with their lower leg, whereas this was never seen with university participants.

These phenomena seem to be generated by the tendency nurses had of sitting further back on the seat than university participants. We thus have a basic fact (distance), and a whole series of consequences on postural behavior at all levels. Although there seems to be a social law related to these observations (nurses have a greater interpersonal distance than university participants), how this law is exemplified varies considerably from one individual to another, from one dyad to another. Those nurses who lean forward maintain a bigger base surface by having both their legs and feet in contact with the chair. In other cases it is mostly arms and hands that compensate for the legs' lack of support. In a case where configurations have such a variance, the notion of signal does not seem to apply.

4. In the school of nursing, students had a tendency to create distance, whereas university students seemed more intrusive, often leaning forward. They seemed to have the strategy of wanting to "extract" information from subjects.
5. The university assistants had a tendency to "freeze" their base posture, whereas the school of nursing teachers seemed more mobile. Furthermore, we know that base surface repertoire was small in the different status dyads in the university setting.

The whole strategy in the dyads differs in the two institutions. In the university, students were more aggressive, whereas assistants did not dare to move too much. In the school of nursing, the students were more respectful and the teachers (who also have a more clearly differentiated status from students) were more at ease. These results are independent of the participants' opinion of the relation between status and bodily behavior.

B. Autocontact

The front of the body is "softer" than the back. This is mostly true for the space that spreads from the throat to the genitals, which can be referred to as *ventral surface*. This surface is discussed in the literature as relevant for phylogenetically inherited dominance behaviors: Exposing these parts of the body often conveys trust or power when one is not in a very "safe" situation. In this experiment exposure of these parts was measured by average ventral autocontact surface: How many parts of this area are touched by another part of the body (mostly hands and arms, or crossed legs for the lower abdomen and genitals)? Mehrabian (1968, 1969, 1981) and Henley (1977), among others, labeled postures with exposed ventral surface as "open" and postures with protected ventral surfaces as "closed."

6. In the school of nursing, all participants used fairly open postures; nevertheless, nurse subjects more often than nurse experimenters had something touching their ventral surface. Experimenters had a fairly "open" attitude toward subjects, as if they wanted to leave space for subjects to answer. This observation is coherent with what we already observed on base posture. Subjects had a tendency to have always at least a hand in front of their chest.

7. Mean ventral autocontact was related to personal style: Comparing experimenters when interviewing fellow students and when interviewing teachers, one could notice that, although there may be strong individual differences, each individual correlated with herself.

8. Mean ventral autocontact had a specific effect: It differentiated role (subject–experimenter), but not status (teacher–student).

9. Autocontact instability did not vary in relation to role, but autocontact instability of the ventral surface did.

10. Leg autocontact instability varied in relation to two variables for experimenters: personal style and the status of the subject.

DISCUSSION

This study showed that body behavior simultaneously adapts itself to several variables in a highly differentiated way: General autocontact mobility is mostly sensitive to the pupil–teacher polarity, ventral autocontact surface and mobility are mostly sensitive to the experimenter–subject polarity, and autocontact mobility of the legs is mostly sensitive to the influence of the pupil–teacher polarity of subjects on experimenters.

A single variable often acts through a coordinated construction of behavior. Nurse experimenters sit as far back as possible from their subjects. This behavior supports a whole series of body regulations that can be related to a general strategy: Nurse experimenters want to show that they are creating a space that the subjects are required to fill. The general attitude, well known in therapeutic ethics, is to be at the service of the other (it is certainly what one tries to teach first-year students). This strategy manifests itself through a large base surface and an exposed ventral surface. In a similar way, the observation that teachers in the school of nursing are more at ease than university assistants is supported by data on both base and autocontact surfaces.

Once such an "attitude" has been developed, one notices that it is rather a system of rules than a signal system: Every individual seems to have the same inner rule, but applies it differently. This is probably due as much to varying personal representations of the rule as to the behavior of others. The important finding here is that all members of a group follow rules that seem to be specific for their group.

Comparing role and status displays in both institutions, one notices that often they did not manifest themselves through the same body variables. Teacher–student and assistant–student differences influenced the same variable, base surface instability, but with reversed rules: Students changed posture more often than assistants, and teachers more often then pupils. Nurse experimenters gave space to their subjects; university experimenters were extracting information from their subjects. Everything happened as if each situation had its rules, its issues, its "core relational" themes, and as if people somehow had access to these rules and found ways to act as a result of them. Students of child development (e.g., Papoušek & Papoušek, chap. 6, this volume) have shown the intense training we all have as infants to develop this capacity for rule interpretation, which is clearly a universal requirement for social life.

CONCLUSION

Institution, status, role, and individual style were found to exert a differential influence on various aspects of postural behavior. The results shown here are only a selection (Heller, 1992), focusing on a single part of the body for a short time sample. Looking at the same samples, not taking individual differences into account, one might generate highly significant results showing that the social variables considered in this study could be correlated to those body signals, through which the persons I observed regulated status display. However, this conclusion could only be arrived at by eliminating most of the observable behavior.

There are too many relevant signals and too many fine distinctions for behavior to be processed by a communication system responding in a univocal way to signs. The data suggest, rather, the construction of a system that allows for parallel communication. My basic hunch is that body signs, as such, have a poor communicative capacity. Signs are used for very precise and simple meanings, toward which the attention of the communicator must be drawn in a dramatic way. Their main function could be that of accentuating a given chord of a communicative score, or of drawing another person's attention to a melody he or she might not notice. I am presenting the concept of body repertoire in a way that suggests that we communicate first of all by choosing a set of repertoires, and only secondarily by signs. Similar suggestions have been made, for example, by Stern (1990) on infant–mother interaction, and Inhelder and de Caprona (1992) on cognitive development. This new way of looking at nonverbal communication may open up interesting perspectives for future research.

REFERENCES

Argyle, M., & Kendon, A. (1967). The experimental analysis of social performance. In L. Berkowitz (Ed.), *Advances in experimental social psychology* (pp. 55–92). New York: Academic Press.

Birdwhistell, R. L. (1970). *Kinesics and context. Essays on body motion communication.* Philadelphia: University of Pennsylvania Press.

Bourdieu, P. (1984). *Distinction. A social critique of the judgement of taste.* Cambridge, MA: Harvard University Press.

Bullinger, A. (1980). *Posture et occulomotricité (Posture and ocular motor behavior)* (pp. 18–20). *Enfance, 4–5.*

Chomsky, N. (1980). *Rules and representations.* Oxford, UK: Basil Blackwell.

Darwin, C. (1965). *The expression of the emotions in man and animals.* Chicago: The University of Chicago Press. (Original work published 1872)

Elias, N. (1991). *La civilisation des moeurs (The civilization of behavior).* Paris: Calmann-Lévy.

Feldenkreis, M. (1981). *Body and mature behavior. A study of anxiety, sex, gravitation and learning.* New York: International Universities Press.

Frazer, J. (1922). *The golden bough.* London: MacMillan.

Frey, S., Hirsbrunner, H.-P., Florin, A., Daw, W., & Crawford, R. (1983). A unified approach to the investigation of nonverbal and verbal behavior in communication research. In W. Doise & S. Moscovici (Eds.), *Current issues in European social psychology* (Vol. 1, pp. 143–200). Cambridge, UK: Cambridge University Press.

Frey, S. (1996). Prejudice and the theory of inferential communication. In I. Eibl-Eibesfeldt & F. Salter (Eds.), *Indoctrinability, Warefare, and Ideology: Evolutionary Perspectives.* Oxford, UK: Berghan (in print).

Gangloff, B., Chan Tak Nam, J. C., & Lepoutre, F. X. (1984). Etude ergonomique des sièges de secrétariat: Définition d'une problématique (Ergonomic study concerning secretarial seats: Definition of a problem). *Le Travail Humain, vol. 47*(4), 329–349.

Hall, E. T. (1963). A system for the notation of proxemic behavior. *American Anthropologist, 57,* 1003–1026.

Heller, M. (1992). *Postural dynamics and social status.* Unpublished doctoral dissertation, Duisburg University, Duisburg, Germany

Henley, N. M. (1977). *Body politics. Power, sex and nonverbal communication.* Englewood Cliffs, NJ: Prentice-Hall.

Hewes, G. (1955). World distribution of certain postural habits. *American Anthropologist, 65,* 1003–26.

Hewes, G. (1957). The anthropology of posture. *Scientific American, 196,* 2, 122–132.

Inhelder, B., & de Caprona, D. (1992). Un parcours de recherche (A research process). In B. Inhelder & G. Cellérier (Eds.), *Le cheminement des découvertes de l'enfant (The steps of children's discoveries).* Neuchâtel, Switzerland: Delachaux et Niestlé.

Jung, C. G. (1964). *Man and his symbols.* London: Aldus.

Lazarus, R. S. (1991). *Emotion and adaptation.* Oxford, UK: Oxford University Press.

Leroi-Gourhan, A. (1964). *Le geste et la parole: Technique et language (Gesture and speech. Technique and language).* Paris: Sciences d'Aujourd'hui, Albin Michel.

Leroi-Gourhan, A. (1965). *Le geste et la parole: La mémoire et les rythmes (Gesture and speech).* Paris: Sciences d'Aujourd'hui, Albin Michel.

Lesko, C., Heller, M., & Haynal, A. (1992). *Facial behavior and suicidal patients* (Research report on laboratory affect and communication). Geneva.

Lévi-Strauss, C. (1962a). *La pensée sauvage (Savage Mind).* Paris: Plon.

Lévi-Strauss, C. (1962b). *Le totémisme aujourd'hui (Totemism).* Paris: Presses Universitaires de France.

Mehrabian, A. (1968). Inference of attitudes from the posture, orientation and distance of a communicator. In M. Argyle (Ed.), *Social encounters. Readings in social interaction* (pp. 103–118). Harmondsworth, UK: Penguin.

Mehrabian, A. (1969). Significance of posture and position in the communication of attitude and status relationships. *Psychological Bulletin, 71,* 359–372.

Mehrabian, A. (1981). *Silent messages.* Belmont, UK: Wadsworth.

Stern, D. (1990). *Diary of a baby.* New York: Basic Books.

14

SIGN LANGUAGE AND GESTURES IN MEDIEVAL EUROPE: MONASTERIES, COURTS OF JUSTICE, AND SOCIETY

August Nitschke
University of Stuttgart

When monks are forbidden to talk, they use a system of sign language, just as deaf-mutes do. As we know the sign language used by monks in the 10th, 11th, and 12th centuries, we have a tool for finding out whether the sign language thus handed down to us is a phenomenon specific to a particular society, or whether it may be encountered among human beings anywhere. We can thus address the question of whether we might expect sign language to change with culture or society, or whether this is a universal.

To begin with, I consider the reasons sign language may be a universal. I then focus on the reasons against this notion. Finally, we see what conclusions may be drawn from this discussion.

SIGN LANGUAGE IN MONASTERIES

In his *Sprache ohne Worte*, Kleinpaul (1888/1973) referred to the language of religious orders in which speaking is not permitted, such as the language of the Trappists: "In the Trappist order one eats by repeatedly moving the first three fingers towards the mouth; one drinks by placing the tip of the thumb on the lips and tilting the fist like a bottle; one fasts by pressing together the lips with thumb and forefinger one gets up by tapping the left palm with a knuckle as if to awaken it" (p. 383).

We now know the lists of signs of medieval monasteries, and they are similar in terms of understandability. The Cluny list describes the sign for bread thus: "Make a circle using both your thumbs and the fingers next to them because bread is normally round" (Jarecki, 1981, p. 121). Another example:

> To make the general sign for book, stretch out your hand, moving it as if turning the page of a book; for the missal, generally make the signs just mentioned, and in addition make the sign of the cross; for the sign of the gospel, additionally make the sign of the cross on your forehead; for the sign of a letter, additionally make the sign of the cross on your chest; for the sign of the book to be read at night, place one hand on your cheek in addition to the general sign and to the sign of the book and the lesson. (Jarecki, 1981, p. 133)

In this way, the combination of the signs for book, reading, and sleeping means "reading at nighttime."

In Germany, von Hirsau slightly varied the signs of the Cluniac monks, but the principle remained the same. For example, the sign for milk went something like this: "For the sign of milk, place all the fingers of your right hand around the smallest finger of your left, and stretch the latter, imitating someone who is milking." Another example, concerning honey: "For the sign of honey, let your tongue protrude for a moment and move your fingers close as if you intended to lick them" (Jarecki, 1981, pp. 169, 171).

However, sign language is not only about concrete things. The Hallelujah can also be represented in this way, although some previous knowledge is required for this. Because the hallelujah is sung by angels, the sign refers to this: "For the sign of hallelujah, raise one hand and move the slightly curved upper side of the fingers in a way that suggests a flying motion"(Jarecki, 1981, p. 132), for angels have wings. Crying is indicated thus: "For the sign of crying, take the index finger, which has been placed below the eye, moving it downward twice" (Jarecki, 1981, p. 219): Here tears are being wiped away.

The language of the Cistercians of the 12th century is basically the same. Balance is indicated by two outstretched hands that, palms facing upward, are each alternately raised and lowered slightly in front of the body (Barakat, 1975). To indicate singing, the tip of the right forefinger is brought to the mouth, but without actually touching it (Barakat, 1975). To demonstrate the word *fire*, one blows on the tip of the forefinger, which is held pointing up (Barakat, 1975). A fish is represented thus: Keeping the fingers together, move the right hand, keeping it straight, in front of the body in a zigzag manner like a swimming animal (Barakat, 1975).

All of this make it sound as though it would not be difficult to develop a universal language, for these signs imitate a figure or an event so well that they can be easily understood. However, already Kleinpaul, a long time ago, ironically remarked that this consensus could quickly be upset by differences in social background. He recounted a sermon in dialogue form that a parson, whose fellow clergyman failed to arrive, conducted together with a shoemaker instead. In the pulpit:

> The parson raises his thumb. Immediately, the shoemaker raises his thumb and forefinger. Next, the parson raises three fingers, the shoemaker his whole fist. Now, the parson takes an apple out of his pocket. The shoemaker, undaunted by this, takes out a bread roll. At that point, the parson gets angry. He rushes back to the parsonage and confesses: "This man is unbeatable in disputation." I said to him: "There is one God." "Yes," he answered, "but with two natures." Then I said: "As three persons," to which he replied: "Three in one being." Then I said: "The apple was the beginning of all sins." He retorted: "Yes, but through the Communion they are healed."—Meanwhile, the learned shoemaker recounts the dispute as follows: "First, he wanted to knock out one of my eyes. But I said to him: "I will knock out both of yours." To which he replied: "I will twist your nose." But I said: "Just wait until I punch you." After this, he wanted to feed me like an animal. But I said: "In my home, we eat bread. (Kleinpaul, 1888/1973, p. 383)

If one looks more closely at the signs, characteristic differences become evident. The sign for drinking that seemed so simple in monastic language—thumb approaching lips, fist tilted like an upraised bottle—may be expressed very differently by American Indians, Australians, Spaniards, or Italians. The thumb may be brought to the lips with the other fingers tightly closed, forming a fist. But it can also be brought to the lips with the other fingers kept straight. It can be brought to the lips with the middle fingers bent and the little finger kept straight, or with the last fingers bent and the forefinger kept straight (B. J. Bäuml & F. H. Bäuml, 1975). Conversely, we know of a number of expressions in which the fingers were brought up to the lips, just like the sign for eating in the monasteries. Elsewhere, however, they signaled admiration, attention, or leave taking. When the lower lip was pushed forward a little and pulled down toward the forefinger, this signified ignorance. One finger placed between lips and teeth could be interpreted as regret (B. J. Bäuml & F. H. Bäuml, 1975). The fact that the signs that originated in European monasteries may have been more readily understood by Europeans of that time does not tell us anything about their general understandability. All of this is discussed in the careful, comparative, and partly lexicographical works of Bäuml and Bäuml (1975) and Key (1975, 1977).

SIGN LANGUAGE IN COURTS OF JUSTICE

A separate sign language is used in court. We know of some early traditions, for example from illustrations contained in the 13th century Code of the Saxons (*Sachsenspiegel*; Koschorreck, 1970). In the Middle Ages, Roman law, too, was illustrated with miniatures (Ebel, Fijal, & Kocher, 1988). Again, some gestures have obvious meaning: gestures of showing, pointing, and commanding, which are depicted by hands with an outstretched forefinger (von Amira, 1905). Other gestures are more difficult to understand. An inability, for example, may be represented by a gesture: A situation in which a sentenced person cannot pay his or her debts, a person under interrogation who does not know how to answer, or a person who shows general incompetence, is indicated by depicting the wrists placed crosswise one on top of the other (von Amira, 1905). It has been said that this shows a prisoner bound by the wrists. This is possible, although it cannot be immediately recognized, and, as a "sign" belongs to a society that dealt with prisoners in this way.

It is already more difficult to interpret the gestures in the courts of justice of the Germanic tribes during the period of the migration of peoples. For a long time, legal historians believed that juridical gestures were bound up with traditions. Consequently, they deduced from the miniatures in the Code of the Saxons the modes of expression of earlier centuries (von Amira, 1905; Nitschke, 1989b). Since then, however, it has been shown that there have been several breaks in tradition. Gestures changed accordingly (Nitschke, 1989b).

Our first result, then, is the following: We know of sign languages that are characteristic of occupations—the sign language of monks, and the gestures of persons in a court of law in the 7th or 13th centuries. In replacing words, these sign languages relied on fairly simple means; but these signs originated from within groups of persons whose relationships with one another were based on shared activities. In this way, every sign language developed in relation to an estate or an occupation. Many peculiarities are found only in one of the estates, which means that they cannot simply be transferred to other realms of society.

Still, these signs, which are relatively simple and imitative, and simulate certain activities, may vary considerably. As a result, the range of variability may give rise to misunderstandings. On the other hand, we know of signs that are similar in appearance, but may have a different meaning. (Such variants occur mostly outside Europe.) All this should lead to caution in assuming that a universal sign language has been found.

The problem becomes even more complicated when we consider how the hand gestures made by persons ought to be related to their simultaneous body movement. It may well happen that an identical hand sign will change meaning in conjunction with a different body motion. As we have seen, signs made with the hand generally transmit information: They refer to bread or vegetables, drinking or eating, singing or sleeping, and communicate the intentions of the person "talking" in sign language. However, the body motions performed at the same time are not merely informative. In general, they characterize the forms of communication typical of a society or a whole epoch.

GESTURES

Whereas sign languages convey information (e.g., relating to bread, water, fish, singing and sleeping, drinking and eating) gestures and body motions tell us something else. Neumann (1965) attempted to distinguish two kinds of gestures (*Gesten* and *Gebärden*): "*Gesten* (semiotic gestures) are outwardly directed, consciously controlled, intentional movements which, as communicative signs, involve an active, dialogic function. *Gebärden* (expressive gestures) denote involuntary, self-contained, and self-explanatory body movements. Such *Gebärden* are emotional manifestations and, like a monologue, reveal the inner existential sentiments of a human being in a particular situation" (pp. 1f). However, this distinction has not been generally adopted. Instead, researchers study the particular gestures of a time and the changes from one epoch to another.

For instance, Sittl (1890/1970) described the gestures of the Greeks and Romans, treating both *Gesten* and *Gebärden* and sign language information in the same way. Likewise, in her study of greeting scenes shown on Attic vases, Bogen (1969) studied all types of gestures, but without distinguishing among them. The argument against such a distinction would be that expressive gestures, too, serve the purpose of communication and, for this reason, do possess a "dialogic function" (Neumann, 1965, pp. 1f). However, even assuming we did introduce this distinction—which might prove difficult in certain cases—we could not show that either type of gesture is identical for all peoples and times. There is already an observable difference between the gestures of the Archaic and of the Classical Greek periods (Nitschke, 1989a). In this analysis, I use only the general concept of gesture.

Gestures changed during the Middle Ages. Habicht (1959) did a separate study of each gesture in English Medieval literature, and Schubert (1991) examined the nonverbal expressions contained in *La Chanson de Roland*, the *Aeneas* epic, and *Tristan*. Similarly, Peil (1975) analyzed the gestures in *Chrétien, Hartmann, and Wolfram*. Roeder (1974) described gesture in Medieval drama, for example, in the *Easter plays*, and Suntrup (1978) pointed to the importance of liturgical gestures and movements in the period from the 9th to the 13th centuries. Research has revealed a continuous flow of new distinctions. For the Renaissance and Early Modern age, there have been several studies on gesture. The number of works dealing with the present has also tended to grow, and there has been a sudden increase since the mid-1950s (Engels, 1976)

Meanwhile, significant contributions have been made also in ethnology (E. E. Boesch, 1983; Eibl-Eibesfeldt, 1984; Goodenough, 1964; Honigmann, 1973). These insights have permitted a differentiation of three basic types of communication. These can be easily recognized in the forms of gymnastics, but they also occur in everyday life:

1. People can respond to ongoing movements in their environment and continue these. We are observing this in the Chinese, Japanese, and other Far Eastern peoples in their gymnastics and martial arts (Nitschke, 1991b).

2. People can let their movements be changed by movements. They can either adopt the other movement or let the other movement make them perform new movements. These two options—the adoption of another movement and the acceleration of one's own movement by another movement—are sometimes interrelated. In-

dian women dancers, for example, respond to the movements of their god(s) with new movements, and the Germanic warriors adopt the movements of their god.

3. With the help of gestures, people can convey their intentions to others and, through their gestures, seek to influence the gestures and movements of others. This was customary among the Greeks and Romans in the Classical period, and also among Europeans since the 8th century (Nitschke, 1975b; 1989a).

People living in different societies thus employ a language of movements that either continues other ongoing movements, is open to being transformed, or is representative and prevails in a dialogic context (Nitschke, 1991a).

Owing to a sign language that uses the hands, information can, of course, be transmitted within all three types of communication. However, the informative hand gestures will have to be combined with gestures indicating the kind of dialogic situation in which people find themselves as representatives of their societies.

GESTURES AS INDICATORS OF EMOTION, STATUS AND SOCIAL ORDER

Within each of these three forms of communication, some variants occur, most of them bound up with the surrounding society. One need not look further than Europe to come to the following conclusion: Also among Europeans, we can find very diverse gestures involving particular sign languages for representation and social influence. Here, different types of body motions may be combined with different hand movements. I give three examples:

In pictures from the Ottonian period (the 10th century), people mutually influence one another. They attract one another's attention by stretching out their arms in front of themselves, giving the impression of a stream running from the neck along the shoulders, down to the elbows, wrists, and extending beyond the fingers. Attention should be on the fingertips, which are depicted in elongated form, creating the appearance that the stream continues beyond them. Whenever a person wants to convey something to a lower placed person, he or she can, by holding the palm of the hand upward, grant something or, by holding the back of the hand upward, give a direction or command. Conversely, a person placed in a lower position can request something from a higher placed person by means of the same gesture, which is holding the palm upward and slightly raising the arm. By way of such gestures, human beings show that they are used to influencing others by addressing them in a giving, commanding, or requesting mode (Nitschke, 1975b).

From the middle of the 11th century, these gestures, which used to be part of a "flow," tended to become bent and protruding. The human beings so depicted tend to flex their shoulders, elbows, wrists, and hips and point or go forward in a certain direction with every part, or, more specifically, limb of their bodies. In this way, lively dialogic scenes are created in which all persons seem to be oriented toward one another, and at the same time nearly all of them seem to be reaching out beyond themselves.

In this gestural language, people reveal the forces residing in the various parts of their bodies, which make the bodies project outward. In this way, they represent their respective estates—as well as their states of mind: joy or grief and at the same time, by means of their directional gestures, an order structured from the top down (Nitschke, 1989a).

In Italy, in the early 14th century, there was a further change. The body as a whole is now often shown as a bell-shaped mass. The arms—owing to the garments—remain connected to the rump, which may be quite massive. Indicating subdued movements, the arms tend to point either upward, downward, or to the side without disturbing the composure of the person concerned. In the context of this gestural language, these human beings represent separate entities, although strangely isolated ones. They are not pointing in different directions, but their measured movements seem to anticipate some place ahead of them (Nitschke, 1992).

Each of these gestural languages has a corresponding behavioral code. In the Ottonian period, people lived in a social framework in which everyone related to both higher or lower placed men and women. People needed contact in order to survive (Nitschke, 1989a). From the middle of the 11th century, one can observe smaller segments that are separated from one another. People were found in segments of space that were usually vertically organized. Within these spaces, they showed an outwardly directed, goal-oriented activity that denoted their estate. They belonged to estates that characterized by specific modes of action and work—those of knights, traders, artisans, or peasants (Nitschke, 1989). In early 14th-century Italy, individual human beings were becoming isolated. They directed their orientation to places in their environment, showing a tendency to direct their movements to distant places located on higher or lower levels, although for the moment they could indicate this only by their posture (Nitschke, 1992). Here, we see the beginnings of the changes leading up to the Renaissance, in which human beings were finally able to move to different places within a homogeneous space.

In the behaviors just described, additional information may be conveyed with the help of hand gestures. If we look only at the hand movements, we can see that they involve pointing to something, giving orders, or eating and drinking. However, if we study the (expressive) body motions, we can see that they are used by people to convey their wish to influence one another. The particular body movements that are used for this purpose change with the succession of historical epochs in Europe. In the Ottonian era (the 10th century), people could exercise influence by adapting their body motion to the "flow" leading to other human beings. In the High Middle Ages (11th and 12th centuries), the same aim could be achieved by body movements that fit into small spaces, pushing outward into neighboring spaces. Finally, from the 14th century in Italy onward, the influence took the form of an orientation upward or downward, pointing toward a place within reach for the individual.

Thus, we can conclude by saying that although some hand gestures may constitute universals that can be understood by all human beings, the essential aspect of human social life and communication is expressed through semiotic and expressive body motions, and these motions change from one society to another. Paying attention only to sign language might lead one to assume that the language of the body also is easily and universally understandable. The opposite is the case: The interpretation of the language of human gestures and body motions requires special training on the part of the researcher.

THE QUESTION OF UNIVERSALS

In any comparison of human and animal nonverbal communication, it is necessary to make the same distinction between gestures as the one employed earlier for humans. Thus, the following gestures should also be identified in animals: (a) gestures that are informative, (b) gestures that continue the movement of others, and (c) gestures by which individuals let themselves be changed by the movements of others. The first type involves animal signaling (e.g., of readiness to mate), the second social coordination (e.g., birds flying in formation), and the third one has to do with regulation of social dominance (e.g., through ritualized gestures, such as the response to a gesture of submissiveness).

If we leave aside those gestures and movements that are merely informative, the question is whether the body language of a certain species can be based on the second and third types of gestures: those involving coordination, and power and status relationships. As we saw in the previous analysis, body motion changes with a changing historical context. Thus, there do not seem to exist any "typical" human body movements that could be isolated from the total sociohistorical context and might become candidates for human universals. However, perhaps there is another way of looking at universals: Considering them as various types of predispositions for behavior that will eventually bring about observable patterns of social coordination and organization. Such a view of universals would also allow for different outcomes in different social contexts. The universals would then not reside in the meaning of particular gestures or body motions but rather in the minimally required basic genetic and neurological equipment that, in the proper environment, will generate those capabilities that we associate with particular animal species or humans, and are presumably important for social organization (e.g., for humans, our inborn capacity for social bonding, imitation and feedback; see Segerstråle & Molnár, chap. 1, this volume). From this point of view, it is perhaps even surprising that there seem to exist only a limited number of historical variations of human body motion. Further historical research may give us more clues as to the different ways of expressing social organization through gestures, postures, and body movements.

REFERENCES

Amira von, K. (1905). Die Handgebärden in den Bilderhandschriften des Sachsenspiegels (Gestures in the pictorial manuscripts of the Sachsenspiegel). *Abhandlung der philosophisch-philologischen Klasse der Königlich-Bayerischen Akademie der Wissenschaften, 23*(2). Munich: G. Franz.

Barakat, R. A. (1975). *The Cistercian sign language. A study in non-verbal communication.* Kalamazoo, MI: Cistercian.

Bäuml, B. J., & Bäuml, F. H. (1975). *A dictionary of gestures.* New York: Methuen.

Boesch, E. E. (1983). *Das Magische und das Schöne. Zur Symbolik von Objekten und Handlungen (The magic and the beautiful. On the symbolism of objects and actions).* Stuttgart, Germany: Frommann-Holzboog.

Bogen, K. (1969). *Gesten der Begrüßungsszenen auf attischen Vasen (Gestures of greeting scenes on Attic vases).* Bonn: Rudolf Habelt.

Ebel, F., Fijal, A., & Kocher, G. (1988). *Römisches Rechtsleben im Mittelalter. Miniaturen aus den Handschriften des Corpus iuris civilis (Roman legal life in the Middle Ages. Miniatures from the manuscripts of the Corpus iuris civilis).* Heidelberg, Germany: C. F. Müller.

Eibl-Eibesfeldt, I. (1984). *Die Biologie des menschlichen Verhaltens. Grundriß der Humanethologie (The biology of human behavior. Outline of human ethology).* Munich: Piper.

Engels, H.-J. (1976). *Status und nonverbales Verhalten (Status and nonverbal behavior).* Köln: Peter Hanstein.

Goodenough, W. H. (1964). *Explorations in cultural anthropology.* New York: McGraw-Hill.

Habicht, W. (1959). *Die Gebärde in englischen Dichtungen des Mittelalters (The gesture in English medieval poetry).* Bayerische Akademie der Wissenschaften, Philosophisch-Historische Klasse. Munich: Verlag der Bayerischen Akademie der Wissenschaften.

Honigmann, J. J. (1973). *Handbook of the social and cultural anthropology.* Chicago: Rand McNally.

Jarecki W. (1981). *Signa loquendi. Die cluniazensischen Signalisten (Signa loquendi. The Cluniazensic signalists).* Baden-Baden, Germany: Koerner Verlag.

Key, M. R. (1975). *Paralanguage and kinesics (Nonverbal communication).* New York: Methuen.

Key, M. R. (1977). *Nonverbal communication research: Guide to bibliography.* New York: Methuen.

Kleinpaul, R. (1973). *Sprache ohne Worte. Idee einer Allgemeinwissenschaft,* mit einem Vorwort von Thomas A. Sebeok *(Language without words. The idea of a comprehensive science,* with a preface by Thomas E. Seboek). Paris: Mouton. (Original work published 1988)

Koschorreck, W. (1970). *Die Heidelberger Bildhandschrift des Sachsenspiegels, Kommentarband (The Heidelberg pictorial manuscript of the Sachsenspiegel, commented volume).* Frankfurt: Insel.

Neumann, G. (1965). *Gesten und Gebärden in der griechischen Kunst (Gestures and poses in Greek art).* Berlin: Walter de Gruyter.

Nitschke, A. (1975a). *Kunst und Verhalten. Analoge Konfigurationen (Art and behavior. Analogous configurations).* Stuttgart, Germany: Frommann-Holzboog.

Nitschke, A. (1975b). *Ottonische und karolingische Herrscherdarstellungen. Gestik und politisches Verhandeln (Ottoman and Karolingian representations of rulers. Gestures and political negotiation).* In Beiträge zur Kunst des Mittelalters. Berlin: Gebr. Mann.

Nitschke, A. (1989a). *Körper in Bewegung. Gesten, Tänze und Räume im Wandel der Geschichte (Bodies in motion. Gestures, dances, and spaces in the course of history).* Stuttgart, Germany: Kreuz-Verlag.

Nitschke, A. (1989b). Wandel der Rechtsgesten (The change of legal gestures). In L. Carlen (Ed.), *Forschungen zur Rechtsarchäologie und rechtlichen Volkskunde* (pp. 105–129). Zürich: Schulthess Polygraphischer Verlag.

Nitschke, A. (1991a). Bewegungen als Dialog (Movements as dialogue). *Praxis der Psychotherapie und Psychosomatik, 36,* 90.

Nitschke, A. (1991b). *Die Mutigen in einem System. Wechselwirkungen zwischen Mensch und Umwelt. Ein Vergleich der Kulturen (The couragious in a system. Interdependencies between man an environment).* Köln, Germany: Böhlau.

Nitschke, A. (1992). *The change in space perception in the fifteenth century.* Report Nr. 23/92 of the Research Group on Biological Foundations of Human Culture at the Center for Interdisciplinary Research of the University of Bielefeld, Germany.

Peil, D. (1975). *Die Gebärde bei Chrétien (Chrétien on gestures).* Munich: Hartmann und Wolfram.

Roeder, A. (1974). *Die Gebärden im Drama des Mittelalters. Osterfeiern, Osterspiele (Gestures in medieval drama. Easter celebrations, Easter games).* Munich: C. H. Beck.

Schmitt, J.-C. (1992). Die Logik der Gesten im europäischen Mittelalter (The logic of gestures in medieval Europe). Stuttgart, Germany: Klett-Cotta.

Schubert, M. J. (1991). *Zur Theorie des Gebarens im Mittelalter. Analyse von nichtsprachlicher Äußerung in mittelhochdeutscher Epik. Rolandslied, Aeneasroman, Tristan (On the theory of gestures in the Middle Ages. The analysis of nonverbal expression in middle-high-German epic. Roland's song, Aeneas, Tristan).* Wien, Austria: Böhlau.

Sittl, C. (1970). *Die Gebärden der Griechen und Römer (The gestures of Greeks and Romans).* Leipzig, Germany: Georg Olms. (Original work published 1890).

Suntrup, R. (1978). *Die Bedeutung der liturgischen Gebärden und Bewegungen in lateinischen und deutschen Auslegungen des 9. bis 13. Jahrhunderts (The significance of liturgic gestures and movements in Latin and German interpretations of the 9th–13th centuries).* Munich: Wilhelm Fink.

15

NONVERBAL COMMUNICATION AND THE EMERGENCE OF MORAL SENTIMENTS

Robert Frank
Cornell University

MORAL SENTIMENTS IN EVERYDAY EXPERIENCE: TIPPING ON THE ROAD

My topic is how nonverbal communication might have supported the emergence of moral sentiments. I want to introduce the discussion by reference to a simple example: The tip following the meal in a restaurant.

First, you might ask why would there be a tip in the first place? Why not simply include that amount in the waiter's paycheck and ask that he provide good service in return for his fair compensation? The waiter might be happy to perform good service in return for the extra compensation embodied in the tip, but if it were automatically included in his paycheck, his selfish tendencies might get the better of him. If he knew that the owner of the restaurant were out of sight, he might be tempted to shirk. And as as a result the diner would not get the service he or she was willing to pay for. The restaurant owner would have dissatisfied customers and have an incentive to correct the situation. A tip seems a natural solution. It says, in effect, to the diner "We are going to reduce the price of your meal by a little bit and at the end of the meal, if you are happy with the courteous service you received, then you should leave a tip of some amount—let us say 15%, just because 2% would be too little and 30% would be too much." So that custom is announced and customers find the tip does indeed cause the waiter to provide better service than in restaurants that do not have the tipping practice. Restaurants gradually begin to copy this institution because it seems to work so well.

Now, here comes the first question. If the tip comes at the end of the meal as it usually does, why does the diner not renege on the obligation to leave it? Having already received the good service, why not say: "I will not leave the tip, I will walk out and pay my bill and that is the end of it?" Here is where one of the biological theories that tries to explain cooperation and altruism enters in. Many meals are eaten in restaurants where patronage is not a sporadic, one-time affair, but occurs on a regular basis. If we want to think in formal terms, we have something like a repeated prisoner's dilemma represented here. The diner might be tempted to withhold the tip, but he or she knows that in future interactions in that same restaurant, the service will not be as good, and it is this prospect that provides the diner's incentive to uphold his or her part of the bargain. So we have a hard-nosed, economistic, biologically rigorous theory of why the tipping institution holds together and works to the benefit of all involved. Nobody has the incentive to cheat.

But then we observe that tipping occurs not just in local restaurants that people frequent on a regular basis, but also at steakhouses along interstate highways—restaurants where you will stop, run up a $50 or $100 tab and then never expect to eat there again. Under those circumstances, why not walk out and not leave a tip? How can the waiter retaliate? Clearly, the waiter is not in any position at all to do anything if you do that.

Now, confronted with this question, many economists respond, "Well, people probably do not leave tips in restaurants out of town." That seems like a compelling argument. In fact, people have looked at the data, and the interesting thing is that the tipping amount is only marginally lower in restaurants that have a lot of transient trade.

So, the first prediction of the *homo economicus* self-interest model is flatly rejected on the basis of empirical observation. The kin selection model is not much help here either. It is very unlikely that the waiter you leave a tip for on the interstate highway will be a sufficiently close relative of yours to make it worth your while to leave a 15% tip. Nor is Trivers' reciprocal altruism model likely to work here (e.g., Trivers,

1985), for the odds of you receiving a reciprocal benefit as a result of your leaving a tip are vanishingly small. You will either get nice treatment from strangers in the future, or you will not, irrespective of whether you leave the tip—or at least so it seems.

Thus, the puzzle of tipping on the road remains unsolved. Economists might try to patch up the inconsistency by coming up with a slightly modified institutional mechanism for collecting the tip. There is a *New Yorker* cartoon that shows a solitary diner eating his meal. He has a little plate on the table with some coins on it and a sign that reads, "Your tip so far." This would be in the economist's parlance an "incentive compatible" tipping mechanism. It is one where the waiter can size up the tip at the end of each course and see if it is accumulating at the proper rate. If not, then he can withhold his service on the next course and the diner likewise can give step-by-step feedback to the waiter. There is no possibility for an opportunistic act at the end of the meal. Yet we do not see this mechanism of tipping adopted. The reason seems to be not that people just have not thought not to leave a tip in out-of-town restaurants, that people, even when you point to them that they can get away with leaving no tip in an out-of-town restaurant, simply have little inclination really to do that. They do not say, "Oh, I never thought of that. I am going to start leaving no tip from now on." They say, "Well, that is not why I leave a tip. I leave a tip because that is the responsible thing to do under the circumstances. The waiter has provided good service. He has lived up to his part of the agreement; I would feel bad if I did not live up to my part of the agreement." That is a behavior that I hope most of us can identify with from experience, and yet it poses a puzzle for this ruthlessly self-interested vision of what the forces are that mold behavior.

THE INADEQUACY OF SOCIOBIOLOGICAL AND ECONOMIC EXPLANATIONS

Leaving a tip in a restaurant is not the only example of behavior like that. Lenny Skutnik was an employee who worked in the mail room of one of the large government organizations in Washington, DC, and he happened to be present when a commercial airliner went into the Potomac River in Washington, DC. It was just taking off when ice on its wings caused it to lose altitude and crash into the river on a January night in 1982. It had been bitter cold for the last 3 weeks, and there were icebergs in the Potomac River, something rarely seen. Skutnik took off his coat and shoes, jumped into the icy river, swam out into the middle where the plane had gone in, and managed against all odds to swim back to shore with one of the five survivors from the crash out of 105 people who were on the plane. It is very difficult to construct a narrowly self-interested rationale for his having taken that action.

Now, because he got back to shore safely, he probably is better off now than if he had not done it. Ronald Reagan, the President then, honored him in the national State of the Union address. He was present in the gallery and the television cameras showed his face to the applauding nation, so he did receive a lot of credit as a result of performing this act of heroism. However, even if he had gotten millions of dollars of extra wealth in reward for his behavior, the odds of getting back to shore alive were so low that it still would not have been a narrowly self-interested act. Theories of kin selection and reciprocal altruism do not explain behavior of this sort.

One of my favorite examples is the Falkland War, which took place in the early 1980s over the utterly valueless, windswept, desolate Falkland Islands off the coast of Argentina. Argentina invaded them. The British, of course, claimed them as their own territory. There was a small number of British subjects who lived on the Islands, who mostly raised sheep. Somebody calculated that for much less than the cost of sending the fleet down to circle the Islands once just to give a show of force, the Falklanders could have been given generous pensions and retirement homes in the Caribbean. In the 19th century, Britain might have said, "Well, if we let them take the Falklands, who knows where next?" But, in 1982, what might they have been interested in sending a signal about as to their willingness to defend? Gibraltar? Hong Kong? Essentially, there was no empire left to posture about. The Argentine writer Jorge Luis Borges likened the war to "two bald men fighting over a comb" (Woodall, 1996). Economically, it did not pay to defend the Falklands, and yet it is very difficult to find even a single British subject who expresses any regret at the vast financial and human cost of having stood up to the Argentines. Some self-interest theorists have responded by saying, "Well, Thatcher had everything to gain by sending the fleet down because the voters sent her back resoundingly to office as a result of that." But that does not really answer the deeper question of why voters thought it was a good thing that she should spend such a sum to defend the worthless Falkland Islands. Still, we have a motive here, this sense of national pride or honor for which people seemed willing to expend a great treasure for no apparent material return.

There is an interesting series of experiments done in New York City, where the environmental conditions normally thought to foster altruism are generally absent. A sociologist left wallets on street corners to see what people who found them would do. The sociologist scuffed the wallets up to make them look used, put a small amount of cash inside and some identification cards and laundry receipts so that it would look as if real people had lost them. In about half of the cases, these wallets came back in the mail, mostly anonymously returned.

People just seem to be doing what the biologists and economists say they should not be doing: They are trying to do the right thing. We see examples of soldiers who dive atop live hand grenades. When a grenade comes into the trench and there are seven or eight soldiers there, one jumps on the hand grenade and absorbs the blow and saves the others. If you pursue the standard version of the self-interest theory, it is quite easy to see why a soldier might want *somebody* to dive on the grenade, but easy, too, to see why each one might wait, hoping it would be somebody else, and so the prediction under that model is that everyone would wait and finally the grenade would explode and they would all die. There would be no reason not to wait 1 second more, because if any time remained at all, there would always be some finite probability that one of the others would die; but if you dive, you are going to die for sure.

When I present examples like these to audiences where there are a lot of sociobiologists present, I always get the most imaginative attempts to think of indirect ways in which the participants might have gained some advantage after all. It is really quite extraordinary. The theoretical model has such a firm grip on the thinking within this tradition that contrary data are almost inadmissible. They cannot be thought about without engendering such a sense of disquiet that the moment somebody proposes an explanation that is consistent within that framework, it is immediately accepted and no further discussion is attractive, for fear it might raise further questions about whether it really was an adequate explanation. However, let me just remind you that none of those standard explanations seemed the least satisfactory in accounting for behaviors like these.

I will now report the results of some work in which I have tried to argue that the kinds of sentiments that motivate behaviors like these—I call them moral sentiments—could indeed have arisen under the ruthless sort of self-interested pressures of the natural selection mecha-nism.[1] I try to show that people who are motivated by moral sentiments of the sort we commonly recognize in people are much better equipped than ordinary selfish people to solve an important class of problems that we encounter in the material environment. I go on to explain what that class of problems is and give some examples.

There is an indirection to the argument that I want to alert you to at the outset. I am going to argue that in order to pursue your own material interest, it is sometimes necessary to set aside concern about your mate-rial well-being. In fact, I try to show that persons who are known to pursue unselfish goals often are, for that very reason, more likely to achieve selfish goals.

It is as if, by analogy, you had a visit with your psychotherapist, who tells you that your problem is that you are insufficiently spontane-ous. Your social relationships are not working effectively because you are just not spontaneous enough. Now, if a person was told that by his or her psychotherapist and then went out from the session determined then and there to rectify the problem by being as spontaneous as possi-ble at every opportunity from then on, you would have an intuitive sense that the strategy was doomed at the outset. Trying to be spontane-ous is not likely to be a successful strategy for social interaction. I want to argue in a similar way that direct pursuit of material self interest is, in a similar sense, unlikely to yield a satisfying result. In order to really achieve the goal of maximum material wealth it is going to be neces-sary to adopt something of a zen strategy. You have to pursue the goal obliquely, to not have it clearly in mind, but to be focused instead on other goals that do not very much resemble the goal of pursuing mate-rial wealth.

THE COMMITMENT PROBLEM

People with selfish tastes of the sort assumed by biologists and econo-mists have difficulty solving *the commitment problem*. That is the name I use for it and it is nicely illustrated by an example from the American economist, Tom Schelling. He talks about a kidnapper who seizes the victim and then changes his mind. He realizes that the crime was a

---

[1]The material that follows draws heavily on my book *Passions Within Reasons* (1988).

mistake, that he is likely to be caught and punished, and so he wants to set the victim free. The difficulty is that he knows that the victim, once free, has the incentive to go to the police and reveal the identity of the kidnapper. Now, the victim says to the kidnapper, "I promise if you set me free, I will not go to the police." He wants with absolute sincerity to keep this promise. He wants to make a binding commitment not to go to the police because he and the kidnapper both realize that unless he can do that, once he is free he will not have any incentive to keep the promise. He will go right to the police even though he really wanted to promise and keep the promise before he was free. That is a commitment problem. If he could somehow commit himself to keep the promise, then he could be set free by the kidnapper and they would both get a result that they liked better than the alternative, which is what is bound to happen if they think the victim cannot make a commitment: Namely, that the kidnapper will feel he must kill the victim. Otherwise he will be arrested and punished for the crime of kidnapping, which in the United States happens to be a capital offense.

Schelling (1960) suggested an interesting solution to the problem: a commitment device; a device that makes it the interest of the victim to keep his promise once he is free. The device Schelling suggested is that if the victim has commited a crime in the past—if he has stolen some money from his employer, for example—he can give evidence of the crime to the kidnapper and that evidence will provide a bond that gives the victim an incentive to keep his promise once he is free. He will not go to the police because then the kidnapper will reveal this evidence and the victim would suffer. That is a very elegant solution. You could solve the problem in similar ways by signing elaborate legal contracts: I promise to give $40,000 to some cause I do not approve of if I go to the police. There would be ways to change your material incentive so that you will not break your promise once you are set free, but they are often cumbersome. It is difficult to negotiate solutions of that sort under practical circumstances that arise in daily life. I want to suggest that problems like this can be solved instead if people can simply make a credible promise not to go to the police. If the kidnapper somehow knew (and this is going to be the key step) that the victim was somebody endowed with moral sentiments of the sort that would make him want to keep his promise even though it was not in his narrow interest to do so, then the problem would be solved. If you are the kind of person that lives up to your agreements, having made that promise, the kidnapper could feel secure setting you free; and you would both do better than if you could not be recognized as such a person.

Commitment problems are an endemic feature of economic and social life. I give some examples, one of which I work through in some detail. The cheating problem is an ordinary prisoner's dilemma that I am going to go through in more detail later, so I skip quickly by it here. I instead start with another one: The deterrence problem. I brought with me a nice leather briefcase given to me by my wife a couple of years ago as a Christmas gift. Let us say that someone in the audience liked it and thought it would be a nice briefcase to have. If you thought I was a purely rational, self-interested economic agent it would be safe for you to conclude that you could go up after the talk, and walk off with my briefcase. What would I do? I would have to contact the police. I would have to give testimony. I would have to miss my plane back to the United States tomorrow. I would have to come back to Europe and testify and undergo harsh cross-examination and if I were a rational person I would say, "Well, look, that is too bad. My briefcase got stolen while I was in Germany. Next time, I will not bring it to Germany, or I will chain it to my wrist if I buy a new one." The last thing I would want to do would be to retaliate and press charges and get involved in all those costs. It would be thousands of dollars for a briefcase worth only a few hundred dollars. It would be the height of folly to take action of that sort. So if anyone knew me to be a narrow, rational, self-interested person, it would be safe to steal my briefcase.

However, what if I were a "normal" person reacting to the theft of his briefcase? "What do you mean stealing my briefcase? What an outrage! That was a present given to me by my wife." I am going to stay over and will reschedule my flight. If I have to testify for a week, I will do that because when I look back 20 years from now, if I did not do that I would feel like a fool; letting him steal my briefcase and not doing anything at all about it. I would have such a churning feeling in my guts that it just would not be narrowly in my psychological interest not to press charges. That is not rational under the self-interest theory of behavior, but if the potential thief has some reason to presume that that is the way I will calculate when it comes time to make the decision about whether to retaliate, then I am in a much safer position. He is going to find my briefcase a much less tempting target.

THE PROBLEM WHEN COOPERATORS AND
DEFECTORS ARE INDISTINGUISHABLE

I now review a simple frequency-dependent model that shows how a moral sentiment might evolve under natural selection in a population. I am going to begin with the simple prisoner's dilemma model in Table 15.1. If you each cooperate, you get a higher payoff than if you each defect, but if one of you cooperates, the other party does best by defecting. If one of you defects, the other party also does best by defecting. The dominant strategy is for each individual to defect and yet, when each does that, each gets a payoff of two. You could have gotten a payoff of four if you had each cooperated.

Table 15.1

Monetary Payoffs in a Joint Venture

	Cooperate X	Defect
Cooperate	4 for each	0 for Y 6 for X
Y Defect	6 for Y 0 for X	2 for each

That is the basic cheating problem or cooperation problem. Imagine now that we have a population of people and we are by genetic predisposition—possibly combined with some cultural indoctrination—inclined to do one thing or the other when we interact in one of these prisoner's dilemmas. Either we are cooperators, who always cooperate in these interactions, or we are defectors. Now, I do not really want to suggest that it is a simple split like that. People are not all good or all bad; but just for the purpose of discussion imagine that some of us are cooperators and others are defectors and the way we earn our living in this environment is by interacting in pairs and getting paid according to the payoff structure in the example in Table 15.1. I will consider three cases. First, suppose the cooperators and the defectors look exactly alike. If I am a cooperator, of course I would rather interact with another cooperator because then I would get four. If I interact with a defector, I will get zero. However, if all people look alike, then it is just up to chance. I cannot selectively interact with cooperators; I just have to interact and hope it is a cooperator. The likelihood that it will be will depend on the composition of the population.

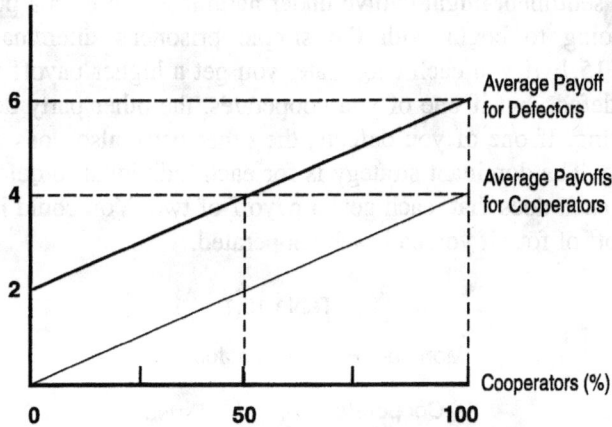

Fig. 15.1.   Average payoffs when cooperators and defectors look alike.

Now, if that is the kind of ecology we have, then it is a very simple matter to construct frequency-dependent payoff schedules for the two types. On the horizontal axis of Fig. 15.1 is the percentage of the popu-lation that is the cooperative type. One hundred minus that percentage is the percentage that is the defector type. Notice what happens. In a population that was 100% cooperators, the cooperators would expect to get four. They would interact at random with other people and they would always have cooperators as partners. Imagine a defector invading that population. He would always get a cooperator as a partner, too, and so he would get six. If you had a population with no cooperators—or virtually none—then the cooperators would always be victimized by de-fectors and they would get zero. The defectors would end up interacting with one another, as that is all there is in the population, and in between the payoffs are just linear interpolations of those extreme values. The more cooperators in the population, the higher the expected payoff for each type. Therein is the wisdom that the world would be a better place if everyone was a cooperator—we would get four each—than if every-one were a defector, in which case we would get two each.

However, the difficulty in the Darwinian framework is that it does not matter whether the world would be a better place if we all did X.

What matters is whether I have more descendents if I do X or Y and here the answer is clear. If I am a defector, I will always have a higher expected payoff and on the simple dynamic rule that population types grow in proportion to their material payoffs, the cooperators would be driven to extinction. No matter where we start, the defectors have a higher payoff, so their share of the population grows, which in the graph means we shrink toward zero. The only stable outcome is the opportunistic one. This model is a crude caricature of the sociobiological model of behavior. It would be nice if everyone were altruistic, but it just cannot be. We would all be driven to extinction.

AN ECOLOGY IN WHICH COOPERATORS
CAN BE COSTLESSLY IDENTIFIED

Now, take a very simple modification of that framework. Imagine that there is some marker that identifies who is a cooperator and who is a defector. Suppose that the cooperators have a birthmark in the form of a red C on their forehead and the defectors have a D to identify them.

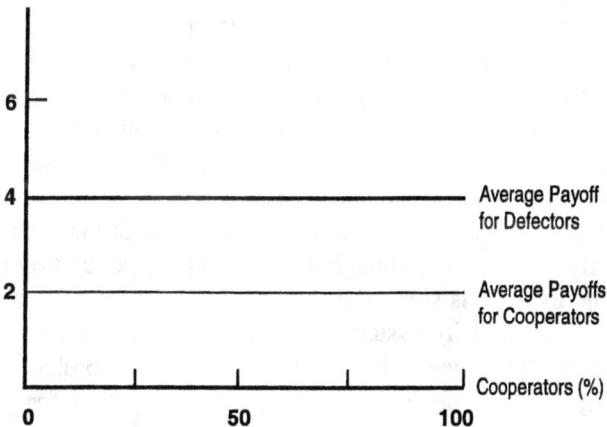

Fig. 15.2. Average payoffs when cooperators and defectors are perfectly distinguishable

More realistically, suppose the cooperators have a sincere manner and the defectors seem furtive and insincere. In that case, it would not matter what the initial frequencies in the population were at all. If I were a cooperator, I would simple walk up to someone with a C on his forehead and offer to interact. He would see a C on my forehead and agree to do so and we would get four. If I were a defector, I would be able to identify a cooperator and propose to interact, but in general I would be told "no" because he would see the D on my forehead. Cooperators are nice; they are not stupid. They will avoid interacting with defectors if they are able to do that. So, in this simple version, you get the degenerate payoff structure in Fig. 15.2, where the cooperators always get four no matter how numerous they are in the in the population. The defectors always get two. Therefore, the equilibrium here is a population consisting only of cooperators. We know, however, that there are many defectors, so we may also reject this second model as a description of the equilibrium that we actually observe in the world.

AN ECOLOGY IN WHICH COOPERATORS ARE COSTLY TO IDENTIFY

Let us just look at a third variant of the model, one that I think is still stylized but captures an important ingredient of the picture. Imagine that you could tell cooperators from defectors, but only after expending some effort. There are symptoms of some kind that identify people's moral character, but they are not observed for free. You have to spend some effort in order to observe them. Stylistically, just imagine that there is a pair of spectacles you could buy at a cost of one unit and that if you had these spectacles you could put them on and see who has a C and who has a D on the forehead. If you do not buy the spectacles, then everyone looks the same. The first question is should you buy these spectacles if you are a cooperator? The answer is that you would buy them only if there were enough defectors in the population to be worth worrying about. It is similar to the decision of whether you should buy an expensive security system for your home. If you live in a village where there has never been a burglary, then it is probably not worth spending $20,000 on an expensive security system for your home. However, if you live in a city where burglaries are common, then it may be worth investing in that extra security. Similarly, if you are in a population where there are hardly any defectors, you would not invest the effort to scrutinize character in other people, but if there were a lot of defectors, then it would pay you to invest.

Consider a numerical example. If there were 90% cooperators and you did not buy these spectacles and just took your chances on interacting with a member selected at random from the population, you would have a 90% chance of getting another cooperator as a partner, and a 10% chance of getting a defector. Your payoff on the average would be 90% of four and 10% of zero or a total of 3.6. If you bought the spectacles, and all the other cooperators did, too, then you could pair off selectively and you would get a payoff of four, but you would have to deduct from that the cost of the glasses and that would leave you with a payoff of only three, so you should not buy the glasses in that case.

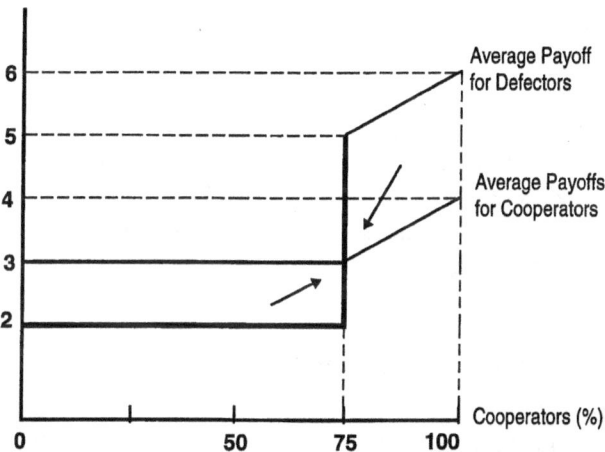

Fig. 15.3. Equilibrium when character is costly to observe

Now work the same example with 10% cooperators in the population and you will see immediately that it does pay to be vigilant under those circumstances. The breakeven point for buying the spectacles in this example occurs when cooperators make up three quarters of the population. At that fraction you expect to do equally well as a cooperator whether you buy the glasses or not. You will get an expected payoff of three if everyone just takes their chances; you will also get a certain payoff of three if everyone buys the glasses. So at any point to the left of 75% cooperators, the cooperators will want to buy these glasses. They will want to be vigilant. In that case, they are going to get a payoff of three (net of the cost of glasses). The defectors will get a payoff of two because they will have only one another to interact with. Whenever we start off with less than 75% cooperators in the population, the cooperators have a higher payoff. If we start with more than 75% cooperators, however, the defectors have a higher payoff. The expected payoff schedules for the two types in this model are shown in Fig. 15.3.

There is a stable ecological niche for both cooperators and defectors. In Maynard Smith's Hawks and Doves Models he gets similar results (Maynard Smith, 1986). The present model has one extra step added. The key point obviously is that there be some mechanism whereby you identify somebody as being a cooperator, or at least with sufficiently high probability to make it worthwhile to gamble on interaction of this sort. It is clear that there will be a ready supply of people who would be eager to mimic this symptom of integrity, whatever it might be. If you can, by seeming sincere, seeming to have integrity, get opportunities to interact with cooperators and take advantage of them, then as long as you can display that symptom at no cost, we are back again in the first version of the model: Everyone looks the same. All the defectors will copy the signal. The cooperators have the real signal, but you cannot tell them apart and so eventually the cooperators go extinct. Obviously the key step in the argument is that there not be the ability for the defectors to instantaneously and costlessly mimic whatever this signal is of cooperation.

THE ROLE OF NONVERBAL COMMUNICATION

With this background in place, I can now finally introduce the role of nonverbal communiction. I am arguing that people are motivated to behave morally not because they have rationally calculated that it is in their material interest to do that, but because they are emotionally predisposed to do so. They have some emotional hardware that they have inherited biologically. Perhaps it is necessary for that hardware to be programmed in specific ways through culture. We do not need to get involved here in a debate about whether it is genes or culture. The present argument suggests a clear role for both genes and culture in sustaining cooperative behavior in equilibrium.

Now, assuming that you have got these emotional capabilities predisposing you to behave honestly, how do others know you have them? That is the question. Darwin's drawing of the emotionally aroused dog (see Fig. 15.4) recaps his notion that you can easily tell what is on the dog's mind when the dog is aroused to do battle. If dogs that were in the attack posture had to willfully summon all the details of that posture in order to get ready to do battle, it would just take too long. They would be defeated by dogs that had a hard-wired link between the relevant muscle groups and the emotionally aroused condition of the brain.

be defeated by dogs that had a hard-wired link between the relevant muscle groups and the emotionally aroused condition of the brain.

Fig. 15.4. The Attack Mode
(Source: Charles Darwin, *The expression of emotion in man and animals,* London: J. Murray, 1872, illus. on p. 52 (*"The Attack Mode"*) (MFY 82-693).)*

Therefore, according to Darwin, the only surviving dogs were those for which there were automatic links between emotional arousal in the brain and the relevant muscular positions in the body. In effect, there is a window to the organism's brain. We can make confident statements about the emotional valence of the dog by looking at observable concomitants of emotion.

Fig. 15.5. Nonverbal expression of emotion.

Several presentations at the conference on which this volume is based dealt with the human face. My argument is based on the observations that Ekman (1985) made. This particular combination of pyramidal and corrugator muscles where you have the eyebrows go up in the middle and fall toward the edge is very hard to summon voluntarily (see

---

*Photography Collection Miriam and Ira D. Wallach, Division of Art, Prints and Photographs, The New York Public Library, Astor, Lenox and Tilden Foundations.

Fig. 15.5). If you are feeling sad or distressed, this configuration appears on your face spontaneously. The emotions really do give a signal that is hard for even a skilled actor to mimic in response to unanticipated stimuli coming at real time.

In this scheme, *sympathy* plays as important a role as it did in Adam Smith's scheme. I am inclined to leave the waiter in an out-of-town restaurant a tip because I feel sympathetic to the waiter's interest. I imagine myself in the waiter's position, having worked hard to provide good service, and how distressed I would feel if somebody failed to tip me. Sympathy is one of the key emotions for supporting the kind of behavior I have talked about in the examples.

Kagan (1984) and others have observed that in very widely disparate cultural childrearing arrangements the capacity to experience sympathy with the distress of another child seems to emerge in children around the age of 2. If a child falls down and gets hurt and starts crying, others in the play group come up and attempt to provide comfort. They seem to recognize that. They know what this feeling is and they seem to evidence concern for the well-being of their playmate. If nurtured, sympathy becomes a very powerful motivating force. The conditions that trigger it are sometimes culturally specific. People are taught not to feel sympathetic for the interests of the enemy during wartime. They are able to do things that they would not be able to do to people under normal circumstances. I do not mean for a moment to say that we are indiscriminately sympathetic and that we are just blindly altruistic irrespective of circumstances. But, again, the constant puzzle in biology and economics has been the question: How could those organisms that were motivated not to take full advantage of egoistic opportunities manage to survive in competition with their adversaries who were more ruthless? Here the argument is very simple. If the people who have those motives are somehow observably different from the purely opportunistic agents, then they can interact selectively and reap the benefits of cooperation.

Can you then identify the character of other people? Here is a very simple thought experiment. Imagine that you have just gotten home from a concert and you have lost $1,000 in cash that was in an envelope in your coat pocket. It had your name and address on it. Can you think of some person you know, not related to you by blood or marriage, who you feel sure would return the envelope with your cash in it? Most people, on brief reflection, say, of course, not just one person, many people. Most people feel they know someone who would return even a stranger's cash if they found it under these circumstances. When people name someone they feel sure would return their own cash, usually they name a close friend. If you believe that you can make identifications of that sort, then you accept the central premise of the argument. If you can do only this, then it is possible for genuinely altruistic behavior to emerge.

What about cheaters—can they be identified, too? We did some experiments to see whether people had the capacity to identify cheaters in simple games where there was a possibility to cheat with no possibility of detection. In one experiment, we recruited groups of students, three to a group, and we put them together in a room by themselves. They had 30 minutes to get acquainted with one another and they knew that at the end of that time they were going to play prisoner's dilemma games with each other for real money. Each dyad in the three-person group was going to play a single prisoner's dilemma game and they were going to get a payoff. The instructions tell you to fill out a form and predict the other player's response and also how sure you are that he or she will cooperate. An answer of 50% means not sure at all and 100% means that you feel really certain. We took elaborate measures to try to preserve the one-shot character of the game so that participants could not know for sure what any of their partners had done under the structure that we designed.

We were actually surprised to discover how good people were at predicting what their partners would do in these games. We matched predictions with the actual responses. The subjects showed remarkable accuracy (56%) in predicting strangers' defection as a result of a very short encounter in a game where the defection rate was about 29%. I was surprised that even on the basis of a quick 30-minute interaction, people seemed able somehow to gain some insight about what other people would do in these anonymous one-shot prisoner's dilemma games. I think there is substantial evidence that people are able to make the kinds of character judgments necessary for the mechanism to work. It seems that nonverbal cues are providing us with the metaphorical spectacles I mentioned earlier. Our sensitivity to nonverbal communication enables us to differentiate between those with the Cs and Ds on their foreheads, after all.

CONCLUSION

The empirical fact of cooperation in one-shot prisoner's dilemmas
played by nonrelatives poses one of the deepest challenges to conven-
tional theories of human behavior in both sociobiology and economics.
I have sketched a commitment model that attempts to show how the
moral sentiments that motivate such behavior could have been favored
by natural selection. The central idea is that people known to have cooperative predispositions are able to solve a variety of commitment
problems that purely self-interested persons cannot. The role of nonverbal communication is central in my account, for it is the observable signals of emotion that enable us to identify cooperative predispositions in
others.

REFERENCES

Ekman, P. (1985). *Telling lies: Clues to deceit in the marketplace, marriage, and politics.*
    New York: W. W. Norton.
Frank, R. (1988). *Passions within reason.* New York: W. W. Norton.
Kagan, J. (1984). *The nature of the child.* New York: Basic Books.
Maynard Smith, J. (1986). *The problems of biology.* Oxford, UK: Oxford University Press.
Schelling, T. (1960). *The strategy of conflict.* Cambridge, MA: Harvard University Press.
Trivers, R. L. (1985). *Social Evolution.* Menlo Park: Benjamin Cummings.
Woodall, J. (1996). *The man in the mirror of the book: A life of Jorge Luis Borges.* London:
    Hodder & Stoughton.

LIST OF AUTHORS

Ulf Dimberg, Department of Psychology, University of Uppsala,
P.O. Box 1225, S-75142 Uppsala, Sweden

Paul Ekman, Department of Psychiatry, University of California,
401 Parnassus Avenue, Box HIL, San Francisco, CA 94143-0984, USA

Christopher S. Evans, Department of Psychology, Macquarie University, Sydney,
NSW 2109, Australia

Robert Frank, Johnson Graduate School of Management, Department of
Economics, 528 Malott Hall, Cornell University, Ithaca, NY 14853, USA

Walter Goldschmidt, Department of Anthropology, University of California, Los
Angeles, CA 90024, USA

Michel Heller, Department of Psychiatry, University of Geneva,
16 Boulevard St. George, CH-1211 Geneva, Switzerland

Jan A. R. A. M. van Hooff, Ethology and Social Ecology, University of Utrecht,
P.O.Box 80.086, 3508 TB Utrecht, The Netherlands

Dacher Keltner, Department of Psychology, 3210 Tolman Hall, University of
California, Berkeley, Berkeley, CA 94708, USA

Peter Marler, Animal Communication Laboratory, Section of Neurobiology,
Physiology, and Behavior, University of California, Davis, CA 95616-8761,
USA

Alexandra Maryanski, Department of Sociology, University of California,
Riverside, CA 92521-0412, USA

Peter Molnár, Department of Medical Anthropology, Institute of Behavioural
Sciences, Semmelweis University Medical School, Nagyvarad sq. 4, H-1089
Budapest, Hungary

August Nitschke, Historical Research in Human Behavior, University of Stuttgart,
Keplerstr. 17 KII, D-70174 Stuttgart, Germany

Hanuš Papoušek, Strassberger Straße 43, D-80809 München, Germany

Mechthild Papoušek, Strassberger Straße 43, D-80809 München, Germany

Signe Preuschoft, Ethology and Social Ecology, University of Utrecht,
P.O.Box 80.086, 3508 TB Utrecht, The Netherlands

Wulf Schiefenhövel, Human Ethology Institute of the Max Planck Society, von-
der-Tann-Straße 3-5, D-82346 Andechs, Germany

Klaus Schneider (†), General and Developmental Psychology, Ruhr University of
Bochum, P.O. Box 10 21 48, D-44780 Bochum, Germany

Ullica Segerstråle, Department of Social Sciences, Armour College, Illinois
Institute of Technology, Chicago, IL 60616, USA

Stephen J. Suomi, Laboratory of Comparative Ethology, National Institute of
Child Health and Human Development, NIH, 31/B2B-15, 9000 Rockville Pike,
Bethesda, MD 20892, USA

Jonathan H. Turner, Department of Sociology, University of California,
Riverside, CA 92521-0419, USA

AUTHOR INDEX

A

Aaron, N. 135, 136, *144*
Adams, J. L. 102, *106*
Adang, O. 177, *186*
Ahlquist, J. 200, *208*
Ainsworth, M. D. 110, 116, *127*, 232, 242
Alexander, R. D. 179, *186*
Alley, R. 134, *144*
Amira von, K. 266, *272*
Anderson, J. R. *188*
Andrew, R. J. 48, *59*, 110, *127*, *206*
Angst, W. 176, 182, 183, *186*
Anisfeld, M. 231, *242*
Arcus, D. *84*, 143, *145*
Argyle, M. 246, 247, *261*
Aureli, F. 182, 185, *186*

B

Bailey, W. *207*
Baldwin, B. 9, *19*
Barakat, R. A. 264, *272*
Barkow, J. 7, 16, *17*, *18*
Barnes, D. M. 76, *78*
Baron, G. 194, *208*
Bastian, J. 200, *206*
Bates, E. 239, *242*
Bateson, G. 14, *17*, 227, 228, 236, *242*
Bäuml, B. J. 265, *272*
Bäuml, F. H. 265, *272*
Beard, C. 195, *206*
Beningni, L. 239, *242*
Benson, P. *207*
Berard, J. 132, *144*
Bernstein, I. S. 184, 185, *186*
Bertalanffy von, L. 91, *105*
Bever, T. G. 191, *207*
Biben, M. 137, *144*
Birdwhistell, R. L. 4, 5, *17*, 25, 26, 28, 29, 38, *43*, 247, *261*
Bischof, N. 181, *186*
Blest, A. D. 117, *127*
Blue, J. 40, *43*
Blurton Jones, N. G. 174, 177, 182, *186*
Boesch, C. 139, *144*

Boesch, E. E. 268, *273*
Boesch, H. 139, *144*
Bogen, K. 268, *273*
Bone, E. 201, *206*
Bornstein, M. H. *17*, *18*, 83, *84*, 102, *105*, *106*
Bourdieu, P. 250, *261*
Bowlby, J. 10, *18*, 83, *84*, 110, 116, *127*, 232, *242*
Boyce, W. T. 143, *144*
Boysen, S. 97, *106*
Boysson-Bardies, B. *105*
Brakke, D. *208*
Brazelton, T. B. 11, *18*, 83, *84*
Bretherton, I. 239, *242*
Brooks-Gunn, J. 118, *128*
Brooks, V. 118, 134, *144*
Brown, D. E. 7, *18*, 65, *78*
Bruner, J. S. 38, *43*
Brunswik, E. *84*
Buck, R. 49, *59*
Bugental, D. B. 40, *43*
Bühler, C. 116, *127*
Bullinger, A. 247, *261*
Burling, R. 205, *206*
Byrne, R. W. 184, *188*

C

Caan, W. 9, *20*
Cacioppo, J. T. 54, *60*
Cadell, T. E. 134, *145*
Camioni, L. 239, *242*
Cantfort, T. 191, *207*
Caro, T. M. 162, *168*
Carstensen, L. L. 35, *45*
Caryl, P. G. 175, *186*
Caspi, A. 239, *242*
Caudill, W. 237, 239, 241, *242*
Caul, W. F. 184, *187*
Cavalli-Sforza, L. L. 96, *105*
Champoux, M. 134, *144*, *145*
Chan Tak Nam, J. C. 250, *262*
Chan, A. *44*
Chapais, B. 181, *186*
Chapman, A. J. 64, *78*
Charnov, E. L. 162, *168*

SUBJECT INDEX

For Product Safety Concerns and Information please contact our EU
representative GPSR@taylorandfrancis.com
Taylor & Francis Verlag GmbH, Kaufingerstraße 24, 80331 München, Germany